ALFRED MYNN AND THE
CRICKETERS OF HIS TIME

Also by Patrick Morrah

THE GOLDEN AGE OF CRICKET

ALFRED MYNN
and the cricketers of his time

Patrick Morrah

CONSTABLE · LONDON

Published in Great Britain 1986
by Constable and Company Ltd
10 Orange Street London WC2H 7EG
Copyright © 1963 Patrick Morrah
First published 1963 by Eyre & Spottiswode
ISBN 0 09 467020 X
Printed in Great Britain by
St Edmundsbury Press
Bury St Edmunds, Suffolk

CONTENTS

*

*

ACKNOWLEDGEMENTS

*

Acknowledgements and thanks are due to the
Sussex County Cricket Club for the signed
ticket for the Alfred Mynn Testimonial Match;
to Mr John Best-Shaw for the photograph of
Alfred Mynn's tombstone; to William Blackwood & Sons Ltd for the drawing from *Seventy-
One Not Out*; to Eyre & Spottiswoode Ltd, for
the Hampstead Cricket Club menu; and to the
M.C.C. for all the other illustrations.

ILLUSTRATIONS

*

INTRODUCTION

*

To most followers of cricket the history of the game begins with
W.G. Grace. It was he, one of the most eminent of Victorians,
who brought it out of its 'middle ages', swept it into the public
eye, and transformed it into the great national institution that we
know today. By his force of character, as much as by his skill as a
player, the great doctor created modern cricket.

Yet there were giants before Grace; and pre-eminent among
them, a giant alike in stature and in personality, was Alfred
Mynn.

The foremost batsman of the 'middle ages' was Fuller Pilch.
The finest bowler, probably, was William Lillywhite. But as an
all-round cricketer Mynn shone above them all. He was a hitter
who could send the ball vast distances, and he was one of the
fastest bowlers who ever bowled. But it was the lovable nature of
the man himself that so endeared him to his contemporaries.
Never was any cricketer more popular both with those who
played with him and with those who only watched or read about
him. 'Kind and manly Alfred Mynn' was W.J. Prowse's
description in his famous poem. 'Dear, genial Alfred,' said his old
friend Edward Hodges. 'A more delightful man never lived.'

I had long wondered why nobody had considered Mynn
worthy of a biography. The present study was written more than
twenty years ago. Since writing it I have learnt a little more
about him, but nothing that alters the general picture. I have
therefore done no revision; the book is presented as originally
compiled. I can only hope that it will induce in a few readers
something approaching my own enthusiasm for one of the most
notable characters who ever stepped on to a cricket field.

PATRICK MORRAH
Brighton, 1986

FOREWORD

*

As Alfred Mynn died in the latter half of 1861, it is extremely unlikely that there is anybody living who spoke to him or saw him play; I have been able, therefore, to make no use of personal reminiscences. I have, however, received most valuable help from a considerable number of people to whom I should like to express my gratitude.

To friends in Kent I owe my warmest thanks. Mr and Mrs John Best-Shaw, Mr and Mrs D. P. Evans, Sean Fielding, who tragically died while my book was in the press, and Mrs Sean Fielding not only gave me hospitality, but partook of my enthusiasm and drove me round the countryside in search of Mynnian tracks. Sir John Best-Shaw helped me with Kentish lore, and the incumbents of Goudhurst, Bearsted, Harrietsham, Hollingbourne and Hellingly (Sussex), Mr Carden of Lenham and Mrs White of Thurnham, most kindly put parish records at my disposal.

I have received valuable assistance from officials of the Kent County Cricket Club, particularly Mr A. O. Snowden, who invited me to inspect the Mynn relics in the pavilion at Canterbury besides putting me on the track of many aspects of Mynn's career. Mr Knell, the St Lawrence groundsman, showed me over the pavilion, and Lord Harris and Mr Nevill Christopherson were good enough to answer my searching questions. Mr Roger de Grey went to great personal trouble to show me the original records of the Old Stagers.

The pavilion at Lord's is of course a treasury of cricket history, and I am greatly indebted to Miss Diana Rait Kerr, who could not have been more helpful in enabling me to study the documents I asked to see and also in suggesting others. Mr L. E. S. Gutteridge, with his unrivalled knowledge of cricket books, gave me immense help; while Major Rowland Bowen supplied most important information, in particular the details of Alfred Mynn's arrest for debt in 1845. Mr Robert H. Goodsall traced for me the bankruptcy record of the same year, in addition to other details. Mr Gerald Brodribb not only put me right on a number of points, but allowed me to read the proofs of his book on Felix, which had not then appeared. Mr R. L. Arrowsmith traced the record of Mynn's marriage, which had long eluded me.

Others who have helped me are Mr John Arlott, Mr Sidney Loweth, Mr A. W. Warland, Mr F. I. Watson, Mr Bertram Wakley, Miss Molly E. Hide, Mr R. N. Rothwell and Miss Anne M. Oakley; and I would particularly like to thank Mr Irving Rosenwater for compiling the index.

To these and any others whom I may have inadvertently omitted I am glad to record my gratitude.

PATRICK MORRAH

CHAPTER I

ROUNDARM REVOLUTION

*

Jackson's pace is very fearful; Willshire's hand is very high:
William Caffyn has good judgment, and an admirable eye;
Jemmy Grundy's cool and clever, almost always on the spot;
Tinley's slows are often telling, though they sometimes catch it hot;
But however good their trundling – pitch or pace, or break, or spin –
Still the monarch of all bowlers, to my mind, was Alfred Mynn!

In the middle of the reign of George IV there was living near
Sutton Valence, in Kent, a country gentleman named John
Willes. He was a wealthy landowner in Kent and Sussex, part
of his property later becoming the site for Lancing College. He
was also an individualist characteristic of his period, with something of Squire Osbaldeston in him, something of John Mytton:
a fine athlete, an all-round sportsman, a first-class shot, a devil-
may-care rider. His nephew Edward Hodges, to whom we owe
most of our knowledge of him, had some stories to tell of his
uncle that give the full flavour of the man.

Hodges, who was born at Bellringham, his uncle's house,
remembered being shown a place where Willes, on returning
across country from a visit to a friend, had jumped his grey
mare over a high stile, down very steep and irregular stone
steps between twenty and thirty feet deep, into a very narrow
lane. 'How any horse could have done it with safety I cannot
think,' commented Hodges; 'at the time it seemed to me that
my uncle did it in order to break his neck.' On another occasion
there was brought to him a horse so vicious and intractable
that neither its owner nor the grooms could handle it. Willes
succeeded in mounting it, whereupon it galloped up the hill
and then tried to smash its rider's leg by beating itself against a
wall. Willes resisted all the animal's attempts to unseat him, and

13

then set off on a wild ride across country to Boxley Abbey, nine miles away, the seat of his friend Colonel Best. Half-way there he lost his hunting whip, but still kept control of the horse; he 'got him close to a hedge, pulled up a hedge-stake, and every time he wanted to go the wrong way gave him a smack on the head'. When he arrived at Boxley he paid his respects to Colonel Best and then, without dismounting, set straight off on the return journey; when he reached Bellringham the horse was thoroughly broken in.

Another story, for the truth of which Hodges could not vouch from first-hand knowledge, concerned a different kind of adventure. Willes knew a young lady at Harrietsham, and one day he said to her: 'If I drove up in a coach-and-four, would you run away with me?' The lady said she would, and a few days later Willes appeared before her house with his coach-and-four. In popped the lady, and away drove Willes as fast as the horses could cover the ground. Unfortunately, however, the lady's father had seen what had happened, and leaping upon his horse he gave chase. He quickly gained on the runaways, whereupon his daughter decided that it would be better to surrender than be caught. Having persuaded Willes to draw up she got out and ran to meet her father, while her dashing swain, in no mood to face an angry parent, whipped up his horses again and made for home.

When Hodges had heard this story he innocently asked his uncle if it was true. Willes blazed with fury and demanded to know where his nephew had got it. When told that it was from another lady friend of his, he was not mollified.

It is, however, with cricket that we are here concerned. And John Willes holds a very special place in cricket history. He left little mark as a player, though he was good enough to appear in the first Gentlemen v. Players match in 1806; but he more than any other man was concerned in one of the most momentous movements in the evolution of the game: the introduction of roundarm bowling.

In the early days of cricket all bowling was underhand, and till almost the end of the eighteenth century nobody attempted any other method. At first it was all along the ground; 'sneaks' or 'daisy-cutters' were the order of the day. Then the Hambledon

men, led by Richard Nyren and 'Lumpy' Stevens, began to bowl
to a length, and so brought about the first great revolution in the
form of the game. A straight bat was introduced in place of the
curved club that had served for swiping the daisy-cutters, and
scientific batting made its appearance, culminating in the graceful hitting of 'Silver Billy' Beldham, the first great stylist in
cricket history.

But as has often happened at later periods the balance between
bat and ball was upset. Beldham and others mastered the best
the underhand length bowlers could produce; bowlers found it
harder and harder to get wickets, and they began to look around
for new methods whereby they could regain their supremacy
in attack.

The first to experiment to this end with a higher action was
Tom Walker, one of those delightful characters of the old
Hambledon eleven so marvellously brought to life for future
generations by John Nyren. Nyren's description of Tom and
his brother Harry is well known but will always bear re-quoting:

And now for those anointed clod-stumpers, the Walkers, Tom
and Harry. Never sure came two such unadulterated rustics
into a civilized community. How strongly are the figures of
the men (of Tom's in particular) brought to my mind when
they first presented themselves to the club, upon Windmill-
down. Tom's hard, ungain, scrag-of-mutton frame; wilted
apple-john face (he always looked twenty years older than he
really was), his long spider legs, as thick at the ankles as at
the hips, and perfectly straight all the way down – for the
embellishment of a calf in Tom's legs, Dame Nature had
considered would be but a wanton superfluity. Tom was the
driest and most rigid-limbed chap I ever knew; his skin was
like the rind of an old oak, and as sapless. I have seen his
knuckles handsomely knocked about from Harris's bowling;
but never saw any blood upon his hands – you might just as
well attempt to phlebotomize a mummy. This rigidity of
muscle (or rather I should say of tendon, for muscle was
another ingredient economized in the process of Tom's con-
figuration) – this rigidity, I say, was carried into every
motion. He moved like the rude machinery of a steam-engine

15

in the infancy of construction, and when he ran, every member seemed ready to fly to the four winds. He toiled like a tar on horseback. The uncouth actions of these men furnished us, who prided ourselves upon a certain grace in movement and finished air, with an everlasting fund of amusement, and for some time they took no great fancy to me, because I used to worry, and tell them they could not play. They were, however, good hands when they first came among us, and had evidently received most excellent instruction; but after they had derived the advantage of first-rate practice, they became most admirable batters, and were the trustiest fellows (particularly Tom) in cases of emergency or difficulty. They were devilish troublesome customers to get out. I have very frequently known Tom to go in first, and remain to the very last man. He was the coolest, the most imperturbable fellow in existence; it used to be said of him that he had no nerves at all. Whether he was only practising, or whether he knew that the game was in a critical state, and that much depended upon his play, he was the same phlegmatic, unmoved man – he was the Washington of cricketers. Neither he nor his brother were active, yet both were effective fieldsmen. Upon one occasion, on the Mary-le-bone grounds, I remember Tom going in first, and Lord Beauclerk giving him the first four balls, all of an excellent length. First four or last four made no difference to Tom – he was always the same cool, collected fellow. Every ball he dropped down just before his bat. Off went his lordship's white hat – dash upon the ground (his constant action when disappointed), calling him at the same time 'a confounded old beast'. 'I doant care what ee zays', said Tom, when one close by asked him if he had heard Lord Frederick call him 'an old beast'. No, no; Tom was not the man to be flustered.

Such was Tom Walker, 'Old Everlasting', mainly a batsman though hardly a sparkling one. But he bowled as well, and however slowly his rustic mind may have moved it was apparently to him that the idea of roundarm bowling first occurred. He tried it out somewhere about 1790, and his performance created such a stir that a special meeting of the Hambledon Club, then still the generally accepted governing authority for cricket, was called to discuss it. The result was condemnation; the new style was declared to be foul play and was outlawed from all grounds.

Tom was not the man to fight such a decision. He might be independent in his attitude to his fellows; he might treat the tantrums of Lord Frederick Beauclerk with sturdy contempt; but his station in life was too humble, and his temper too placid, for him to conduct a campaign for reformation against established authority. In any case it is doubtful if he cared very much. He had tried an experiment and it had failed; so with characteristic philosophy he took to bowling slow lobs. They were highly successful.

There, for the time being, the matter rested. But it was inevitable that the question of the height of the bowling arm would be raised again before very long. When this came to pass the protagonist was a man of very different temper from the phlegmatic Tom Walker: he was John Willes.

Willes's innovation owed nothing to Walker's example. On the contrary, according to the well authenticated story, it was, almost literally, petticoat influence that led to the final vindication of roundarm. Willes was thorough in all his sporting activities; when he took to cricket he practised all the year round: in his barn when conditions made outdoor play impossible. To help him he recruited two members of his household: his sister and his dog. The dog was brilliant in the field, and it became a local joke to claim that Willes, his sister Christina and his dog could beat any eleven in England.

Christina did the bowling, and it was she who turned out to be the most important of the trio. The voluminous looped skirts worn at the turn of the century made it impossible for her to bowl in the conventional underhand manner; she had to raise her arm at least above the level of the hip. She must have made herself into a very fine bowler indeed, for her brother found her more difficult to play than the bowlers against whom he batted in important matches. This gave him food for thought; if he could bowl like his sister he might topple the pride of the greatest batsmen in England. And so roundarm bowling was re-born.

Doubts have been cast on this version of the story. But

Edward Hodges related it as fact, and as the lady in question was his mother his testimony would seem to be final.

Exactly when Willes started bowling roundarm we do not know, but it seems to have been within the first few years of the nineteenth century. At first it was in small local matches in Kent, but by 1807 his reputation as an innovator was becoming known. In July of that year a match was played on Penenden Heath between thirteen of All England and twenty-three of Kent, described in the press as the greatest match that had been played in Kent for upwards of twenty years; Willes was in the Kent side, and the *Sporting Magazine* reported: 'The straight-arm bowling, introduced by John Willes, Esq., was generally practised in the game, and fully proved an obstacle against getting runs in comparison to what might have been got by the straight-forward bowling.'

There is no suggestion here of any resentment being aroused by Willes's methods. But during the following years the rumble of controversy reverberated round the cricket world. We are told little about Willes's style of bowling, but doubtless his pace was considerable. It is difficult to imagine a man of his dynamic temperament being a slow bowler, and the complaint against the new 'throwing' bowling, as it quickly came to be called, was that it was dangerous to life and limb. Such it may well have been. No batsman had yet thought of wearing pads or gloves for protection, and the wickets of the early nineteenth century were atrocious. It was hardly surprising that Willes came to be looked upon by the conservative opposition as little better than a wilful murderer. Charles Box, author of *The Theory and Practice of Cricket*, published in 1868, tells of the reception accorded the new bowling, and of Willes's reactions to it:

Among the great bulk of cricketers the new comer met with a sorry reception. Both Mr Willes and his offspring were frequently 'barred' in the arrangement of a match, and thus for a time they were kept in abeyance. There are persons yet living who remember Mr Willes playing in a match on Penenden Heath amidst much uproar and confusion from players and spectators, John Crawte being especially noisy on the occasion. Mr Willes was not the man to be daunted by what he considered silly ejaculations, clumsy cajoleries, or empty threats of personal violence, so on he went until the 'ring' was broken in, the stumps uprooted, and the game brought to a dead lock.

Other bowlers followed Willes's lead, and in the second decade of the century the uproar rose to its climax. The new bowling had its supporters, but its opponents were both more vociferous and more influential. Lord Frederick Beauclerk took a characteristic attitude: when playing on the same side as Willes he defended the roundarm style; when playing against him he denounced it as unfair. At length, as in the case of Tom Walker, authority decided it must take action, though in this case the action was less decisive. Hambledon was no more, and the Marylebone Cricket Club was now the accepted legislative body for the game. It was William Ward, the leading amateur batsman of the day and with Lord Frederick one of the two most forceful personalities in cricket, who took the initiative. He was a staunch conservative and hater of innovations; what was more to the point was that he had faced the new bowling and found that he could not play it. So he persuaded the M.C.C. to call a meeting and frame a law which would make it quite clear that roundarm bowling was illegal. The law (Law 10) was duly passed, in 1816, and this was its wording:

> The ball must be bowled (not thrown or jerked) and be delivered underhand, with the hand below the elbow. But if the ball be jerked, or the arm extended from the body horizontally, and any part of the back of the hand be uppermost, or the hand horizontally extended when the ball is delivered, the Umpire shall call 'No ball'.

The late Colonel R. S. Rait Kerr, in his admirable book *The Laws of Cricket*, quotes this as 'an example of how not to frame a law'. Umpires found it impossible to understand, let alone administer; and roundarm bowling proceeded as before. Sometimes the bowler was no-balled, sometimes not; it all depended on the individual interpretation the umpire placed on the cumbersome new law.

19

The climax came in 1822. Although Willes and his imitators had for some time now been bowling roundarm with only spasmodic molestation, nobody had yet ventured to try the new style at Lord's. To realise what this signifies we must recall the pre-eminence that Lord's then held among cricket grounds – a pre-eminence far greater even than that it holds to-day. There was as yet no defined distinction between 'first-class' and other matches, but there was a very definite distinction between those played at Lord's and those played on other grounds. This is remarkable in view of the fact that at this time Lord's had been in existence for less than forty years, and on its present site for less than ten. Yet so quickly had the M.C.C. established its supremacy that its ground had acquired a prestige that set its matches apart from all other cricket. Anything that happened there carried the stamp of authority.

Willes, therefore, decided that to set the seal on his chosen style of bowling, and to win recognition for it as a legitimate mode of play whatever the law of 1816 might say or mean, he must try it out at Lord's. If the umpires passed it, roundarm would be established as an integral part of cricket. A match was accordingly arranged; Willes undertook to raise a Kent eleven (there was not yet a Kent cricket club) and take it to head-quarters to play the M.C.C.

The match, played on July 15 and 16, aroused great interest; it was generally known that this would be the great test of the new bowling. The M.C.C. fielded a strong side which included Lord Frederick Beauclerk, William Ward, E. H. Budd and Benjamin Aislabie, the secretary of the club. Willes for his part brought, in addition to himself, another roundarm bowler named Ashby, a carpenter from Rochester; the difference between them was that Ashby did not turn his hand over as prohibited by the law of 1816. The umpires were Noah Mann, junior, son of the old Hambledon bowler, and Harry Bentley.

The great moment came almost as soon as the match began. The M.C.C. won the toss and opened their batting with R. Lane and F. Nicholas. Willes put Ashby on to bowl first, and Mann allowed all the four balls that then constituted the over. Then Willes, with renewed confidence, himself bowled from the other end – and was promptly no-balled by Bentley. That was enough; for the irascible Willes it was the end. He hurled the ball down, strode off the field, leaving his team to carry on without a captain, and jumped on his horse, swearing he would never play again. In the words of H. S. Altham he 'rode away out of Lord's and out of cricket history'.

However, Willes's part in cricket history did not quite end with this unedifying scene at Lord's; he had another service to the game to perform, and it is at least arguable that this service was a greater one than anything he had done before. Roundarm bowling would have come in any case, even if Miss Willes had never puzzled her brother in a Kentish barn; but had it not been for John Willes in his later days one of the grandest cricketers who ever stepped on to a field might never have risen above the level of the village green.

Willes settled down at Sutton Valence, where he devoted himself mainly to hunting and shooting; he kept his own pack of hounds, which according to his nephew were known all over the county for their fine breed. True to his word he played in no more cricket matches; but he did not lose his interest in the game. The district in which he lived was the most enthusiastic in Kent for its cricket. This was doubtless partly due to the influence of Willes himself; also partly to the fact that nearby was Lees Court, the seat of Lord Sondes, one of the most generous patrons of the game. Village cricket was far from general in the early years of the century, but Sutton Valence and the neighbouring villages of Leeds and Harrietsham all raised teams of their own, and Leeds in particular boasted a flourishing cricket club, under the auspices of Lord Sondes.

John Willes interested himself in the doings of the Sutton Valence cricketers, helping them with advice and entertainment. When they were returning late from an away match he would leave bottles of whisky and brandy, with glasses and a pail of water, outside his hall door for them to help themselves. The team would then serenade him, and Hodges remembered them singing the old hunting song:

There was Spero, Spendigo, Bonny Lass and Truelove,
And Ruler that never looked behind him.

He used also to watch the village boys playing on the local

greens, and would sometimes give them hints and practical coaching. And it was here that, in the middle of the 1820s, his attention was attracted by the size, strength and keenness of two lads newly arrived in the district. Their name was Mynn, Walter and Alfred, and they were the sons of a farmer at Harrietsham. Both were over six feet in height, broad and powerful. Walter, the elder, was stiff and awkward in his movements, though determined to make himself a batsman; but Alfred had a natural grace remarkable in so large a youth. His ambition lay in bowling, and his asset was sheer pace. Like many another young aspirant before and since he took an enormous run and hurled the ball down with all his great, though largely wasted, strength; it was liable to go in almost any direction, but wherever it went it went there fast. He was of a happy and imperturbable temperament, and accepted success and failure with a good humour that endeared him to all.

Willes watched him, and saw the magnificent material of which he was made. If he could be carefully coached, and his impetuosity curbed, he might reach the greatest heights of the cricket world.

First, however, it is worth glancing at Alfred Mynn's antecedents and the background to his cricket life. He was born in the parish of Goudhurst, one of the most charming of Kent villages, his birthplace being Twysden Lodge on the road to Kilndown. The house still stands; additions have been made during the last hundred years, but even at the beginning of the nineteenth century it must have been a solid, substantial dwelling for a reasonably prosperous farmer.

Where the family previously lived is not known. Mynne was a well-known name in the seventeenth century, first in Shropshire and later in Hertfordshire and Surrey, but whether the Mynns of Goudhurst had any connection with George Mynne, who made a fortune by highly dubious means in the reigns of James I and Charles I and enriched his relations at the expense of the Government, it is impossible to say. On the face of it it seems unlikely, though the status and fortunes of a family could easily be reversed in the course of a century.

It does not seem probable that there was ever much wealth

in the Kentish Mynn family, but Alfred's immediate forbears were of sturdy, independent yeoman stock, the stock that has often been described as the backbone of England. In their case the backbone was as sound and as tough as could be desired. They are said to have been renowned for at least two generations before Alfred for their great stature and physical strength. As two generations are all that have so far been traced, we know of no Mynn who did not live up to this standard.

The family connection with Goudhurst apparently began about the middle of the eighteenth century. The first relevant record in the parish register is of the burial on October 4, 1756, of Elizabeth, wife of John Mynn. Some time during the next few years John Mynn re-married (presumably in some other parish), his second wife also being named Elizabeth; for John and William, sons of John and Elizabeth Mynn, were christened on December 10, 1762, and December 30, 1763. Four years later the first John Mynn, who, it seems probable, was still quite young, died and was buried at Goudhurst. His widow married Richard Ratcliffe in 1772 and died, still at Goudhurst, in 1798. The assumption must be that the Ratcliffes and the young Mynns all lived together at Twysden.

This is all we know for certain of Alfred Mynn's grandparents. But on a ground-floor window-pane at Twysden there is clearly scratched the name 'Mynn' in what appears to be an eighteenth-century or early nineteenth-century hand. The initial before it is difficult to decipher, but I think it is 'J'; underneath there are a few more words, but these are illegible. It is at least possible that here we have the signature of the first John Mynn who lived at Goudhurst; but there were two subsequent Johns in the family, and the mark may equally well have been made by one of them.

John Mynn's elder son seems to have left home as a young man and settled down at Hellingly, near Hailsham in Sussex, where he raised a family and lived to his eighty-ninth year. William, the younger, grew up to take over in due course the management of the Twysden farm. On April 5, 1790, he was married at Goudhurst to Ann Clarke of Cranbrook, who proceeded to bear him a large family in quick succession in the approved manner of the age. The eldest, Elizabeth Ann, was christened on January 15, 1791, followed by William on May 22, 1792, and John on Christmas Day, 1793. Then came two disasters: Thomas Parker, christened on June 22, 1795, was buried on October 15 of the same year, and Joseph, christened on September 12, 1796, died almost at birth, being buried on September 18.

These were the only two who failed to grow up, and in so large a family and in an age of high infant mortality this fact alone is evidence of the healthiness of the strain. The next child, Mary, was christened on May 18, 1799; Matilda on September 19, 1801, and Eliza on April 12, 1803. Walter Parker (Parker was evidently a family name) was born on November 24, 1804, and christened on June 6, 1805, and Alfred, born on January 19, 1807, was christened on July 31. The eleventh and youngest of the family, Emily, was born on August 2, 1809.

An incidental curiosity is that Walter and Alfred, the two cricketing brothers, were both six months old when they were baptised. This was unusual at that period, particularly in a country parish, and may indicate that William Mynn was a little lax in his religious duties.

Alfred is said to have been 'educated privately'. This phrase may be something of a euphemism; it is unlikely that he had much schooling, and there is no evidence that at any time of his life he bothered his head about the cultural side of life. From first to last he was an outdoor countryman; the Mynns had a reputation for athletic prowess, and Alfred doubtless learned to play games with his elder brothers on the Kentish village greens, though cricket in these early days does not seem to have been one of them.

Hodges in his boyhood knew all the brothers. 'John, the eldest,' he said to F. S. Ashley-Cooper, 'was an even finer and more handsome man than Alfred.' And he added, as of something almost beyond belief: 'Think of that!'

When Hodges gave this interview he was eighty-eight years old and within a month or two of his death. So, although in most respects his memory was excellent, it is not surprising if in some details it played him false. For William, not John, was the eldest of the brothers. Perhaps he confused the names, perhaps the order of seniority; in any case there is no means of knowing which brother it was who was the Adonis of the family. Whether it was William or John, we can only regret that he never achieved fame in the cricket field.

Of John Mynn we hear little more, except that for a time he lived at Chart, near Tunbridge Wells, before moving to London. Of William we shall catch occasional glimpses as our story proceeds. The first such glimpse is contained in the last Mynn entry in the Goudhurst parish register before the family left the village. It amounts to no more than a single handful of wild oats; on January 2, 1814, Thomas, illegitimate son of 'William Mynn, junior, farmer', and Elizabeth Crump was baptised in the parish church.

The move to Harrietsham took place about 1825. Why William Mynn, senior, decided to leave his comfortable farmhouse at Goudhurst there is no indication; he must have retained his love for the village of his birth, for when their time came both he and his wife were taken back to be buried there. It would seem that the whole family moved, though the two elder sons were now in their thirties and Walter was married just about this time; Hodges, who knew all the brothers, is hardly likely to have met them at Goudhurst. But whatever the reason the transfer was providential so far as what was to be the prime interest of Alfred's life was concerned. Goudhurst was not one of Kent's cricketing villages; there is no record of any Goudhurst team at this time, and in the early nineteenth century cricket was not necessarily part of a boy's upbringing. But Harrietsham was in the centre of the cricket world; it was close to Leeds, and only a few miles from Sutton Valence.

So here it was that Alfred Mynn learned to play cricket; and if, as seems probable, he had never touched bat or ball before the age of eighteen, his progress was remarkably speedy. When he first attracted the attention of John Willes his play was indeed anything but polished, and his friends roared with laughter to see him bowl, with his enormous run ending in the ball hurtling down anywhere but in the region of the wicket. But Willes saw his possibilities. The young man's natural athletic aptitude was striking and his physique of formidable proportions; he was six feet one inch in height, with the shoulders of an ox, and his strength was gigantic. Some years later, at the height of his cricket career and in the peak of condition, he weighed eighteen stone, and he was probably little less at the time he began to play at Harrietsham. His even temperament and friendly disposition were another asset in his favour.

So Alfred Mynn, soon to be the terror of batsmen throughout the country, began to learn the art of bowling. In spite of Willes's rebuff at Lord's, roundarm was on the increase, and it was clear that sooner or later it must be generally accepted. But the bowlers who followed the pioneer were mostly of slow or medium pace; no fast roundarm bowler of quality had yet appeared. Willes set himself to train young Mynn to be the first who would combine great pace with the new style. The first thing was to get him to bowl straight and not to waste his strength. The long and exhausting run was ruled out; Alfred was taught, probably to his chagrin at first if general human nature is any guide, to be content with six steps to the wicket: the famous approach which, when he had perfected it, so impressed all observers with its stately majesty. This, Willes convinced him, was enough. His great strength of arm and shoulder, combined with the rhythm of the movement, was quite sufficient to give him all the pace he needed.

Accuracy was more difficult to achieve. There is no style of bowling so liable to deviate from the straight and narrow path as roundarm. In both underhand and overarm the natural route of the ball is straight to the wicket, provided the initial impetus is correct; but the ball slung horizontally from wide of the body gives a much bigger margin of error. Thus it was that in the early days of roundarm wide balls provided a much larger proportion of a side's scores than was the case either before or since, and another problem faced the legislators in giving an exact definition of a wide: a problem that had not been raised when wides were few and far between. Mynn when Willes took him in hand was wildly erratic. Only hard work and constant practice could correct the fault. For this he was quite ready; he was devoted to cricket, and was prepared to give it every spare moment he had. But it was hard going, and for a long time after he began to appear in matches Alfred Mynn continued to bowl a proportion of wides that would lose a modern bowler his place in a side after a couple of overs.

About his speed there was never any doubt, particularly among batsmen who came up against him. He soon became the terror of the neighbourhood, and players who faced him successfully in practice boasted of their prowess. Willes was proud of the progress shown by his nephew Edward Hodges, and once before a game at Maidstone he had the stumps brought out and asked Mynn to bowl to the boy, who was then in his teens. The first ball was very fast but pitched to leg (perhaps intentionally), and Hodges managed to hit it right away. Willes then decided that that was enough for glory, and that the first ball should be the last. He had no desire to lose a promising nephew.

Within a few years of arriving at Harrietsham Mynn was playing regularly in local matches. His first appearances were doubtless in village games of which no record has survived; but he soon joined the Leeds club, and the first match recorded in *Scores and Biographies* in which his name appears was Leeds v. Meopham and Gravesend at Leeds Park on June 30, 1829. He was then twenty-two years old; the match was of little importance, and Mynn did not distinguish himself; but as it was his first recorded match the score deserves to be given in full:

LEEDS	*1st Inn.*		*2nd Inn.*
G. Hopper, c Nordish	7	st Nordish	0
W. May, b Harenc	2	b – Andrews	2
E. Beard, c Mullinson	0	b Harenc	9
T. Shirley, c Harenc	4	b – Andrews	0
B. Roper, Esq., st Nordish	1	st Nordish	9
J. Roper, Esq., not out	72	c Briggs	21
Alfred Mynn, Esq., b F. Andrews	1	c Dorrington	3
R. Thomas, Esq., b F. Andrews	33	b – Andrews	2
– Paine, c Dorrington	2	c Dorrington	1
H. Bates, c Dorrington	0	c Gooding	1
J. Lefeaver, b – Andrews	2	not out	1
Byes, etc.	10		0
	134		49

MEOPHAM and GRAVESEND	*1st Inn.*		*2nd Inn.*
– Banstead, b Bates	3	c J. Roper	3
– Buggs, b Bates	0	b Bates	0
– Dorrington, b Lefeaver	1	b Bates	3
T. Nordish, b Lefeaver	0	b Bates	1
C. G. Whittaker, Esq., run out	1	b B. Roper	0
– Pottick, run out	2	absent	
– Mullinson, c Bates	2	b B. Roper	0
C. Harenc, Esq., c B. Roper	6	b Bates	6
F. Andrews, Esq., b Bates	6	not out	6
W. Andrews, Esq., b Lefeaver	1	b Bates	5
– Gooding, not out	1	absent	
Byes	0		2
	23		**26**

Not much can be deduced from this record, which to judge
from the number of initials missing from the visiting side must
have been taken from the Leeds score-book (perhaps only the
home team kept the score). The fact that Mynn's name does
not appear as dismissing any batsmen does not necessarily mean
that he took no wickets, since at this time when a player was
caught or stumped only the fielder's name appeared on the
score-sheet. He cannot, however, have taken more than one in
each innings; while the fact that there were no wides in either
suggests that he did not do much bowling. It is tempting to
speculate that the absence of Pottick and Gooding in the second
innings might have been due to their final refusal to face Mynn's
bowling a second time, but the figures suggest no such thing. In
any case it was a resounding victory for Leeds, particularly as
two prominent Kent players, 'Dorrington' (probably the father of
the later county wicket-keeper whose name is more usually given
as Dorrinton) and the bowler C. Harenc, were playing for
the opposition. Against Harenc's bowling J. Roper's 72 not out
and 21, big scores for those days, must have been the result of
very fine batting indeed.

Scores and Biographies records three other matches in 1829 in
which Mynn's name occurs. The first was the return match
between Leeds and Meopham and Gravesend, played this time
at Meopham. Leeds won again, though by a much narrower
margin; Mynn made 8 and 1 not out, and again, though the

home team made only 15 in their first innings, is not reported to have taken any wickets. But in Leeds's two matches against Maidstone he did better. At Leeds Park, where Maidstone won in an innings, he bowled four batsmen and caught one; to Leeds's scores of 35 and 41 he contributed 6 and 2. Maidstone also won the return match, by 46 runs, Mynn bowling one Maidstone batsman in the first innings and bowling two and catching one in the second. His scores were 0 and 12, and as the Leeds second innings total was only 52 he was quite successful with the bat.

In 1830 he played in no game big enough to catch the vigilant eye of Arthur Haygarth, the industrious compiler of *Scores and Biographies*. But he certainly played in minor games, and his name was in the Leeds team announced in the *Maidstone Journal* for the 'Grand Match of Cricket', Hawkhurst Club *v.* Leeds Club, to be played on Hawkhurst Moor on August 2. The scores of this game, as doubtless of many others, have not survived. In the following year he is recorded to have appeared in only one match, Leeds and Bearsted *v.* Town Malling, making 8 and bowling two. Only one Leeds and Bearsted innings was completed.

Mynn evidently played little cricket in these two seasons. Perhaps domestic cares prevented him; he was married at Trinity Church, Newington, on December 15, 1828, to Sarah, daughter of Dr James Powell of Lenham. He was only twenty-one at the time and his bride was certainly under eighteen. Of Sarah Mynn and of their married life the record is a complete blank. It is hard to imagine Alfred Mynn, who was so loved by all who knew him, being anything but an affectionate and considerate husband, though Sarah must often have been a cricket widow. No doubt she was a retiring and unobtrusive person, whose activities were confined to her home and her family. In providing the latter she did her duty assiduously, but if Alfred hoped for a cricketer among his offspring he was destined for a series of disappointments. Mrs Mynn ran to daughters, producing five in quick succession at Harrietsham. Sarah was born in 1829, Mary in 1830, Frances in 1831, Eliza in 1833 and Laura in 1835.

A significant detail regarding these entries in the Harrietsham parish register is that at the time of the baptism of his eldest daughter, Sarah, Mynn is described as 'farmer'. In all subsequent entries he appears as 'gentleman'; the inference is that he had already given up his profession. Up till 1830 he was presumably working with his father on the Harrietsham farm; later in life he became a hop merchant. But for a long time he seems to have had no regular calling and to have left himself time to play as much cricket as he chose. He played always as an amateur, but it was common knowledge that he received financial assistance, both from the wealthy cricket patrons who admired him and from the clubs for which he played. But he can hardly have been so helped thus early in his career. What then was he doing, and how did he live? The answer must presumably be that he was supported by his father. Old William Mynn was an outdoor man and an athlete himself, and he was doubtless proud of his youngest son's growing prowess as a cricketer. He was evidently a prosperous farmer, and we may guess that, while Alfred no doubt gave his father casual help when he could, he was allowed a free hand to devote himself to cricket without the worry of having to earn his own living.

This would account for the fact that, after the birth of his first two daughters, Alfred began to play regularly in important matches. So far he had done nothing to set the cricket world on fire, but he was coming to be known as a dangerous, if somewhat wild, fast roundarm bowler. The height of his arm aroused no controversy, for in the meantime the new bowling had come to be generally accepted, albeit grudgingly by stalwarts of the old order, who denounced it as 'throwing'. The hot-tempered Willes had given up the struggle too precipitately; in the years that followed his discomfiture at Lord's the matter was thrashed out once and for all. More eminent cricketers than Willes adopted his style and improved on it; notable among them were William Lillywhite and James Broadbridge of Sussex. Lillywhite, the 'Nonpareil', who in the opinion of most good judges, himself included, was for many years the best bowler in England, was slow-medium in pace; he was probably the most accurate bowler who had yet appeared, and with a keen cricket brain he brought a new subtlety into the art of bowling. Broadbridge was rather faster and also a dangerous bowler, if not in the same class as the Nonpareil. He was also a fine, hard-hitting batsman.

With these two bowlers leading the attack, Sussex in the 1820s became the best county side in England. But in some quarters it was still considered that their pre-eminence was unfairly earned. The issue was fought out in 1827. Among the supporters of the new bowling was Mr G. T. Knight, an influential member of the M.C.C. Under his auspices it was arranged in this year that three 'experimental matches' should be played between Sussex and All England with the express purpose of testing the respective merits of the old and new styles of bowling.

The matches were to be played on three different grounds, and the first took place at Sheffield on June 4, 5 and 6. England fielded an all-professional team of moderate strength; Lillywhite and Broadbridge dominated the game, which was won by Sussex by seven wickets. For the next match, at Lord's, the M.C.C. strengthened the All England side, bringing in three leading amateurs – William Ward, H. Kingscote and G. T. Knight who had arranged the matches. Another member of the side was Ashby, who had opened the bowling with Willes in the momentous game of 1822. Both Knight and Ashby took wickets, but there is no mention of their having bowled roundarm. Perhaps, as the game was intended as a trial of rival methods, they restricted themselves to underhand. Sussex again won, this time by three wickets.

The reaction to the result shows the high feeling engendered by the new bowling. Although the three games had been specially arranged to provide an opportunity for a balanced judgement on roundarm, the eight professionals on the beaten side (Ashby astonishingly included), together with W. Caldecourt, who was perhaps one of the umpires, issued the following declaration:

> We, the undersigned, do agree that we will not play the third match between All England and Sussex, which is intended to be played at Brighton in July or August, unless the Sussex bowlers play fair – that is, abstain from throwing.

The declaration had been drawn up in the heat of the

moment, immediately after the defeat at Lord's. Wiser counsels prevailed. The players cancelled the declaration and apologized to the promoters of the match, and the final game took place at Brighton as planned. A few more changes were made in the England side, among the newcomers being the famous Squire Osbaldeston. This time the previous results were reversed; All England, dismissed in the first innings for 27, eventually won by 24 runs. But the effectiveness of the new bowling was more than ever vindicated, for Knight himself bowled roundarm and played a big part in the victory.

During the following months the battle raged in the columns of the *Sporting Magazine*; Knight vigorously defended the new bowling, while his chief opponent was William Denison, author of *Sketches of the Players* and other cricket books. In 1828 the M.C.C. capitulated. Law 10 was again altered, and the hand was allowed to be raised as high as the elbow; the back of the hand permitted to be uppermost, and the arm to be extended horizontally. The hand was still supposed to be below the shoulder, though how, if the arm be straight, the hand can be on a level with the elbow and not with the shoulder must be left to anatomists to elucidate.

Roundarm was now established, and the diehards were defeated. They continued, of course, to prophesy disaster; to them cricket was doomed, developing as it was into a rough-and-tumble brawl of brute strength and broken limbs. William Ward was one of the most voluble among them. Another was Thomas Lord, the founder of Lord's and the M.C.C., now in his middle seventies. He had seen the match at Brighton and left the ground in a fury, denouncing the new bowling and every-body connected with it. But the most outspoken of all was John Nyren, the chronicler of Hambledon. To him it was the end of all things. 'I am decidedly of the opinion,' he wrote, 'that if it be not stopped altogether, the character of the game will become changed. I should hope that such powerful and efficient members of the Mary-le-bone Club, as Mr Ward, etc., will determine, not only to discountenance, but wholly and finally to suppress it; and instead, to foster and give every encourage-ment to genuine, bona fide bowlers – men with a fine delivery.' In a more violent passage on 'the modern innovation of throwing instead of bowling' he prophesied that 'the elegant and scientific game of cricket will degenerate into a mere exhibition of rough, coarse, horseplay'.

After nearly a hundred years of overarm bowling it is easy to ridicule these champions of an earlier order. But it is natural for old players to love the game as they knew it in the days of their glory, and roundarm was after all a major revolution that was bound to give cricket a vastly different aspect. Yet the irony of it all is that, by modern notions, it was the old underhand bowlers who 'threw'. The objections to roundarm were purely to the height of the arm and hand; there was no word of bent arms or of jerking. Yet these were precisely the devices to which the greatest of the underhand bowlers resorted to impart extra pace or spin. Consider Nyren's description of David Harris, 'the best bowler ever known':

> It would be difficult, perhaps impossible, to convey in writing an accurate idea of the grand effect of Harris's bowling; they only who have played against him can fully appreciate it. His attitude when preparing for his run previously to delivering the ball, would have made a beautiful study for the sculptor. Phidias would certainly have taken him for a model. First of all, he stood erect like a soldier at drill; then, with a graceful curve of the arm, he raised the ball to his forehead, and drawing back his right foot, started off with his left. The calm look and general air of the man were uncommonly striking, and from this series of preparations he never deviated. I am sure that from this simple account of his manner, all my countrymen who were acquainted with his play will recall him to their minds. His mode of delivering the ball was very singular. He would bring it from under the arm by a twist, and nearly as high as his arm-pit, and with this action *push* it, as it were, from him. How it was that the balls acquired the velocity they did by this mode of delivery I never could comprehend.

It is hard to visualise this action, and still harder to see in it the grace with which Nyren endowed it. But it clearly could not have been performed without a jerk. However blasphemous the thought, one is forced to conclude that David Harris would certainly be no-balled by an umpire of the 1960s.

Similar testimony comes from that prolific cricket writer, the Rev. James Pycroft. Discussing William Clarke, Alfred Mynn's older contemporary and the finest underhand bowler of his day, and others of similar type, Pycroft writes in *Cricketana*:

> Clarke's bowling was delivered from the hip, with a little chuck or fling from the hand. Mr Budd's bowling, against which I have often played, was delivered the same way; as also was that both of Lambert and Warsop of Nottingham; and of Warsop, Clarke spoke very highly. The same delivery had also old Tom Walker, of the far-famed Hambledon Club, whose style was described to us by Tom Barker . . .

To us of a later day it must therefore seem that the revolution of the 1820s, so far from legalising throwing, ushered in a purer style of bowling. For it is now generally accepted that the essence of bowling, the factor that distinguishes it from throwing, lies in the straightness of the arm.

Alfred Mynn was never involved in these controversies. From first to last there was no criticism of the correctness of his action; his arm was described as being 'as straight as a piston-rod', and he never raised it above the shoulder. His tremendous speed came from his great strength and his ease of delivery; he needed no dubious devices to make him the fastest bowler in England.

The air, then, had largely cleared when, in 1832, Mynn made his first real impact on big cricket. It was the year of the Reform Bill, but if he ever gave a thought to representation of the people no hint of such preoccupation has come down to us. His dreams lay in a different sphere; his first ambition was to send bails flying from cricket stumps as often as he could and with the fastest deliveries he could achieve; his second was to hit the ball out of sight whenever he found himself at the receiving end.

The cricket season in those days started later and finished later than now; the plague of football starting in mid-summer had not to be reckoned with, and more attention was paid to the realities of the English climate. The first match in 1832 in which we find the name of Mynn took place on June 4: a one-day drawn game at West Peckham between the Gentlemen of the

West Peckham Club and the Gentlemen of Hadlow. Mynn (no initials were given in the *Maidstone Journal*, but it seems safe to assume that the player was Alfred) turned out for Hadlow, and bowled one batsman in West Peckham's first innings and bowled one and caught one in the second. His scores were 25 and 7, and in the first innings no other Hadlow batsman reached double figures. Details are lacking, but evidently he was becoming a formidable batsman as well as a bowler.

Six days later he appeared for Leeds Park against Hawkhurst. Both clubs were among the most distinguished in Kent, and the match was of much higher standing than might appear. It was honoured with a substantial account in *Bell's Life in London*, the leading sporting journal of the day, which now took notice of Mynn for the first time. The writer said:

On Friday, the 8th instant, a match was played on the Moor, Hawkhurst, Kent, between the celebrated Hawkhurst Club and the Leeds Park Club. From the well-known celebrity of the former Club, comprising amongst its members some of the best players in the counties of Kent and Sussex, a great display of skill was expected, in which the large assemblage of spectators was not disappointed. The bowling on both sides was beautiful, particularly on the Leeds side – their bowlers, Messrs Betts and Mynn, promising to become equal to the first-rate bowlers of the day (this being their second season only); and when it is considered they had to contend against some of the best bats in England (viz. the Messrs Mills and Messrs Wenman), they proved very effective. The fielding was excellent, and Clifford at the wicket was particularly admired, as he made woful havoc with his opponents' wickets. It being a friendly game, one day's play was considered sufficient to try the respective merits of the Clubs, and night coming on during the second innings of the Leeds Club put an end to this interesting game. The return match will be played at Park Gate, Leeds Park, near Maidstone, Kent on Tuesday next, when the lovers of cricket may expect a very great treat. The score at the conclusion stood thus: – Leeds Club, first innings, 39; 2nd ditto, only four wickets down, 39. Hawkhurst Club, first innings, 31.

There is little in the score sheet to bear out Mynn's effectiveness, as only one victim, Harding, is recorded as having fallen
to his bowling, while his companion, G. Betts, bowled four. But
as usual we cannot say how many wickets he took; he caught
R. Mills, and this may have been off his own bowling, while it
is possible that some of the four men stumped by W. Clifford
should be credited to him. If so, Clifford must have been a fine
wicket-keeper. Mynn was not the sort of bowler to expect many
stumping successes in the days before such refinements as pads
and wicket-keeping gloves.

His batting was not noteworthy. He made 4 in the first
innings, and was 5 not out in the second when night descended.

The return match duly took place at Leeds, but this time
Bell's Life did not deign to notice it. It was again unfinished,
but Mynn bowled three men in Hawkhurst's first innings. He
also stumped one, thus proving his versatility. He was certainly
never a regular wicket-keeper, but in those less formal days any
player might take up any position as convenience dictated.

He next appeared in two matches for Leeds and Bearsted
against Town Malling without doing anything spectacular.
Town Malling won the first by 33 runs and the second, at
Malling, more decisively. Leeds and Bearsted were all out for 45
(Mynn failed to score), and then Mynn bowled the first Malling
man, Hillyer, for 0. That was the last success for the visitors; the
great batsman Fuller Pilch, who played in both games for Malling
as a 'given' man, joined Lawrence, and the pair raised the score
to 112 without being separated, a big stand for the 1830s. At
this point Leeds and Bearsted gave up the match, as was not
infrequently done in the days when no rigid hours of play were
laid down. Pilch had made 72 and Lawrence 35. These were
the first matches in which Mynn and Pilch both played; they
were to be long and closely associated in the future.

Alfred's next appearance was in the first recorded of his many
single-wicket matches – against Thomas Hills, who had challenged him. Mynn won by a wicket, and later in the season he
beat Hills again.

But the greatest event of the season for the young Kentish
player took place at the end of August, when he was selected to
play for the Gentlemen against the Players. It was a remarkable

triumph for one so new to big cricket, and at this time of day it seems a little difficult to understand how he had achieved it. He had certainly done nothing spectacular, but in those days mere figures were perhaps taken less account of than to-day. Plainly the quality of his bowling, and possibly of his batting too, had greatly impressed the pundits and induced them to try him out in what was then the most important match of the season. It was not only his first appearance for the Gentlemen; it was his first match at Lord's.

He justified his selection. The Players won by an innings and 34 runs, but in their one innings Alfred bowled four of them out and had at least one caught off his bowling; his victims, more-over, were Marsden, Searle, Pilch, Beagley and Freemantle, all except the last being among the foremost batsmen of the day. It is significant that there were 19 wides. Going in number nine, Mynn made o in the first innings, but in the second his was the top score, even though it was only 10. The Gentlemen were all out for 57 and 60.

In only two other matches this season does his name occur. The first was Leeds and Bearsted v. Dartford at Bearsted, and this time Pilch was playing as given man for the home side, three other prominent players, Wenman, Cobbett and Mills, being given to Dartford. This was the first match in which Walter Mynn is recorded as playing; as he failed to score in either innings, he hardly enhanced the family reputation. Alfred did better. In the first innings he made 29; W. May made 30 not out, and nobody else more than 9 in the total of 105. Dartford replied with 92 (including 12 wides); Mynn bowled two batsmen, but the most surprising thing about the innings was that no fewer than six were bowled by Pilch, who was not renowned as a bowler. Leeds and Bearsted were skittled out for 18 (Alfred made two more than his brother), and the match was left unfinished with Dartford 24 for seven, giving promise of a keen finish.

Two incidents are recorded in this match. Pilch dismissed Richard Mills in Dartford's second innings with a 'wonderful catch' at long leg. The second incident occurred in the same innings when the result hung in the balance and excitement was mounting. Haygarth tells the story in *Scores and Biographies*:

37

In the second innings of Dartford, Mr E. Winter was in fifth man, seventeen runs to fetch, and the wickets dropping fast. Mr Winter cut at an off ball, and struck the top of the stumps so violently that the whole of the three wickets were nearly in an horizontal position. In striking, however, the end of the bails had been driven so fast into the grooves of the stumps that all held firmly together. The blow was heard, and the effect on the wickets perceived, by the numerous interested spectators, but who were not aware of the fact of the bails not having fallen. Their indignation was uncontrollable when Mr Winter continued his innings – nor could the match be proceeded with till the explanation was fully made!

The last match was another of high quality, Gentlemen of Kent (with Wenman, Mills and David) against Gentlemen of England (with Lillywhite, Pilch and Cobbett) at Chislehurst in September. In addition to the given men there were top-class cricketers playing for both sides: G. W. Norman, Herbert Jenner and C. Harenc for Kent, and William Ward, H. Kingscote, H. E. Knatchbull and R. Kynaston for England.

Mynn held his own in this illustrious company. The match was hotly contested, the Gentlemen of Kent eventually winning by nine runs. Alfred's scores were 14 and 3 out of totals of 68 and 80. In the Gentlemen of England's first innings of 76 he bowled three (only Pilch with 32 reached double figures) and in the second of 63 he bowled four and caught two.

Clearly by the end of this season he was gaining in confidence as well as in skill. Henceforth he was a major figure in the cricket world.

CHAPTER II

TRIUMPH AND DISASTER

*

Richard Daft is cool and cautious, with his safe and graceful play;
If George Griffith gets a loose one, he can send it far away;
You may bowl your best at Hayward, and whatever style you try,
Will be vanquished by the master's steady hand and certain eye;
But whatever fame and glory these and other bats may win,
Still the monarch of hard hitters, to my mind, was Alfred Mynn!

To say that at the time of Alfred Mynn's first appearances in big cricket the game was in a state of transition is to state the obvious; in a constantly developing game all ages are ages of transition. Yet the phrase 'middle ages of cricket', applied by many recent writers to the period between, roughly, 1820 and 1870, has a real meaning. The ancient heroic days of Hambledon, illuminated by the glittering pen of Nyren, had become a memory, and the headquarters of cricket had shifted from Hampshire to London; while the age of test matches and the county championship, and the transformation brought about by the career of W. G. Grace, were still in the future. Moreover the introduction of roundarm bowling did, as we have seen, bring about a fundamental change in the game. The period which embraces the whole of Alfred Mynn's career really was an age of its own.

What, then, was cricket like in the 'middle ages'? In its main features it had assumed the form we know to-day. Except for the limitation that the bowling arm must not be lifted above the shoulder the laws were much as they are now, though many amplifications and minor emendations were to be introduced in the years to come as experience dictated. The implements of the game too had largely assumed their permanent form. The original two stumps and single bail, developing from the 'wicket

39

gate' of rural life, had given place to three stumps and two bails well back in the eighteenth century; the straight bat had succeeded the old curved club when length bowling came in. The bats of 1830 were longer and heavier than those in use now, but their shape was similar. Pads, batting gloves and wicket-keeping gloves had not yet appeared, but it would not be long before they were made necessary by fast roundarm bowling such as Mynn's. For a long time yet, however, there would be many batsmen (one of the last was C. I. Thornton, born in 1850) who would scorn to protect themselves even against the fastest bowling.

Cricket was a rustic game. Most grounds were in small villages, generally in the loveliest settings, and there was high feasting in the neighbourhood when one of the not over-frequent matches took place. Cricket followers swarmed into the village from miles around, coming on horseback or on foot, the gentry in their carriages, their gigs, phaetons and tilburies. Taverns did a roaring business, and the landlord of the nearest inn to the ground would advertise a 'good ordinary' for all and sundry. Spectators sat on benches or on the grass under the trees, pots of ale by their side. Partisanship was fierce, and sometimes passions ran high. Rowdy scenes were not infrequent, and it was far from unknown for a match to be interrupted, and even abandoned altogether, owing to angry spectators invading the field of play.

These were the less amiable manifestations of the spirit of the day. But more often than not good sportsmanship prevailed among players and supporters alike. The countrymen who made up both bodies were unsophisticated, independent of spirit and vehement in their loyalties, and sometimes these loyalties, helped by good ale, got the better of them. But first and foremost they were out for enjoyment, and they had no wish to spoil the enjoyment of others. Many are the tributes to the good humour with which cricket was generally played and watched, and the whole atmosphere portrayed is one of rural carnival and simple pleasure sadly missing from the more formal and solemn contests that take place in deadly seriousness in crowded towns at the present day.

Lord's, for all its grandeur as the headquarters of the game, fully partook of this rustic atmosphere. St John's Wood was not yet a built-up area, and there was not a single house in the immediate neighbourhood of the ground. The Tavern was there from the date of opening in 1814, but the pavilion, which had been burned down in 1825 and since rebuilt, was little more than a large shed. There were two ponds on the ground, and penned in one corner was a flock of sheep, whose duty it was to keep the grass cropped. Rollers were as yet unknown.

Certain rules were enforced. Hodges remembered seeing Lord Frederick Beauclerk at Lord's with a fox-terrier and being told that Lord Frederick, who was a law unto himself, was the only person allowed to take a dog on to the ground. Horses were in a different category. Noblemen and gentlemen rode or drove into the ground, and stabling was provided. Here, however, things did sometimes get out of hand, as we learn from a passage in *Bell's Life* in 1834. The paper's reporter concluded his report of the Kent and England match in that year with a stern reproof:

> We have frequently observed, with regret, that gentlemen, despite of repeated cautions, continue to make a horse-road over that part of the ground, at Lord's, which their own sense, if they had any, would at once tell them must be in violation of the rules, from the fact of it proving extremely injurious to the ground. At the conclusion of the play on Tuesday, two persons in a gig actually drove through the *centre* of the ground, but were justly *backed astern* by Dark, the proprietor, amid the cheers of the gentlemen present.

Cricket was ruled by the wealthy patrons of the game, most of whom were pillars of the M.C.C. It was they who had raised it from the village green, and before the time of Hambledon such men as Frederick Prince of Wales, the second Duke of Richmond and the second Duke of Dorset, with his brother Lord John Sackville, had used their money and influence to support cricketers and get together the finest teams that could be assembled. Later came the third Duke of Dorset, the Earl of Tankerville and Sir Horace Mann, patrons of Hambledon itself.

On these rich lovers of the game the prosperity of cricket depended. Many of them were fine players themselves, and the first professionals were their retainers. A promising cricketer

41

would be given a post as gardener or gamekeeper on the estate of a cricketing nobleman, his nominal duties being subordinated to his main one of playing in his employer's team; from there it was an easy step to being paid for playing cricket alone. Clubs and players alike were financed by the patrons, though at least up to Mynn's time most professionals, if they were not groundsmen or ground managers, had some additional trade to support them.

By 1830 there were many such patrons. Lord Sondes has already been mentioned, and another Kent magnate was the Earl of Darnley, whose seat was Cobham Hall. The Blighs were keen cricketers for many generations, and the fourth Lord Darnley, a great eighteenth-century magnifico, was a liberal supporter till his death in 1831 and a player of moderate ability; his brother, General Edward Bligh, was a far finer cricketer, a leading batsman at the turn of the century.

Other prominent patrons were the Earl of Winchilsea, Squire George Osbaldeston, Colonel Lowther and Lord Grimston. But by far the most influential figure in cricket in the 1830s was the Rev. Lord Frederick Beauclerk. This remarkable cleric, fourth son of the fifth Duke of St Albans and a descendant of Charles II and Nell Gwynn, was vicar of the town from which the family title came, but there is little evidence that he ever let his calling or his parochial duties influence his conduct. Cricket was his life; it was also one of his sources of income, for he gambled on every match and left no stone unturned to ensure that he won his bets. He was the greatest cricketer of his day, a brilliant hitter and a wonderfully accurate slow underhand bowler; born in 1773, he played till he was over fifty, and to the end of his life (he died in 1850) his voice carried more weight in cricket counsels than that of any other man. He was as much the supreme arbiter and elder statesman of the game as Lord Harris a hundred years later or Sir Pelham Warner in recent years. His character, however, was very different from theirs.

Lord Frederick was generous to others as well as to himself, and as a patron his name stands high. At the same time it is a little difficult to understand the general respect in which he was held; for throughout his career his conduct was almost uniformly outrageous. Stories abound of his tantrums on the field, his unscrupulous wagers, his utter lack of what would be regarded as sportsmanship to-day. His reaction to Tom Walker's batting and his attitude to roundarm bowling have already been recorded. It is also related that he frequently refused to run for his batting partner's hits, being interested only in his own, and that he tried to bribe the scorer to cook the score when his side or he himself was doing badly. A typical anecdote concerns a single-wicket match of 1810, in which he backed himself for a considerable sum, with T. C. Howard for partner, to beat Squire Osbaldeston and William Lambert, the best professional cricketer of his time. Osbaldeston fell ill on the morning of the game, but Beauclerk refused to postpone it, demanding that Osbaldeston should 'play or pay'. For once he was outmanoeuvred; Osbaldeston, though a passenger, made a nominal appearance on the field, and Lambert took on the opposition virtually single-handed. He finished off the game by bowling wides (which did not count in the score) until Lord Frederick flew into one of his characteristic rages and threw away his wicket.

One cannot but feel that these episodes were not the whole story. Obsequiousness to high rank and admiration of his play cannot in themselves have been enough to counteract behaviour which would have led to ostracism at a not so much later date. The fact remains that Lord Frederick was held in affectionate regard by many cricketers high and low. There must have been some magnetism in his personality that was uncommunicable by the written word; he must, in fact, have been a 'character', an attractive rogue whose indefinable personal qualities forced his friends to overlook his consistently disreputable actions.

A less spectacular but more admirable figure was William Ward, wealthy banker and member of parliament for the City of London. Ward was a many-sided man, but cricket was one of his main interests. He was one of the finest students of the history of the game and formed a great collection of records, most of them unfortunately lost when the Lord's pavilion was destroyed by fire. As a player he was in the first rank. A big man and a fine hitter, he used a bat weighing four pounds, with which he made some of the biggest scores of the early nineteenth century. Born in 1787, he went on playing in minor matches almost up to his death in 1849; but his fame depends chiefly on two great feats. In 1820, playing at Lord's for the M.C.C. against Norfolk (then a very strong county), he made 278; not only was this the highest individual score recorded up to that time, but it was not excelled at Lord's for more than a hundred years. Five years later he made the first century for the Gentlemen against the Players, 125 at Lord's; this achievement can be measured by the fact that up to 1860 only three centuries were made in this match, both the other two being for the Players (by Beagley and Saunders).

Ward, while a dictatorial figure, was the most generous of patrons, and to him cricket owes as great a debt as to any man in the history of the game. For it was he who saved Lord's from obliteration. Thomas Lord, founder of the M.C.C., was a Catholic Jacobite whose family had been financially ruined after the 1745 Rebellion. He was a keen cricketer, but he started the club and ground as a commercial speculation, for which cricket patrons put up the initial money. The venture had its ups and downs, but by 1825 Lord decided that it was time to sell out. He was actually negotiating for the sale of the ground as a building estate when Ward stepped in and asked him his price. 'Five thousand pounds' was the answer; Ward signed a cheque there and then and became the owner. In his custody Lord's was safe.

The gratitude of the cricket world was expressed in some anonymous lines, typical of the pleasant doggerel that was then a feature of sporting literature:

> And of all who frequent the ground named after Lord,
> On the list first and foremost should stand Mr Ward.
> No man will deny, I am sure, when I say
> That he's without rival first bat of the day,
> And although he has grown a little too stout,
> Even Matthews is bothered at bowling him out.
> He's our life-blood and soul in this noblest of games,
> And yet on our praises he's many more claims;
> No pride, although rich, condescending and free,
> And a well informed man, and a city M.P.

Cricket's dependence on private capital and on wealthy

sportsmen had one unfortunate result. Not all those who laid out their money on the game were disinterested patrons; the gambling fraternity exerted an influence at one time that, had it not been checked, could have been irretrievably disastrous. It was not betting itself that was the trouble, but the evil practices to which it led. The same problem has arisen in other sports, and the doping of racehorses that has aroused so much comment in recent times had its counterpart a hundred and fifty years ago in the buying and selling of cricket matches.

Mr H. S. Altham has described the whole unedifying business in *A History of Cricket*. Large sums were wagered on individual matches, and the bookmaker came more and more into the picture. The worst place was Lord's, and the worst time soon after the turn of the century. The bookmakers sat in front of the pavilion to take the odds, and the punters thronged about them, caring nothing for the game but only for the stakes. Mary Russell Mitford gave a vivid description of these men: 'There they stood, railed in by themselves, silent, solemn, slow, playing for money; making a business of the thing; grave as judges, taciturn as chess players – a sort of dancers without music'.

The result was inevitable. Bookmakers and punters alike, anxious to safeguard their money, turned their attention to individual players. Young professionals up from the country, living beyond their means in London, were easy game. Leading batsmen were bribed to throw away their wickets, leading bowlers to bowl for runs instead of for catches. In days when first-class players were few and sides unevenly balanced a substantial outlay on one or two men might make the result of a match tolerably certain.

Fortunately the evil, if not nipped in the bud, was checked before it had grown to such proportions as to make reform impossible. 'The rogues,' as Mr Altham says, 'overreached themselves.' As their activities became more blatant they fell out among themselves, and their squabbles provided the concrete evidence that the M.C.C. wanted. Lord Frederick Beauclerk, who was always ready to denounce the vices of others, took a leading part in stamping out the corruption, and the climax came in 1817, when William Lambert, the greatest professional batsman in England, was convicted of selling matches and warned off Lord's for ever. He was a great loss to cricket, and his fate reminds one of that of Bobby Peel eighty years later; but on a long view his fall did untold service to the game.

By Mynn's time the worst was over. Lambert's fate had a salutory effect, and the gamblers became more circumspect. But probably an even more potent fact was the all-round improvement in the standard of play. As the game grew in popularity, more players appeared who were worthy to take their places in representative elevens, and teams in big matches no longer consisted of one or two great players and nine or ten nonentities. To make sure of a match the gamblers would have to bribe the whole team and this was fortunately as a rule not financially worth while, besides laying the culprits open to almost certain detection.

Yet it was some time yet before this evil completely disappeared. Some of the wealthier spectators still attempted to corrupt the honour of the leading professionals, and occasionally amateurs too. Pycroft, on the authority of Felix, tells an illuminating story of an approach by an unnamed sporting baronet to (of all people) Alfred Mynn. He presumably knew of Mynn's habitually impecunious condition, but he grievously mistook the character of his intended victim. The story is particularly interesting as being the only instance recorded of Mynn's losing his temper. The baronet approached him with 'a foul proposal', which in Pycroft's context can mean only one of selling a match. Mynn blazed. 'Get out of my sight,' he exclaimed, 'or, Baronet as you are, I am sure I shall be knocking you down.'

There Pycroft's account ends. It would be nice to know with how much alacrity the tempter withdrew himself. To be knocked down by Alfred Mynn was not a fate to recommend itself to even the boldest bad bart.

Perhaps the greatest difference between the conditions of modern and 'medieval' cricket lies in the state of the pitch. Wickets in the first half of the nineteenth century were, by present-day standards, appalling. Little care was expended on them, the grass was cut by any primitive method available, and as the turf was cut up by the play so was it left. Some grounds of course were better than others; Lord's was one of the worst. The M.C.C. have always, and rightly perhaps, been a conservative body, and in the early days all modern improvements were looked on with the deepest suspicion. There seems to have been an idea that any alleviation of the natural hazards of 'the noble and manly game' would be an effeminacy unworthy of cricket headquarters. The rough sheep-cropped wicket that had been good enough for the first M.C.C. players was good enough for their successors. Consequently, in a period of low scores, we find those at Lord's among the lowest. Which makes William Ward's great innings in 1820 all the more remarkable.

On such pitches fast bowlers were a terror; the wonder is that the batsmen, without any form of artificial protection, managed to stand up to them at all. One ball might get up head-high, the next shoot straight along the ground. Pycroft recorded of Lord's:

> So far did this hardness and roughness affect the bowling that I have known a ball from Mr Mynn rise over batsman and wicket-keeper into the long-stop's hands; and I have seen Beagley, so celebrated as a long-stop, with a man to back him up; nor can I forget Caldecourt, when ordered to play on an emergency, saying that he would as soon stand up for a fight, for the blows he expected.

The long-stop of course was universal, and not only for the fast bowlers. The wicket-keeper invariably stood up to the wicket, without pads or gloves, but with a few exceptions he did not attempt to take balls on the leg side, and it would be many a year before he felt able to dispense with his auxiliary. Long-stop was in fact considered one of the most exacting positions in the field; it was a place of honour, allotted to the brave and the strong, and great long-stops such as Beagley, Dean and Walter Mynn were heroes of the day.

Even before the advent of roundarm fast bowlers had their terrors. The word 'lob' nowadays signifies innocuous bowling, but some of the old underhand men achieved tremendous pace. Squire George Osbaldeston and George Brown, who ran his own ground at Brighton, were in the opinion of many, including Pycroft, as fast as any who came after them. Of Brown it was related that once in practice he was bowling with a man stopping the ball behind the wicket with a coat in his hand; one of his

47

fastest balls went through the coat and killed a dog on the other side.

It would be a mistake, however, to imagine that bowling at this time was sheer speed and nothing else. The best batsmen learned to cope with brute force even on the roughest wickets, and the mere slingers were not the most successful. Bowlers like Mynn certainly relied mainly on pace, but length and accuracy played their part. Men such as Lillywhite and Clarke, moreover, proved that slow bowlers could be as devastating as fast. Where the ground was so unpredictable they placed comparatively little reliance on spin; it was subtlety, variation of length and the psychology of studying a batsman's weakness that got them their wickets. Accuracy and intelligence were the bowler's weapons; the pitch supplied the rest.

Batting, like bowling, was simple and straightforward. A batsman, as a general rule, was either a forward or a back player; he seldom ventured to vary his play in accordance with circumstances. Here again it was not the mere rustic hitter who did best. Keeping the ball out of the wicket on the rough pitches called for infinite skill and resource, and there were great stylists like Pilch and Guy as well as great defensive players.

The principal scoring strokes were drives and cuts. The pull and the hook were frowned upon as in rather bad taste; a generation later E. M. Grace was to scandalise the purists by shameless immorality in this respect. But there were two strokes, indulged in by the best batsmen, which have long disappeared from cricket. One was the draw, which can best be described as a leg glance made between legs and wicket, although occasionally it might also have been a tap more in the direction of square leg. It was rendered possible only by the normal stance of the day, the batsman standing up straight with his padless legs well away from the bat. With the introduction of pads, the consequent narrowing of the gap between legs and bat, and possibly too the general increase in the speed of bowling, the stroke fell into disuse; as early as 1871 we find it alluded to as the 'old-fashioned draw'. But in the thirties and forties it was much admired as one of the most skilful and stylish strokes in the game.

The under-leg stroke was a variant of the draw, made by

lifting the front foot and gliding the ball underneath. It was obviously a risky stroke, and probably never so widely used as the draw, but among those who employed it is said to have been Alfred Mynn.

Scoring was slow compared with that of the 'Golden Age' some seventy years later, though not when judged by the standards of the present day. There was big hitting, but the need for watchful defence on difficult wickets made it hard to score off a high proportion of balls, and thirty runs an hour for an individual batsman was considered a very good rate.

Grounds were unenclosed and there were no boundaries. Every hit had to be run out; if the ball went among the crowd the fielder had to chase it, and there were occasional fisticuffs when he was too rough in doing so, or when he suspected a too partisan spectator of deliberately baulking him. The absence of boundaries was another factor conducing to low scores; having to use his legs to register every run tired the batsman and called for more stamina than the conditions of later days. Yet cricketers were tough; they played for long hours, as long as the light lasted, and no player regarded himself as a tottering veteran at the age of forty. Games were of varying duration. The usual arrangement for a big match was two days, but if the match was not finished, and the players not needed elsewhere, a third and occasionally a fourth was employed.

The dress favoured on the field is familiar from old prints. The knee-breeches and stockings of Hambledon had almost died out; the famous amateur E. H. Budd and the Nottinghamshire fast bowler Samuel Redgate are recorded to have been the last to wear them. The new generation wore long trousers, unpressed and supported by belt or braces; white or coloured shirt with stiff collar and sometimes a flowing cravat; black or brown shoes or boots and top hat. The hat was at this date usually a white beaver; the black silk variety came slightly later. But it was not long before the less unwieldy straw hat came into vogue. Charles Wordsworth, captain of Oxford in the first University Match in 1827, was said to be the first to introduce the new fashion, and Alfred Mynn was among those who followed him.

Those who have regularly worn a top hat know how comfortable it can be, but it would certainly seem a rather cumbrous headgear for cricket. Bowlers are usually shown wearing it, but it is to be presumed that at any rate the fast men took it off when they bowled. And for batsmen it had its hazards; there are at least two instances of a player being out 'hat knocked on wicket'.

There was no regular programme of matches. Games of major importance were normally arranged by private negotiation; teams were often far from representative and sometimes bore little relation to the name under which they took the field. The system of 'given men', prominent players put in to strengthen a club or county side, was general; but often a member of a team who was not described as 'given' had little connection with the side for which he was playing. If he was available he was just asked to play.

A few big matches had become regular annual events. The most important was Gentlemen v. Players, which was first played in 1806, not again till 1819, but thereafter regularly except in 1826 and 1828. This match, always played at Lord's, carried more prestige than any other; it was the only annual representative game in which the greatest players in England were assembled. Yet at this time it was hopelessly one-sided. There were good amateur players in the country, but they were few compared with their opponents and they could not compete on equal terms. Various devices were tried to make the game even; sometimes the Gentlemen were 'given' two or three of the best professionals, sometimes they played with sixteen or seventeen men against the Players' eleven; and in 1832 the experiment was tried of giving them smaller wickets to defend. But even so the Players usually won.

There was no University Match. It had been played in 1827 and 1829, but then came a gap. The next game did not take place till 1836, and it was another two years before the unbroken series began.

Odds were given in many matches, eleven men against fifteen, eighteen, twenty-two, occasionally even more. Freak experiments were sometimes tried, and there is one case known of two men playing eleven and beating them.

Of the teams that regularly played throughout the season the most important was the M.C.C. The club put up a side composed of its members (though occasionally there were given men); M.C.C. teams were not just sides of leading cricketers chosen by the club committee. Marylebone was an aristocratic institution; amateurs of humble station such as Alfred Mynn never aspired to membership. But most of the upper strata of leading cricketers belonged, and it was the regular team for some of the best amateurs of the day. William Ward still played occasionally, and so did E. H. Budd.

Budd, though now past his best, was still the finest amateur all-rounder in the country. He was a brilliant hitter, who once hit a ball clean out of the first Lord's ground in Dorset Square and on another occasion drove a ball for nine without an over-throw; a successful medium-paced bowler, something between underhand and roundarm, and a splendid field. He was a great athlete, one of the fastest runners of his day and excelling at tennis, boxing and shooting. Budd was the bosom friend of George Osbaldeston, who was also sometimes still seen in M.C.C. teams at this time.

A much younger M.C.C. player was Sir Frederick Bathurst, who first played for the club in 1831, at the age of twenty-four, and soon made his name as a fast roundarm bowler, one of the best who had yet appeared; he was also a dangerous hitter. Other prominent members of the side were the Grimston brothers, headed by the eldest, Lord Grimston; Roger Kynaston, a strong cover-point hitter, and Henry Walker of Southgate, a left-arm bowler and the first cricketer in the family his nephews were to make famous.*

A name that often appears in M.C.C. sides is that of Benjamin Aislabie, secretary of the club. Aislabie, who is immortalised in *Tom Brown's Schooldays*, was one of the great characters of cricket. He became honorary secretary of the M.C.C. in 1822, and never was a club secretary more popular. He was an enormous man, who weighed nearly twenty stone; when batting in his later days he always had a runner, who however seldom had much to do. Aislabie radiated charm and good humour, was the author of a number of cricket songs, and used to sing them at club dinners. He seldom made a run, never took wickets, and was much too bulky to be of use in the field; but he was so

* See below, page 181.

devoted to the game that he played whenever he got the chance, and went on playing till he was sixty-seven. His achievements were summed up in some contemporary verses, in which affection shines clearly through the ridicule:

'Tis Aislabie's boast to form most of the matches
In this way at cricket; he makes but few catches,
But still he's contented some money to pay
For the sake of encouraging excellent play.

He doats on the game, has played many a year,
Weighs at least seventeen stones, on his pins rather queer;
But he still takes the bat, and there's no better fun
Than to see him when batting attempting to run.

Another popular character at Lord's who may be mentioned here was William Caldecourt, who came from Hampshire and was a fine hitter and medium-paced bowler; also a famous long-stop. He became a ground boy at Lord's at the age of nine and a practice bowler at fifteen, in 1818. For the rest of his life he was closely associated with the M.C.C. He occasionally played as a given man, but in the main he was noted as a coach and a groundsman; he was also the most celebrated umpire of the time. No professional cricketer was more highly respected.

The M.C.C. met all manner of opponents: counties, clubs, schools, and such scratch teams as 'the Bs', a team composed of players whose names began with B. As a random selection we find them about this time playing against Middlesex, the East Surrey Club, Suffolk, Norfolk, the Gentlemen of Kent, the West Kent Club, Norwich, Bury St Edmunds, Harrow School, Oxford University, the Bs and Cambridge Town. In 1831, with Pilch and Lillywhite as given men, they played All England, losing by an innings and 47 runs.

Most big cricket was club cricket. The M.C.C. was only one, though by far the most influential, of the many clubs which could field a first-class team. County clubs were only just coming into existence, but all the cricketing counties had their clubs with their star players. Kent was particularly rich in such clubs. Best known from the social angle was the West Kent, with its excellent ground at Chislehurst, patronised by that most prolific of cricket families, the Normans. The West Kent

could meet the strongest teams on equal terms; so could
Benenden, where the redoubtable Edward Gower Wenman was
in charge. Town Malling boasted a ground which was to
achieve great fame a few years hence, and other strong clubs
were Leeds Park, Dartford, Hawkhurst, Penshurst and Sevenoaks.

In Surrey there was the East Surrey, which had a more or less
regular fixture with the West Kent. Others were Reigate, Epsom
and Godalming. The leading Sussex club was at Brighton, where
George Brown was in charge of the ground; there were also
Duncton and Midhurst. The East Hampshire used to play the
Surrey clubs, while in East Anglia the chief centres were
Norwich, Bury St Edmunds and Cambridge. In the North and
Midlands the principal clubs were Sheffield Wednesday, Man-
chester, Liverpool and Nottingham.

Matches tended to be localised. In the days before railways
it was no easy thing to transport a team a long distance to a
match, and it happened only when the game was of exceptional
importance or when some wealthy patron was prepared to bear
the whole expense. In general clubs played only their close
neighbours, and the leading players of one county would seldom
set eyes on those of equal fame in some other part of England.

Yet though county clubs were mainly in the future, and the
county championship still more so, county matches did take
place with tolerable frequency. They were semi-impromptu
affairs, with the teams selected by local patrons or officials of
the various clubs; no central organisation existed. And here
again most contests were local. Kent, Surrey, Sussex, and
occasionally Middlesex and Hampshire, played each other;
Norfolk, Suffolk and Cambridgeshire; Yorkshire and Nottinghamshire. There was little contact between the three groups.

The connecting link, such as it was, was the Marylebone
Club. M.C.C. teams, amply financed and composed of the rich
and leisured, travelled all over the South and East Anglia to
play their cricket; less often to the North.

Sussex were at this time probably the strongest county:
chiefly, but not entirely, owing to the predominance of Lillywhite and Broadbridge. Lillywhite, the 'Nonpareil', stood out
among all bowlers in England. He was born in 1792, so in the

53

1830s he was already past his first youth; but he was to go on for many years yet, still taking more wickets than any other man and with no diminution of skill or subtlety. He was accuracy personified, and Arthur Haygarth in *Scores and Biographies* opined that in the whole of his long career 'he did not deliver more than half-a-dozen wides'.

The word of 'Lilly' was law at Brighton. He was a little man, five feet four inches in height, but in the high Gladstone collar and top hat in which he always played he was a figure of colossal dignity. He firmly declared himself to be the best bowler in England, and even if anybody had felt inclined to dispute the point he would not have dared to contradict the great man to his face.

In addition to Lillywhite and Broadbridge Sussex had another great bowler in George Brown, lessee of the Royal Brighton Cricket Ground. As he was nine years older than Lillywhite, it is surprising to find him playing in the 1830s, but he still turned out for Sussex teams for some years to come, and still apparently continued to bowl at great speed. He was, with the possible exception of Osbaldeston, the fastest of all the old underhand bowlers, and a dashing hitter to boot. He was six feet two and a half inches tall and weighed fifteen to eighteen stone; it was written of him:

> The one Brown, a tailor, yet strong and complete,
> No ninth of a man, and stands more than six feet;
> A free slashing hitter, who holds it a crime
> To get any less than six runs at a time;
> And a capital bowler – some people will say
> The fastest and surest we have in our day.

Another great Sussex player, now at the start of his career, was Tom Box, the wicket-keeper. He was born in 1809, and by 1832 he had made his name as just about the best stumper in England, his only rivals being Wenman and Jenner, both Kentishmen. He was also a more than useful bat.

Sussex, Surrey, Kent and Hampshire can claim the longest history of the cricketing counties. To Surrey belongs the honour of the earliest unquestionable mention of the game, dated 1598; though Kent, with a 1610 reference, is not far behind. In the early eighteenth century Kent produced the finest eleven, though Richard Newland, the first great batsman of recorded history, was a Sussex man. To Hampshire, where cricket was played as early as 1729, belongs the glory of Hambledon: a glory to some extent shared by Surrey, since many of the Hambledon players were actually Surrey men.

At the time when Alfred Mynn began his career, however, only Sussex and Surrey of these four figured prominently as county sides. Matches were played between them in the early 1830s, and Surrey played England in 1831. Thomas Sewell was the best Surrey bowler, and among the batsmen were two talented cousins, William Searle and James Saunders; Saunders, however, a splendid left-handed stylist, died in 1832 at the age of twenty-nine.

But probably the finest, and certainly the most interesting, cricketer who played for teams in Surrey at this time was an amateur, also left-handed, a schoolmaster of Flemish origin named Nicholas Wanostrocht, who always played under the name of 'Felix'. Although he was born in 1804 he had not yet come to his full stature, but was already known as a brilliant cutter and a fair slow underhand bowler. Much more will be said about him in due course.

Kent, although cricket had never ceased to flourish there, was in a temporary decline so far as the county side was concerned; it is a curious fact that no Kent county match is recorded between 1829 and 1834. There were of course plenty of fine cricketers playing for the various clubs, of whom the most celebrated were the batsman and wicket-keeper E. G. Wenman, his amateur counterpart Herbert Jenner, the hitter William Dorrinton and the bowlers William Hillyer and Charles Harenc, the latter of whom was at this time an Oxford undergraduate. Their merits will be fully discussed when we come to deal with Mynn's own county.

Hampshire played a number of matches, but their great days were over. They had, however, a great batsman in Thomas Beagley, maker of the first Gentlemen v. Players century, now past his best but still a power to be reckoned with. Caldecourt also sometimes assisted them.

Middlesex played few matches as a county. When a team

was raised it usually consisted of M.C.C. members and London professionals; among the latter the slow bowler James Cobbett, a native of Surrey and a member of the Lord's staff, was most consistently associated with Middlesex.

Among the East Anglian counties Suffolk were the least distinguished, and no player of distinction appeared for them at this time. Cambridgeshire had two fine batsmen in Francis Fenner* and Daniel Hayward; Fenner was also a good fast roundarm bowler. Hayward, the first cricketer to bear that famous name, was a very good player indeed, a splendid hitter and a brilliant field. He was born and played his early cricket in Surrey, the county to which his famous grandson was destined to return as one of the greatest professional batsmen of all time.

Norfolk were stronger than their two rivals, but this was chiefly owing to the fact that they possessed, in Fuller Pilch, by far the finest batsman in England. Pilch was the youngest of three cricketing brothers, all tailors, and he first came into the public eye in 1820 when, at the age of seventeen, he was a member of the Norfolk team against which William Ward played his great innings of 278 at Lord's. Fuller made only 0 and 2 and was overshadowed by his eldest brother Nathaniel, who scored 52 out of Norfolk's second innings of 72, but he dismissed one M.C.C. batsman in the first innings and three in the second with his slow roundarm bowling. Yet his batting must even then have been notable, for it cannot have been long after this match that the inevitable poet penned his prophetic lines:

Another bold tailor, as fine a young man
As e'er hit a ball and then afterwards ran,
Is from Bury St Edmunds, and Pilch they him call,
In a few years 'tis thought he'll be better than all.

At present his batting's a little too wild,
Tho' the 'Nonpareil Hitter' he's sometimes been styled;
So free and so fine, with the hand of a master,
Spectators all grieve when he meets a disaster.

* He opened, in 1846, the Cambridge University ground which bears his name.

The spectators at Lord's in 1820 must have grieved twice, but the prophet's prediction soon came true. During the next ten years Fuller Pilch brought batting to a perfection never yet realised. Beldham of Hambledon had been hitherto accepted as the model of a classic batsman, but even the old brigade were generally agreed that Pilch was Beldham's master. He was a fine figure of a man, a little over six feet tall and well proportioned. His style was the best type of forward play; he made the most of his reach and drove with commanding ease. In an age of small scores his were consistently high.

The northern counties were as yet largely cut off from those of the south, but there were great cricketers to be found there. Even at that time Yorkshire could put a formidable side into the field. Their best player was Thomas Marsden, a dynamic left-hander, a very fast underhand bowler and a slashing hitter. A younger and less spectacular cricketer was James Dearman, a fair bat and, although he was only five foot two inches in height and ten stone in weight, a fast roundarm bowler.

Lancashire's great days were in the future, but Nottinghamshire could boast two of the best bowlers in England. William Clarke was as much the dictator of his county as Lillywhite was of Sussex, and as distinguished among underhand bowlers as Lillywhite among roundarm. What he did not know about cricket was not knowledge, and his craft in plotting the downfall of batsmen was inexhaustible. Although he was born in 1799 and had been playing in big cricket since 1816, he was hardly known as yet to southern cricketers; but in the north he was a giant. He was not universally popular, for he was domineering and cantankerous and he always knew best. But he was held in respect if not in affection. In some ways he reminds one of Wilfred Rhodes of a much later date.

Nottinghamshire would have been a terrifying side to batsmen with Clarke alone, but there was also Samuel Redgate. Redgate was three years younger than Alfred Mynn, but he made his name in the north as early as Mynn did in the south, and he was the only roundarm bowler who rivalled him in pace. His speed was indeed tremendous, and though less consistent than Mynn he was probably at his best the more dangerous of the two. Lord Verulam (the former Lord Grimston) was asked in later life which was the faster, Mynn or Redgate, and his reply was: 'I was hit by both and I really cannot say which hurt the most.'

Such was the scene, and such the principal actors, when Alfred Mynn took his place among the finest cricketers in the land. That was his position by 1833, and in his first recorded match that year he showed his quality. He was playing at Lord's for the Gentlemen of Kent against the M.C.C. and was largely responsible for the visitors' victory by an innings and six runs. The M.C.C. were dismissed for 57 and 49, four of them in the first innings and six in the second being bowled by Mynn. Out of the Kent total of 112 Mynn made 19, and as Lillywhite was playing as a given man for the M.C.C. this was a creditable score. The *Sporting Magazine* reported that his batting 'was much admired'.

The return match was played at Chislehurst and Mynn again put up a good performance, bowling five batsmen in the M.C.C.'s first innings and one in the second and making 29 (out of 117) and 0. The Gentlemen of Kent won again, this time by eight wickets. The most surprising thing about the M.C.C.'s two innings was that Fuller Pilch failed to score in either; he was caught at slip in the first innings and at the wicket in the second, but we are not told off what bowler or bowlers. In his immediately preceding game, a single-wicket match against Marsden, he had overwhelmed the Yorkshireman by scoring 78 and 100.

These were Mynn's best matches, but he bowled well throughout the year. He was again chosen for the Gentlemen, and so, for the first time, was his brother Walter. The choice at first sight seems surprising, for Walter had made no big scores, even by the modest standards of the time, but he was making his name as a steady bat, whose solidity and lack of nerves probably made him a more useful cricketer than his scores suggest. He and Alfred often went in first together, a hitter and a plodder being then considered the ideal opening partners. Neither brother, however, distinguished himself in this particular match.

The most interesting game this season was All England *v.* Sussex at Brighton in August; 'more exciting play,' said the

Sporting Magazine, 'was seldom, if ever, witnessed'. England went in first and scored 89, William Ward with 22 and Pilch with 14 being the highest scorers; Alfred Mynn was run out for 0. When Sussex batted Alfred, bowling very fast, quickly demolished the first four batsmen. The later men played better, particularly Tom Box, who mastered Mynn by playing forward to him and made 13 not out. Towards the end of the innings, which closed for 52, a very fast ball from Mynn got up suddenly and hit Marsden, fielding behind the wicket, in the mouth. Marsden left the field, but was able to bat and field in the second innings.

England went in again and this time it was the turn of old George Brown, the Sussex fast bowler. He hit the wicket with the first ball of the innings, and England were soon all out for 30. Mynn emulated Pilch in an earlier match by being leg-before-wicket for 0; it was twenty-four years before he again achieved the ignominious 'spectacles'.

Sussex were thus left 68 to get to win, and when their ninth wicket fell they were still 16 behind. Goad now joined Lillywhite and the last pair, amid great excitement, brought the score to 66. With one run to tie Mynn sent a fast ball, wide of the wicket, down to Goad. It passed the wicket-keeper and the batsmen ran, but the injured Marsden picked up cleanly and threw in to the wicket-keeper, who put the wicket down. Lillywhite had not made his ground, but there was an appeal to the umpire at the bowler's end on the ground that the ball had been a wide. It was decided in favour of Mynn, however, and England were declared the winners by one run.

During the following two years Alfred Mynn's reputation continued to grow. *Scores and Biographies* records thirteen matches in which he played in 1834 (as well as two single-wicket matches), a bigger number than in any previous year. He did little with the bat, but he bowled consistently well, while one entry of 'st. Mynn' shows again that he occasionally kept wicket. Kent played as a team once more, and Mynn was in the county side that met England at Lord's. He was again playing for England when they beat Sussex at Lord's by 183 runs, and he bowled five men out and made 10 and 14 not out; the hero of the match was Pilch, who made 105 not out in England's first innings of

59

229. In the return match at Brighton Mynn for some reason did not play, and an entry in *Bell's Life* shows what his absence from a representative game had come to mean. 'Long before the commencement of the present contest', the paper recorded, 'betting was greatly in favour of England; but, as the time approached, and the fact became known that Mr Harenc (who, as a bowler, stands pre-eminent) and Mr Mynn (also an excellent bowler) were not to play, the odds dwindled down, and settled at 2 to 1'.

He was still playing in plenty of local matches in Kent, and doing the brunt of the bowling. The *Sporting Magazine*'s cricket commentator, in his summing-up of the 1834 season, wrote:

Mr Mynn, *one* of the best of our *amateur* projectors of the ball, has improved greatly of late in both *that* art and in hitting. The average of his wide balls is greatly reduced; and, though still far from a safe wicket, he has added some degree of steadiness to his powerful hitting, and bids fair to become 'Alfred the Great' in skill as well as in stature.

The following year saw two changes in the Laws of Cricket. The barren argument about elbows and shoulders had continued to rumble, and the M.C.C. decided to amend the rule and settle the matter (they hoped) for good and all. The amended Law 10 read as follows:

The ball must be bowled. If it be thrown or jerked, or if the hand be above the shoulder in the delivery, the umpire must call 'No Ball'.

The second innovation was the introduction of the follow-on. The side batting second were to follow their innings if they were 100 or more runs behind. No option of enforcement was allowed to the side leading.

Alfred Mynn had a good season, taking wickets consistently. He played for the Gentlemen, and regularly for Kent. His best performance was for the county against Benenden, when he bowled eight batsmen, caught one, and made 19 and 44. Kent won by three wickets.

Alfred was now, at the age of twenty-eight, at the height of his form, and it will be well at this point to take note of what contemporaries had to say about his style of play. Apart from brief remarks in the sporting papers we have no description actually written as early as 1835, but one of the first is from the pen of William Denison, who had known Mynn well from the beginning of his career. Writing in 1846, he said of his entry into big cricket:

> Not merely was he an excellent and powerful bat, but his bowling came upon the mass of the cricket public with startling effect. There was not anything like it either for extraordinary rapidity of pace with the uphand bowling, or accuracy of length and general steadiness. Ere the batsmen who did not know him could oftentimes get their bats down to play his bowling, the stumps were shivered, or the ball was in the hands of, or past, the 'long-stop'. There had been no bowling, never any of the same character, for several years, which demanded that vast quickness of play requisite to make any stand against the 'great bowler'. . . .
>
> For some time after Mr Mynn had come out, his bowling was occasionally distinguished by wildness, a vice which he has long since overcome by practice, and a better exercise of judgment; and the result is that whilst in his earlier days, *speed* would appear to have been his first aim of attainment, and hence the 'wide balls', in the last few years his bowling has been constantly *at* or near the wicket, but at a lessened pace, and of course with fewer 'wides'. Nevertheless he is still the fastest of our public bowlers.

All writers agree on the grace of his bowling action and his dignity on the field of play. The Rev. Edward Bligh, of the famous Kent cricketing family, wrote:

> It was a treat to see his stately march, ball in hand, some six or seven long yards up to the wicket, and then deliver about the fairest and fastest ball ever trundled; this broke in generally from the leg a bit, but the peculiarity was the rapidity with which the ball rose after pitching; grass was longer in those days than it is now, and an occasional shooter when looking out for your head or body made such a bowler at times very difficult. As a bowler few have excelled him.

Richard Daft, who played with him in later years, said that in spite of his great weight there was nothing 'clumsy or awkward in any of his movements, which were, on the contrary stately and dignified at all times'. Another notable description appeared in a memoir published after Mynn's death in the *Sporting Life*:

How perfectly grand was the advance of Mr Mynn to the wicket to deliver the ball – the very earth seemed to tremble under his measured, manly, and weighty stride, as, with form upright, his vast chest expanded, 'thud' would come down the left foot on the sward, the right arm would shoot out, and, with a majestic sweep, round, low, and as fair as law X itself, away shot the ball, as if propelled from a Whitworth gun, and, if straight, woe to the unlucky wicket opposite.

Perhaps the striking tribute to his bowling came from Fred Gale, 'The Old Buffer'. 'I must see another man who stands six feet two,' wrote Gale in *Echoes from Old Cricket Fields*, 'of gigantic but symmetrical figure, standing up his full height, taking six stately steps to the wicket, and bringing his arm round well below the shoulder, and sending the ball down like a flash of lightning dead on the wicket, before I can ever believe that there is or has been a greater cricketer than Alfred Mynn.'

Mynn always bowled round the wicket, as did most bowlers before the introduction of overarm. William Caffyn in his *Seventy-One Not Out* gave a plan of the field he set. The wicket-keeper stood up to the wicket, as was the custom even with the fastest bowling; of course there was a long-stop. Mynn had only two slips, one close in and one almost level with long-stop; point was slightly forward and cover-point almost behind him; mid-on and mid-off were level with the bowler's wicket and nobody was behind them. Short-leg, almost square, and long-leg completed the field.

One curious report regarding Mynn's bowling remains to be considered: the story that his fastest balls 'hummed like a top'. This could be set down as part of the posthumous legend that grew up with the memories of his tremendous speed, but for the fact that at least three contemporaries, two of whom were first-

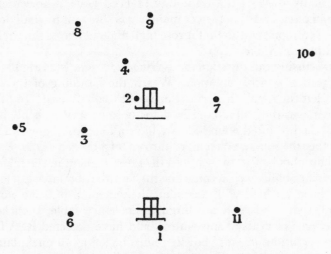

*Field as placed for the fast bowling of Alfred Mynn
(No. 1). From Caffyn's Seventy-One Not Out.*

class cricketers and all sound judges of the game, recorded their conviction of its truth.

One of these was V. E. Walker, the most eminent of the seven brothers whose joint efforts established the Middlesex County Cricket Club. Walker was quite definite on the matter when discussing Mynn with A. W. Pullin ('Old Ebor') at the close of last century. 'There was a distinct hum as the ball left his hand,' he said. 'I suppose that was due to the way in which he held the ball. I have never observed the same hum in the bowling of any other man. Some people have thrown doubts upon this peculiarity of Alfred Mynn's delivery, but what I say is quite correct.'

Edward Dowson, the old Surrey player, was equally emphatic; Mynn, he said, used to impart a peculiar spin to the ball which made it hum. And he added: 'I have often mentioned this matter to some of my old cronies, and one or two have borne me out, but others have said they never heard it. All the same, I maintained that Alfred Mynn could, and did, make the ball actually hum in its flight through the air.'

Finally there is the testimony of Fred Gale, who watched Mynn often and closely over many years: 'he sent the ball down like a cannon shot, so that it rose high and cut across the wicket, and hummed like a top.'

Discussing this question in his *History of Cricket* Mr Eric Parker suggests a possible solution. 'Was it the handling of the ball as it left the hand.' he writes, 'or was it the ball itself? In other words, was the ball altered in shape in some way, possibly by a scratched or lifted seam? . . . we have all heard, at one time or another the sound, when hit or thrown, of a broken cricket ball.'

This may be the answer, and the improvement in the making of cricket balls may account for the fact that no later cricketer has been credited with a similar phenomenon. But one would think that, had such a solution been conceivable, such keen observers as Walker and Gale would have detected it. Alfred Mynn's 'humming-top' bowling must be left as an unexplained mystery.

His bowling had one bad effect on contemporary cricket. Young bowlers who watched him were inspired to emulate his speed, for which many of them were physically quite unsuited. Mynn's height and strength made him a natural fast bowler; smaller men who tried to bowl as fast succeeded only in being wild and dangerous and in lending justification to the gloomy predictions of the old-time pessimists that with roundarm bowling cricket would degenerate into a vulgar spectacle of brute force. The danger was exaggerated; but for a time the game suffered, and wide balls proliferated just at the time that the chief figure was curing himself of bowling them.

No batsman felt very comfortable against Mynn when he was at his best and fastest, but two amateurs are recorded to have mastered him more often than most. One was William Ward, and the story of how he did it shows how earnestly he took his cricket even in his later years. When he was to play against Mynn he would practise by getting one of the professionals to bowl fast to him from a distance of nineteen yards. After that he felt able to face Alfred at twenty-two.

The second batsman was the Hon. Robert Grimston, who would take two bats to the wicket, a heavy one to face Mynn and a lighter for the other bowlers. This he found most effective.

He was a jovial character, and Gale records how, when asked to play for the Gentlemen of England against the Gentlemen of Kent, he said that he would and that he would 'bang old Mynn, and would make him run after the ball'. Gale continues the story:

> ... He did play and did 'bang old Mynn', driving him right away to Dark's corner at Lord's, and scored five off the second ball he had, and Mynn had to run after it himself, as his balls were so crushing that a long field was hardly ever needed.
>
> 'Do you know the name of my heavy bat, Mr Mynn?' he asked.
>
> 'No!' said the Kentish giant.
>
> 'This is Mynn's master'.
>
> Good-natured Alfred Mynn laughed and got punished again more than once, and F. Fredericks (the Rev. F. Fagge), a medium dodgy bowler, was put on and got Mr Grimston's wicket.
>
> On returning to the pavilion a little chagrined – for he hated slows – he put down his bat and said, 'wish that Fred Fagge was dead'.
>
> 'What a bloodthirsty expression!' exclaimed one of his friends.
>
> 'Well! I don't wish him *dead*, but I wish they would make him a Bishop and we should see him no more'.

So there was one batsman at least who was capable of knocking Mynn off his length.

Of Mynn's batting we have fewer descriptions. He was of course above all a hitter; but he was not a mere slogger. While primarily a driver he had a good range of strokes, and with his keen eye and great reach he was feared by bowlers. Pycroft tells us that his 'great stature and enormous strength made a bat quite a feather in his hands; therefore his hand, beyond that of any other player, rivalled the quickness of his eye, and he could hit by sight certain short lengths which no one else could attempt'. And he adds that Hillyer and Redgate, great bowlers both, considered him the most dangerous hitter they had ever encountered.

The *Sporting Life*, in its obituary memoir, said that 'Mr Mynn always appeared to us as never putting forth his huge strength to its full tether, but to merely "tap" the ball;–but such tapping, they used to deepen the field for him when hitting, as they *now* do for Griffith'.

Edward Bligh also mentioned this 'tapping'. 'As a bat,' he wrote, 'if not so sure a scorer as Pilch, his defence was thoroughly sound and good, while he had a trick of lifting the ball out of most ordinary cricket grounds, or giving it a quiet tap for four, equal to a big hit for most men, under his leg or otherwise, which was always useful. Alfred Mynn was, in fact, one of the best bats of his time, as well as bowler.'

Fred Gale says that he was a brilliant cover-point hitter. According to both Daft and Caffyn he was much better against fast bowling than slow, and Caffyn adds that he had not sufficient variety of stroke to deal with the best slows.

As a fielder Mynn, who bowled through many an innings, was generally in the slips, and in that position Fuller Pilch said there was never a better: 'one hand was good enough for Alfred, for his fist was about the size of a small shoulder of mutton.'

But when all is said it was as a personality of the cricket field that Alfred Mynn really shone. In old prints of elevens of the time it is his majestic figure that immediately catches the eye. And so it was to his contemporaries. It was not simply a matter of size; Walter Mynn was almost as big a man as his brother, and George Brown was probably bigger. The stateliness of his bearing doubtless had something to do with it; 'he mingled with the players like a king amongst them all'. But there was more to it than that; somehow the commanding and endearing character of the man made itself felt as soon as he stepped on to a field. Wherever he went he was followed by a crowd of hero-worshipping small boys, and when a Frenchman visited Lord's out of curiosity his excited cry was heard when the great man appeared: 'Voilà le grand Mynn'.

His popularity was immense; so was his devotion to cricket. He was always ready to bowl all day, and when his opinion was asked on the advisability of increasing the number of balls to the over (then four) he drew himself up – 'in his Porthos-like manner,' says Lord Harris – and said: 'For myself I should like 100 balls to the over.'

His kindness and geniality were equalled by his convivial love of the good things of life. Wherever Mynn was there were laughter and beer. His tastes were simple but ample, and his friends were constantly amazed at his capacity for eating and drinking. His recipe for a cricketer's diet was 'beef and beer'. And when asked if that were all he thought for a moment and then added: 'Well, perhaps beer and beef.' The words recurred again and again in his talk. Once he came upon his young contemporary, Caffyn, drinking tea; he was shocked to the core. 'My boy,' he said sternly, 'beef and beer are the things to play cricket on.'

The late Alfred Cochrane, in an interesting article in an early number of the *Cricketer*, pointed out that Mynn was a new type of amateur. In the early years of last century most amateurs were men of wealth and position, and though relations on the field were habitually cordial there was a great social gulf between the 'gentlemen' and the 'players'. Mynn in his own person bridged that gulf. He aspired to no higher rank than yeoman or 'gentleman farmer', and he was on the easiest and friendliest terms with his professional colleagues. Yet in that age of rigid class distinctions his cricketing fame and his sunny nature made him a favourite with men far above his station in life. Noblemen such as Lord Frederick Beauclerk, Lord Sondes and the Hon. Frederick Cavendish were proud to call him their friend.

The season of 1836 was the year of Alfred Mynn's greatest triumph – and his greatest disaster.

In the earlier part of the season he was in good form, but did nothing spectacular. He took, as usual, plenty of wickets, including those of many of England's best batsmen, but he made no scores worthy of mention. He did well for the Gentlemen and played as a given man for the M.C.C. And he was an automatic choice for the two great games of the season, the North *v.* South matches.

This was a new venture. The fame of the great Yorkshire and Nottinghamshire players had been spreading, and the M.C.C. decided the time had come for a test of strength between two representative sides, the first game to be played at Lord's and the second in an as yet undecided centre in the north.

The matches excited enormous interest. The northern champions were unfamiliar to southern spectators; William Clarke in particular, though now thirty-seven years old, had never yet played at Lord's. The first game was played on July 11 and 12 and resulted in a win for the North by six wickets; the South's scores were 97 and 69, and the North's 109 and 58 for 4. Mynn's part was not particularly distinguished. He made 0 and 8 not out and took no wickets in the first innings; in the second, however, he took three of the four wickets that fell. In this year, for the first time, catches and stumping were credited to the bowler in the score sheets at Lord's, though the custom was not yet general; there was still no detailed analysis kept. James Dark had recently taken over the proprietorship of Lord's from William Ward and was busy introducing all sorts of improvements, re-decorating the pavilion and planting trees round the ground.

The North's victory made the excitement even greater as the date of the return match approached, and the interest was enhanced by a first-class row that blew up over the location of the game. The principal promoters of the two matches were Lord Frederick Beauclerk and Benjamin Aislabie, acting for the M.C.C., and Captain R. Cheslyn, a Leicestershire cricketer, for the North. Leicestershire had put a fair side into the field about ten years earlier, but at this time the county could boast no prominent cricketers and was of little account in the cricket world. Leicester had, however, an excellent ground, with reputedly the best wicket in England. Captain Cheslyn saw the possibility of so important a match encouraging a revival of interest in Leicestershire cricket, and as he had done most of the work on the northern side in arranging the games he considered himself justified in proposing to the M.C.C. that the second game should be played at Leicester. Beauclerk and Aislabie agreed, and the fixture was arranged for August 22.

The result was an explosion from Nottingham. Five Nottinghamshire players, headed by Clarke and Redgate, had been in the North's team at Lord's, and the county considered that there was only one suitable place for the second match, the Forest ground at Nottingham. Clarke took the matter up at Lord's, but without success. Thereupon the *Nottingham Journal* jumped into the fray, denouncing the insult to the city and proclaiming that 'it is the general opinion of those who understand the game of cricket that Nottingham can not only play any county in England, but might venture to enter the field against the combined counties south of the Thames'. The *Leicester Herald* answered with spirit, and soon a full-blooded newspaper war was in progress.

Passions rose higher and higher; the climax came on July 26, when a public meeting was held at Nottingham with the mayor, Mr Thomas Wakefield, in the chair. The enormity of the affront to Nottingham was discussed with the utmost solemnity, and a resolution was passed 'that, as the town of Nottingham has, for a long series of years, by the liberality of its contributions, supported the practice of the game of cricket, by which the present players have been enabled to attain to the highest skill, this meeting has heard with great regret that Leicester is spoken of as the place where the return match between the Northern and Southern counties is to be played (although six Nottingham men are engaged, and not a single player from the County of Leicester has been chosen), and this meeting therefore earnestly requests the Noblemen and Gentlemen who superintend the arrangements to do an act of courtesy and kindness by selecting the Nottingham ground as the place for playing the return game on August 22nd.'

A copy of this resolution was sent to the M.C.C., with a letter from John Hicklin, on behalf of the New Forest Club, demanding that the match should be at Nottingham. Aislabie, however, replied as follows:

Sir, – In answer to your letter of the 26th inst. (to which is annexed a copy of certain resolutions passed on that day at Nottingham) I am desired by the parties who made the Northern and Southern matches to observe that a promise having been made to the proprietors of the ground at Leicester to play the Return Match there, it cannot under any circumstances be broken.

I shall be very happy if, upon some future occasion, a match of equal interest may be made to be played at Nottingham.

This was decisive, and nothing more could be done to soothe

the ruffled feelings of the citizens of Nottingham. But the slight continued to rankle, and matters were not improved by the jubilant crowings of the *Leicester Herald*, particularly in its detailed account of the match itself.

Curiously enough it seems never to have been suggested that the game should be played at Sheffield, the other great centre of northern cricket. Perhaps the town was considered too far from London to be a practical proposition.

A week before the great game was due to be played the M.C.C. played Sussex at Brighton, and it was here, in a splendid match, that Alfred Mynn flashed into form as a batsman that he had never approached before. The M.C.C. side was hardly representative of the club as it included no fewer than five given men: the brothers Mynn, E. G. Wenman, Tom Barker of Nottingham and Fuller Pilch.

The M.C.C. won the toss, and the two Mynns opened the batting. Walter had improved greatly as a batsman and the brothers scored 60 before they were separated. Alfred had some luck, being missed twice, but he hit finely while Walter defended. One of Alfred's hits met catastrophe; the handle of his bat snapped right off, and, as *Bell's Life* put it, 'away went bat after ball, while, to the great amusement of the company, he ran with the handle and touched the crease'. Walter was first out, having scored 15, and three runs later Alfred followed with 45 to his credit. The excellence of the Mynns' batting was shown by the collapse that followed. Pilch made 14, but he was never comfortable against Lillywhite, and the rest made only 14 between them. With five extras the M.C.C. total was 93.

Sussex batted more consistently and made 140, Broadbridge being top scorer with 32 not out. Alfred Mynn was in his best form with the ball and took four wickets, all bowled. He was described as making 'sad havoc with the wickets'.

The M.C.C. went in again at one o'clock on the second day, and again the brothers Mynn made a fine stand. It was an hour before the first wicket fell, Walter being bowled by Broadbridge for 18. James Dark then made 15 and Pilch a quick 20, but Alfred Mynn far outshone all his colleagues. He was seeing the ball beautifully and seemed to do just what he pleased. His leg hits were magnificent, and even Lillywhite could do nothing against him. He was in for nearly five hours and scored 92, much the biggest score he had yet made in any sort of match. The M.C.C. total was 176.

This left Sussex 130 to get to win, and the final innings was exciting. Eight wickets were down for 63, Alfred again bowling splendidly; but Thwaites and Lillywhite made a fine stand for the ninth wicket which nearly brought victory. Thwaites made 31 and Lillywhite 24 not out, but at last Alfred Mynn brought the innings to an end and the M.C.C. won by seven runs. Alfred took five wickets, three bowled.

And so came the great game at Leicester, with Mynn at the height of his reputation. The teams had been announced a week before, and the name of Clarke was conspicuous by its absence. Rather curiously, no contemporary writer comments on this; the obvious reason would seem to be, particularly in view of his belligerent temperament, that he had refused to play because the match was not at Nottingham. However, if such had been the case it is hardly to be credited that the *Leicester Herald* would not have made some capital out of the matter; so perhaps there was some other explanation. The North were to miss his bowling sadly before the match was over.

The North had a strong team, with Pilch, Redgate, Dearman, Barker and Marsden. The leading South players were Alfred Mynn, Lillywhite, Beagley, Hillyer and E. G. Wenman. As with the majority of games in this era, we are given no indication who the captains were. One may hazard a guess that they were Pilch and Lillywhite; the convention that the captain should always be an amateur was still in the future.

August 22 was a Monday, and by Sunday night Leicester was full to capacity. Every form of conveyance had been be-spoken a week before; hundreds of Nottingham enthusiasts walked the whole way between the two towns, and at the end of each day tramped off to Loughborough to find somewhere to sleep. By ten o'clock on Monday there were five thousand people on the ground, including a large number of ladies. Lord Frederick Beauclerk and Aislabie were there, and so was William Ward; 'so great an assemblage of Cricketers,' wrote the *Leicester Journal*, 'from all parts of the Kingdom, were seldom or ever known to be collected together.'

Everybody was eager to see the Titan who had just performed such prodigies at Brighton, and who was now the most celebrated cricketer in England. He had never played in the North before, and when he came out to practise the crowd gathered round to watch.

Here it was that disaster occurred. There were no nets in the 1830s, and practice took place on the field of play. Mynn was batting to the bowling of Dakin, a Leicestershire professional, when he hit a ball hard on to his right ankle. The blow was painful, but did not at first appear to be serious. Soon, however, the ankle swelled up, and Mynn came reluctantly to the conclusion that he would not be able to turn out that day. His ankle was bound up by a local doctor, and he was taken off to his quarters at the Anchor Inn.

This was a big disappointment to the crowd, but as it happened he was not needed that day. The South won the toss and went in to bat. Redgate got two quick wickets, but Mills, E. G. Wenman and Taylor played steadily, particularly Wenman, and the South score mounted. The dinner interval was at three o'clock, and soon after play was resumed it began to rain. Play was abandoned for the day with the South score at 97 for 6, Milliard of Sussex and the veteran Beagley batting.

Mynn felt better after his day's rest, and next morning he came to the ground. Beagley was out soon after play began, being succeeded by J. G. Wenman, and a little later Milliard, after making some good hits, was caught by Pilch for 31, the best score of the innings. And now, with eight wickets down and to the delight of the crowd, in came Mynn. He was limping a bit, but did not seem badly hurt; he was allowed to have a runner, Taylor of Sussex, who had lost his wicket the day before.

His innings started with a minor comedy that kept the spectators in good humour. Lillywhite had remarked to his neighbours that once he started hitting Mynn would forget all about his leg and his runner, and so it proved. Mynn hit the ball away, and he, Wenman and Taylor all charged up the pitch. The muddle was sorted out, but the same thing happened again several times before the end of the innings. Mynn was in great form, and after Wenman was out he and Lillywhite had a lively last-wicket stand before Lillywhite was run out. The innings closed for 165, with Mynn 21 not out.

The North now went in and lost five wickets for 14, Pilch and Marsden failing to score; but Garratt, Dearman and Redgate pulled the game round and kept their side in the game; the final total was 110. Lillywhite bowled well, E. G. Wenman kept wicket brilliantly, and the South's fielding was, as the *Leicester Herald* reported characteristically, 'applauded by every person present, except the Nottingham gentry'.

Mynn's innings had done his ankle no good, and he found the strain of bowling too much for him. Yet he did bowl, for he took the wicket of the last man, the amateur Creswell.

The South went in again at five o'clock on Tuesday evening and lost one wicket before the close, Mills being brilliantly caught by Rothera.

Next morning Mynn's leg had swollen to an alarming extent, and it was painful for him to walk. Almost any other player would have dropped out of the match, but Alfred would play as long as he could stand, and he was determined to bat. He was not called upon at once, for E. G. Wenman played a fine innings and was well supported by Hillyer and Taylor; but at the fall of the third wicket at noon, with the score 91, he limped to the crease. Presumably he must again have had a runner, but we are not told anything about it. At any rate there is no mention of his forgetting his injury and running up the pitch. He was in continuous agony, but the form he had found at Brighton, and maintained in the first innings at Leicester, did not desert him now. From the first he attacked the bowling, and it seemed that he could do nothing wrong. Wenman had been batting beautifully and continued to do so; but now he was overshadowed. It was Mynn, Mynn, all the way.

Redgate was bowling his fastest and best, but he might have been a village novice for all the effect he had. 'That was Mr Mynn's day, that was,' he said admiringly later; 'it mattered not what length I bowled him – the better I bowled, the harder he hit me away.'

In increasing pain Mynn went on. Redgate was not the man to take deliberate advantage of a disabled opponent, but bowling at his pace and on a wicket of that day, even on the comparatively smooth one at Leicester, he was bound to hit the batsman fairly often, and Mynn's leg got a terrible battering. Yet he would not retire. Wenman was out, and Taylor, and Clifford, all after making some runs; still Mynn went on hitting the bowling all over the field. 'It is useless for us,' said the *Leicester Herald*, 'to pass any encomiums on the play of this gentleman, suffice it to say that never since Leicester stood, has his equal been seen. A determined hitter, he seemed to do what he liked with the ball. Fast or slow bowling had no effect on him. A lively gentleman player, everyone seemed gratified and satisfied, if we except the Nottingham visitors.'

Amid wild enthusiasm he passed his century, and still he went on hitting. Then at last J. G. Wenman was bowled by Redgate and Lillywhite by Jarvis, and the long but glorious ordeal was over. Mynn had batted without giving a chance for a little under five hours, about the same time as at Brighton, and made the great score of 125 not out, out of 223 put on while he was in.

He staggered towards the tent, and as he did so Lord Frederick Beauclerk came to meet him. Mynn asked him to go with him into the tent, and there he showed him his leg. Lord Frederick was appalled at the extent of the injury; the leg was so swollen and inflamed that it seemed impossible that any man so disabled could have stood up for so long. He sent at once for a fly and told Mynn to get home as quickly as he could and send for the best medical attention. There was a stage coach leaving Leicester for London, but with his huge frame and stiffening leg it was impossible to get Mynn into it. So he was hoisted up and laid flat on the roof of the coach where the luggage should have been; and in that position he travelled from Leicester to London. The roads of the 1830s were not of the best, and one hardly cares to think of the suffering he must have endured on that journey.

By the time he arrived any idea of going on into Kent was out of the question. He could get no further, and was laid up at the Angels Tavern in St Martin's Lane.

The match went into the fourth day, a rare occurrence. The North made a creditable reply, Pilch and Redgate both batting well. But they were all out at 1.30 for 151, and the South had won by 218 runs. The full scores of this great match were:

SOUTH	1st Inns.		2nd Inns.
R. Mills, b Redgate	11	c Rothera	1
W. Hillyer, b Redgate	0	b Redgate	16
J. Cobbett, b Redgate	7	c Creswell	8
E. G. Wenman, b Marsden	30	c Garratt	64
J. Taylor, c Good	12	b Redgate	26
G. Milliard, c Pilch	31	b Redgate	12
W. Clifford, c Baker	7	b Jervis	21
T. Beagley, b Redgate	19	b Redgate	1
J. G. Wenman, b Redgate	10	b Redgate	14
A. Mynn, Esq., not out	21	not out	125
W. Lillywhite, run out	7	b Jervis	0
Byes, wides etc.	10	Byes, wides etc.	26
	165		314

NORTH	1st Inns.		2nd Inns.
T. Barker, b Lillywhite	11	b Lillywhite	21
E. Vincent, c Lillywhite	1	b Cobbett	22
G. Jarvis, b Lillywhite	2	b Lillywhite	7
F. Pilch, b Lillywhite	0	lbw	28
T. Marsden, run out	0	c Beagley	21
W. Garrett, b Lillywhite	16	b Lillywhite	10
B. Good, b Lillywhite	8	b Cobbett	0
J. Dearman, c Beagley	41	b Lillywhite	0
S. Redgate, b Milliard	22	c Milliard	28
C. Rothera, Esq., not out	4	b Cobbett	2
C. Creswell, Esq., b Mynn	1	not out	8
Byes etc.	4	Byes etc.	4
	110		151

The *Leicester Herald* fired a parting shot at Nottingham:

Upon the whole, we feel delighted at the issue, for it has done one thing, lowered the pride of the Nottingham players. – They appeared to us complete second raters, and when watched by the beautiful fielding of the South, had very little chance indeed. They must never again think of calling a public meeting at Nottingham, with the Mayor in the Chair, and talk such nonsense & fulsome stuff about 'the *invulnerable* players of Nottingham'. . . .

Mynn had scored 283 runs in two successive matches – four

innings and only twice out. Such figures would be impressive to-day; in 1836 they seemed almost miraculous. Never had such batting been seen, and the country rang with his praises.

But the hero of the hour lay painfully in bed at a London tavern, while eminent surgeons debated whether it was possible to save his leg, and even his life.

CHAPTER III

AMATEUR ASCENDANCY

*

You may praise the pluck of Burbridge, as he plays an up-hill match;
You may thunder cheers to Miller for a wondrous running catch;
You may join with me in wishing that the Oval, once again,
Shall resound with hearty plaudits to the praise of Mr Lane;
But the Gentlemen of England the match will hardly win,
Till they find another bowler such as glorious Alfred Mynn!

There could be no clearer illustration of the gulf between
1836 and the days of Compton's knee than in the slowness with
which the news of the extent of Alfred Mynn's injury percolated
through the cricketing world. Kent were due to play Sussex at
Brighton on September 12, nearly three weeks after the
Leicester game; yet although the Kent team included Alfred's
own brother they apparently had no idea until the morning
of the match that he would not be turning up. *Bell's Life*
recorded that when the news became known the betting on
Kent was reduced from two to one to three to two.

But in the same issue of the paper there appeared a letter
which revealed the situation:

In your last number I perceive that you have, in your list
of names to play in the great cricket match at Brighton,
inserted that of A. Mynn, Esq, who so much distinguished
himself at the great match at Leicester. I have to inform you
that, in consequence of repeated blows on the inside of the
right knee whilst playing at Leicester, such severe inflam-
mation and sloughing followed, that on arriving in London
he was unable to proceed further, and has been lying at the
Angels Tavern, St Martin's-lane, ever since, not only his
limb but even his life having been at one time almost
despaired of. He has been unremittingly attended by Dr

77

Bainbridge, of St Martin's lane, and Surgeon Lawrence, under whose skilful treatment he has considerably improved, and the limb is now considered safe, although the medical gentlemen state that it will be some months before he will be able to take exercise. I have thought it right to give you this information, that the gentlemen of Brighton may fully understand that it has not been from a want of inclination that he has not been amongst them.

The letter was anonymous, and we can only guess who wrote it. It could have been Lord Frederick Beauclerk, but the most probable author is Felix, who did not play in the Brighton match and who we know was in close touch with Mynn at the time. It was evidently touch and go whether Mynn's leg would have to come off or not; according to some writers the surgeons thought it would be necessary, but Alfred interposed a decisive veto. Pycroft speaks of his 'obstinate determination to keep his leg on', and the author of Mynn's obituary notice in the *Kent Herald* says more specifically that, when the surgeons told their patient that the thigh would have to be amputated at the hip joint, he replied: 'You may amputate my limb, but die I will before I lose the entire limb'.

Felix tells a slightly different story. In a letter written after Mynn's death he relates that he called on the injured man one day after the surgeons had been, and that Mynn told him that they had agreed not to take his leg off, adding: 'When I saw the surgeons enter the room, old fellow, I collected all my thoughts and requested that before they began they would leave the room for a few minutes that I might say my prayers.' Those five minutes of prayer, said Felix, saved his leg, for the surgeons retired and, renewing their consultation, decided to postpone the operation.

Felix was in the best position to know the truth, and we learn from him that Mynn was a sincerely religious man, with the simple and unobtrusive faith of the countryman. In the same letter Felix recalls their comradeship in the days of the All England Eleven. 'Often,' he writes, 'in our travels in the days of the 'Eleven' of England have I gone to his room to awaken him lest we should be too late for some early starting

train, there was his dear old Prayer Book on the Toilet Table
which he always carried with him, no display, no affectation
of Religious bearing, but there was that wish that passed
human show.'

Mynn was apparently taken to St Bartholomew's Hospital
from St Martin's Lane, but how long he remained there is
uncertain. It was nearly two years before he played cricket
again, and a number of writers have jumped to the conclusion
that he was laid up for all that time. Such does not seem to
have been the case. Several times in 1837 he was confidently
expected to take the field, and on May 14 the following report
appeared in *Bell's Life*:

> We rejoice to hear that A. Mynn, Esq, who was so severely
> injured last season, while engaged at Cricket, has so far
> recovered that it is expected he will shortly be able to enter
> the field again, with all his accustomed vigour. All who know
> Mr Mynn, we feel assured, will hail his re-appearance with
> heartfelt delight, for, independently of his superior merits
> as a cricketer, he ranks high in the estimation of numerous
> friends.

In June he was expected to play for Kent against Sussex,
but did not appear; and both he and Walter were absent from
the Gentlemen's side against the Players in the following month.
On this occasion the Gentlemen, in spite of the Players having
to defend four stumps three feet high, were defeated in an
innings, and a correspondent wrote indignantly to *Bell's Life*
asking why such a weak team was fielded. Where, in particular,
were the two Mynns, Harenc, Jenner and Rich? The reply
given so far as the Mynns were concerned was that they had
promised in the previous season that they would play in the
match, and had given no indication that they had changed
their minds, 'although it was pretty generally rumoured that
circumstances would prevent their attending'.

What were these 'circumstances'? Clearly Alfred was now
fit enough to play; moreover his injury would not account for
Walter's absence. We must therefore look elsewhere for the
reason why neither brother made a single appearance in the
cricket field in 1837. And though details are lacking the basic

cause is not difficult to find. For in the early months of this
year the Mynns lost both their parents. Old William Mynn
died at Harrietsham on January 26, at the age of seventy-three,
'deeply regretted and sincerely beloved by his family and
friends'. Three months later, on April 25, his widow followed
him to the grave. 'To her sorrowing and afflicted family,'
said the *Maidstone Gazette*, 'her loss will be long and deeply
deplored.' Both were buried at Goudhurst.

The expressions of regret in the press were, of course, in the
conventional language of death notices. But all the evidence
there is indicates that the Mynns were a closely united family.
At the same time it is unlikely that the loss of their parents in
itself would have kept Walter and Alfred out of the field for a
whole season. But doubtless there were complications. They
had all probably been living together hitherto, but now the
family home was broken up. Walter and Alfred must have
found their hands full in planning for the future, so much so
that they even forgot to notify the M.C.C. that they could not
turn out for the Gentlemen.

All we know for certain is that just about this time Alfred
moved to Bearsted or Thurnham. The boundary between
the two parishes is hard to distinguish, and sometimes his
home is mentioned as being in one and sometimes in the other.
Here he lived for most of the remainder of his life, but whether
always in the same house is uncertain. Denison says that he had
a farm until 1845, but then 'circumstances compelled him to
give it up'. In 1951, through the initiative of Mr Sidney Loweth,
the Kent County Architect, a plaque was placed on the wall
of the house where he is said to have lived; the house is now
called Mount Pleasant, and it stands a few hundred yards up
the hill above the Bearsted cricket ground – and above his
favourite White Horse Inn, which still stands at a corner of the
green. But in Bagshaw's Gazetteer of Kent, published in 1847,
Mynn's house is given as 'Freningham', in 'Thornham Parish',
and this is confirmed by census returns of 1851.

Alfred was living at Thurnham by the end of 1837, for it
was there, on December 5, that Sarah Mynn gave birth to her
first son. Alas, the boy lived only two hours, and was never
given a name. Six years later, on September 4, 1843, another

son was born, and was christened Alfred Thomas. But the Mynns' luck was little better this time; Alfred Thomas died on October 15. Only the daughters grew up.

Walter apparently moved to Thurnham also. Little is known of his private life, but Edward Hodges related that he 'once made a sensation by eloping from Maidstone with the daughter of a retired postmaster'. This was the one startling incident in the life of the unspectacular Walter, and one would much like to know more of an episode so apparently out of character; but the romance is buried in obscurity. Walter was married in 1825 to Susanna Howard, but by 1837 seems to have been a widower, and it is probable that he shared Alfred and Sarah's house.

There is little to relate of the life of the brothers at Thurnham; it was seldom that they got into the news other than on the cricket field. But in 1846 the local press reported that an oast-house fire broke out late at night at Bearsted; the Mynn brothers happened to pass the spot (on their way home from the White Horse?) and 'by prompt and indefatigable exertions, aided by the neighbours', put out the blaze before the fire-engine arrived from Maidstone.

In the same year Walter Mynn won a pigeon shooting match against Mr William Saxby of Leeds, after which 'a good ordinary was provided by Mr Godding, the landlord of the White Horse Inn, and a strong muster of friends met in the evening which was kept up to a late hour in mirth and harmony'. We know from Gale that both brothers were good shots, but that Walter was the better of the two.

Alfred Mynn's absence from the field in 1837, then, was not due to his injury. But that that injury did give him trouble for many years to come is indicated by a remark in the *Maidstone Journal* as late as 1841. Reporting Mynn's innings in the Kent *v.* Sussex match in that year, the writer said that 'in consequence of the immense padding which he is compelled to wear, to protect his 'game leg', he lost his wicket by a ball from Deane, striking his pad and turning in upon his wicket'.

One wonders what form this padding took, since no other contemporary mentions having noticed it. It was perhaps some kind of protection worn next the skin, like the early pads devised by Felix, and not normally visible under the rather baggy trousers then in fashion. The Maidstone reporter probably knew Mynn well, and saw what had happened.

The subject of the introduction of pads and gloves, with particular reference to Alfred Mynn, deserves a brief digression. It was certainly the fast bowling of players such as Mynn and Redgate that led to their use, but apart from the special protection mentioned above there seems to be no strictly contemporary reference to Alfred himself ever wearing either. Fred Gale, however, in his book *The Game of Cricket* has a story of a pair of pads that had belonged to Alfred Mynn being presented to W. G. Grace. 'The Old Buffer' was usually an accurate chronicler, but he claimed no first-hand authority for the story and his book was published in 1887, twenty-six years after Mynn's death. If this incident really occurred, what happened to the pads? One would think that 'W.G.' might have presented or bequeathed them to the Kent County Cricket Club, and Lord Harris in *A Few Short Runs* has a passage that at first sight seems to suggest that this was the case. 'Batting-gloves and pads,' he writes, 'have not undergone much change, and were in regular use when I first saw first-class cricket; but Alfred Mynn's pads – which are in the pavilion at Canterbury – cannot have given much protection . . .'

But if Mynn's pads were really in the Canterbury pavilion in 1921, when Lord Harris's book appeared, they have disappeared now. There is indeed an old pair of pads there, but they are labelled as having belonged to Fuller Pilch. Moreover they do not fit the description; they are remarkably modern in appearance, and one would say that they must have given very good protection indeed. Lord Harris's words would apply more accurately to the early wicket-keeping pads, said to have belonged to E. G. Wenman, which are kept in the pavilion at Lord's.

The possibility that Pilch did wear pads of this highly developed kind at an early date is borne out by the following letter which appeared in the magazine *Cricket* in March 1886:

Sir, – I should be glad if you or any of your correspondents would tell us in your columns when pads first came in.

The first time I saw them was in the year 1833 or '34, when I went down with the Kent Eleven under Knatchbull and Herbert Jenner to play Norfolk at Dereham.

Fuller Pilch came out of the tent, to my astonishment, with the identical sort of pad that is now worn, up to and above the knee. He made a hole with his heel in the turf, stuck his foot there firmly and defied the leg-balls, which we had to jump and dance to get away from, and which at that time were often purposely driven in at the legs two or three times running and perhaps into the stumps the fourth time, when the *ruse* had caused unsteadiness. The case made a great impression upon me, because I actually hit him on the legs once, but my slow ball did not make as much impression through his pads as a flea bite would have done.

After Pilch had got about half a hundred runs, Herbert Jenner, the best all-round cricketer of the day, the conductor of our match, and our wicket-keeper, put me on to bowl. I never was a regular bowler, but often got a wicket by a catch or over-reach and stump when put on with slow left-handed rounds after swift underhand cannon balls.

The first ball I gave pitched well, the great man was drawn, the ball was missed, went over the shoulder of his bat, and in its parabola pitched exactly on the top of the bails and – did not knock them off!

Herbert Jenner threw his hands up in the air, and with an expression which I need not repeat, rolled the ball back to me, while the umpire looked to the bails and gave them a shake to see if all was right. Pilch's leg was up, he was actually out of his ground! Of course a child would have stumped him – the best gentleman wicket-keeper in England failed to do this simply because he saw the ball was going to hit and did hit the wicket.

. . . The next ball Pilch hit for six, the third ball for four, the fourth he meant to have sent for six but missed it altogether, and it hit him on his unmoved padded leg, and I had not even the satisfaction of feeling at least that I had given him a stinger. . . .

Many more will remember Alfred Mynn and his peculiar action and delivery. I think I can mention one fact in proof of the pace with which the balls were driven by his giant arm. In 1834 when I played against the players, I was put as extra man, very deep, to cover long-slip if the ball was hit, and to cover long-stop and guard the Pavilion if the ball was missed, and so I was kept at it all the match, and have the pace fully impressed upon my memory.

I am, Sir,

Your obedient servant,

SEPTUAGENARIAN.

Eton Eleven, 1830-1-2. Cambridge, 1833-4-5. Gentleman v. Players, 1834.

There is no difficulty in identifying the writer of this letter. The only member of the Gentlemen's team of 1834 who was at Eton in the years mentioned was C. A. Wilkinson, who afterwards went up to Cambridge though he did not get his blue. But the letter itself is puzzling. There is no record of Kent playing Norfolk at Dereham in 1833, 1834 or any other year, and in 1835 Pilch transferred his allegiance to Kent. It looks, therefore, as though 'Septuagenarian's' memory was a little hazy about dates and details, and we cannot accept his letter as evidence that Pilch wore pads of the modern type as early as 1834. Pycroft wrote that in 1836 'pads and gloves were quite unknown as articles of commerce', though he and others had improvised their own.

At the same time there is no need to discount Wilkinson's story altogether; no other correspondent challenged him, and no more recollections about pads followed. Leg guards of some sort began to be worn during the 1830s, and Pilch was evidently one of the first to wear them. But Wilkinson's letter implies that at first they were somewhat frowned upon, and probably for several years it was considered rather unsporting, or at least cowardly, to make use of them. Perhaps that was why some cricketers wore them under the trousers, decently hidden from view. The inventive Felix was here a pioneer. In *Felix on the Bat*, published in 1845, he wrote:

Always, whether in practice or whilst engaged in matches, wear paddings; for the uncertainty and irregularity of the present system of throwing bowling is something dangerous;

and one violent blow in the beginning of the season may incapacitate or discourage you for the rest of the year. False pride will actuate many to discard this means of preventing pain; but this pseudo fortitude will pay dearly for its obstinacy. The padding which I recommend as most becoming in its appearance and most effective in its intentions, is to have longitudinal sockets, made (inside the legs of the trousers) of linen, half an inch apart, extending down from two inches above the knee-pan down to the lower part of the trousers. Long slips of Indian rubber, half an inch thick, can always be inserted therein, and taken out as they go or come from the wash.

Batting gloves made their appearance at about the same time. Here again some of the earliest were designed by Felix. Lord Bessborough (the Hon Frederick Ponsonby in his cricketing days) recorded that the first man he saw wearing gloves was Caldecourt: 'they were of leather padded with wool, and when rubber was first used it was arranged in such a manner that the tops of the fingers were left to the mercy of any vicious ball.'

Alfred Mynn was back in the field in 1838, and his injury seemingly had little effect on his form. He demolished James Dearman of Sheffield in two single-wicket matches* and he took many wickets both for the Kent eleven and in local matches in the county. Yet he may still have been hampered by his private affairs, for he missed the two most important matches of the season. He was absent from Gentlemen v. Players, as was Walter, and also from the 'Grand Coronation Match', North v. South, which opened at Lord's on June 25 in honour of the coronation of Queen Victoria. If he had been available he would surely have been selected for the South, for in addition to its special significance this was the game in which he had scored his great triumph two years before. In spite of his absence the South won by eight wickets.

In the following year he was in the Gentlemen's team once more, and this was the first of fourteen consecutive seasons in which he played in the greatest match of the year. During that

* See Chapter V.

time the tide turned. In the past it had been taken for granted that the amateurs could never win unless given odds in some form or other; now not only did they play on equal terms, but for a number of years the Gentlemen had the better of the encounters. That they did so was due above all others to Alfred Mynn. During the years when he was at his best, 1842–1849, the Gentlemen won five matches to the Players' three. The days of amateur teams of sixteen and eighteen, of given men and 'barndoor' wickets, had gone for ever.

It was, as we have seen, in 1832 that Alfred first appeared for the Gentlemen, and justified his selection. In 1833, when the amateurs were allowed sixteen men, and in 1834 he did nothing distinguished; but in 1835, going in when six wickets had fallen, he played a brilliant innings of 53, bringing the innings total to 158. The Gentlemen, for whom Cobbett and Redgate were given men, led by 23 runs, Mynn bowling four of the Players; but in the second innings Lillywhite caused a collapse, bowling seven Gentlemen, and the Players finally won by six wickets. Redgate performed one of his most re-markable feats in bowling Pilch for nought in both innings.

The 1836 match was notable in more than one respect. The Gentlemen won, but as their team had been enlarged to eighteen men their victory, in which Alfred Mynn had the largest share, was rather a hollow one. The most noteworthy feature, however, was that three schoolboys, all from Winchester, were included in the Gentlemen's eighteen. The foremost of these was Alfred Lowth, a fast-medium left-hander with a beautiful action, just eighteen years old but looking younger. He had been bowling so well for Winchester that, as Mr Altham relates, the M.C.C. sent a special deputation down to the school to watch him. The result was that not only he but two of his schoolfellows, N. Darnell and the Hon. W. L. Pakenham, were invited to play for the Gentlemen. Another newcomer to the match was C. G. Taylor, the Sussex amateur, who was also only eighteen and had just left Eton. The presence of these young hopefuls must have suggested to many that better times were in store for the Gentlemen, but their selection does not, perhaps, say very much for the state of amateur talent in general.

The Gentlemen batted first and were given a good start by Walter and Alfred Mynn, Alfred scoring 29 and Walter 20; but thereafter only Lord Grimston, with 21, reached double figures, and the eighteen were all out for 115. This, however, was enough, thanks to Alfred Mynn and young Alfred Lowth, who together swept through the opposition. Lowth was five feet four inches tall and slight of figure, and the contrast between the two bowlers caused great amusement; inevitably the spectators dubbed them 'Alfred the Great' and 'Alfred the Little'. They took four wickets each; the Players' score was 77. There were sixteen byes and thirteen wides, and the next highest score was 9 by Redgate.

Alfred Mynn was again the top scorer in the Gentlemen's second innings, making 30, and again he and Walter, who made 10, gave their side a good start. But they had little support, except once more by Lord Grimston with 15, and the innings closed for 96. Then the two Alfreds repeated their performance. One of the other Wykehamists, Darnell, took one wicket; of the rest Lowth took five and Mynn four. The Players were all out for 99, and the Gentlemen had won by 35 runs. In the Players' second innings there were twenty-two byes, and two no-balls, and in the whole match there were ninety-seven extras. Herbert Jenner, the great Kent wicket-keeper, was playing for the Gentlemen, but it would seem that he had a couple of off days.

The Players won the three matches (there was a return game in 1837) played in the next two years, Mynn being absent, and the 'barndoor' match, which saw the overwhelming defeat of the Gentlemen in spite of the huge wickets defended by the Players, must have seemed the ultimate humiliation.

The 1839 match, played on equal terms, was drawn owing to rain, but greatly in favour of the Players. Alfred Mynn celebrated his return to the match by making 46 (out of 86) and 19, and taking four wickets in the Players' one innings of 235, but he had little support. The *Sporting Magazine* commentator, in his end-of-the-season notes, wrote:

The Match of the Gentlemen against the Players this year was, or would have been if it had been played out, as hollow a thing in favour of the professionals as it has almost always been. It never can be fairly a Match when the numbers and wickets are equal and the strength of each party are really brought into the field; nothing in such a case can give victory to the Gentlemen but mere accident, or an alternative which we will not suppose possible amongst the present generation of cricketers – a generation of whom, if I am correct in thinking the paid portion inferior (as players) to their fathers, I still do not think the Gentlemen *comparatively* superior, although perhaps the very best man now in practice is amongst their number. I allude, as my readers will probably surmise, to Mr Alfred Mynn. If, then, the Gentlemen have not become comparatively better than the paid players, how can they be positively so, since they never could approach them formerly?

He spoke too soon; the turn of the tide was not far off. But for the moment interest in the game was declining. The 1840 match was made possible only by Frederick Ponsonby and C. G. Taylor offering to meet most of the expenses, and the same two amateurs opened a subscription list for the same purpose in the following year. Their public spirit was rewarded. In 1840 the Players won easily, though Alfred Mynn bowled finely, but the 1841 game was close and exciting.

The Gentlemen batted first and made 78. Mynn went in second wicket and scored 18, opening his score with a big hit for five. Only Frederick Ponsonby scored more – 19 not out. Lowth was again playing, and the Players' first innings aroused memories of 1836. The two bowlers were again in great form and between them took all the wickets except that of Pilch, who was run out. But it was Mynn's day; he had seldom bowled better, and took seven of the nine.

The Gentlemen had a lead of 14 on the first innings and scored 109 in the second; Lillywhite, who had taken seven wickets in the first, had another five. The Players needed 124 to win, and with Mynn and Lowth in such splendid form the Gentlemen had a good chance. But Joseph Guy, the young Nottinghamshire batsman, who was such a beautiful stylist that it was said of him that he was worthy to bat in the Queen's drawing room, played a fine innings of 32, and the Players got home by three wickets. Guy played Mynn particularly well, but Alfred had his wicket at last; he took four of the wickets that fell, and Lowth the other three.

The bad days were over; there was no more talk of abandoning the match. A big crowd turned up to watch the 1842 game, and they were well rewarded. The Gentlemen again batted first and scored 78, only Alfred Mynn (21) and Ponsonby (23) reaching double figures. Mynn opened the innings with his brother, and his runs, 'obtained in the most masterly manner', were made out of 29 scored while he was at the wicket. Unfortunately he was again hit on the leg by his old antagonist Redgate, and that evening he was in great pain. But this was not a repetition of 1836; a dozen leeches were applied to the leg, and the swelling went down. But in the second innings he was given a runner.

He had meanwhile taken three wickets in the Players' first innings of 122, and the Gentlemen had lost one wicket for 10. On the Tuesday a new complexion was put on the game. Felix came in, was missed in the slips off his first ball, and proceeded to give a beautiful exhibition of left-handed batting. At 57 for two he was joined by Mynn with his runner, and the two were together when dinner was announced; 'never,' said *Bell's Life*, 'was the sound more pleasing than it was at this time to the fieldsmen.' In the afternoon the two Kent amateurs (Felix was a Kent man now) completely mastered the Players' bowling, and they had put on 99 together when 'Lillywhite gave Mr Mynn one of his *peculiars*, which, hitting the batsman's legs, ran on to the wicket, and never was the falling of timber hailed with greater delight than on this occasion, Mr Mynn leaving a score behind him of 46.' Felix was at last caught at cover-point for 88, 'displaying some of the finest hitting ever witnessed'; nobody else scored much, but the innings reached 206, leaving the Players 163 to get to win.

The final innings saw one of Alfred Mynn's finest feats of bowling. His injury had ceased to trouble him, and he was as accurate as he was fast; the Lord's wicket, notorious for its roughness, made him a terror to the batsmen. He and Sir

Frederick Bathurst opened against Fenner and Box, and Mynn soon bowled Fenner with a tremendous shooter. Wenman got a similar ball, and two wickets had fallen for 14 when Pilch joined Box. The great batsman played with his usual skill, though badly knocked about by Mynn's bowling, but Box was bowled by a 'trimmer' from Mynn and Guy followed almost immediately. Four wickets were down for 23; only Pilch showed any sign of being able to cope with Mynn's bowling, and he was forced to play a wholly defensive innings. Hawkins was the next to succumb, and then Lillywhite was run out. Good followed, but a hit from him was finely fielded by Bathurst and Pilch was run out; he had only made 6, but with his fall all hope for the Players faded. Mynn caught Sewell off his partner, and then bowled Redgate; his bowling at this stage was, said *Bell's Life*, 'at such a pace and at such a length, that it seemed impossible to stop it'.

All seemed over, but the last pair, Good and Hillyer, made a brave though forlorn stand. They played out time, when the score was 52, and the following morning put on another 15 before Good was run out for 14, Hillyer being 11 not out.

The Gentlemen had won by 95 runs. Mynn took six wickets in 114 balls, all of them bowled; his bowling, said *Bell's Life*, 'was the most terrific we ever saw'. He had also caught the batsman who provided Bathurst's only wicket; the other three men were run out.

Only once before had the Gentlemen beaten the Players on level terms: in 1822, when Beauclerk, Ward and Budd were at the height of their careers.

That Mynn was at this time a very great bowler is beyond question. He had quite overcome his early wildness, and the high proportion of victims clean bowled among his total wickets (the name of the bowler was now being more generally recorded on score sheets) testifies to his accuracy. He bowled dead on the wicket, and he could maintain pace and length to the end of the longest day.

Speed and precision, coupled with the roughness of the wicket, would be enough to account for his many wickets; but there is abundant evidence that he imparted spin to the ball as well. It was said that he bowled a ball which pitched on the leg stump and whipped across to take the off. Whether he did more is problematical. It is generally held that the swerve came in much later; but the testimony of Alfred Lowth, even at third hand, should not be disregarded. Mr H. S. Altham, discussing Mynn in *A History of Cricket*, records that 'Mr James Fort, himself a notable figure in Wykehamical cricket, has told me how he remembers hearing "Dandy" Lowth say, "I tell you, sir, I have seen the ball turn in the air from his hand"'.

As to speed, if in fact, as some writers suggest, he was never quite so fast after his injury as before, this seems to have been apparent neither to batsmen nor to the sporting writers. There are innumerable allusions to his tremendous pace; 'ripping' is the adjective most frequently applied to the balls he sent down – not used, of course, in the schoolboy sense, but applied to balls that 'ripped' through the air.

As a batsman too he was in great form. He was still a big hitter, but he was more consistent than he had been before. His 125 not out at Leicester was the only century he ever made, but at a time when even the best players were more likely than not to get out for single-figure scores he made a creditable number of thirties, forties and fifties – substantial scores in that age. The more important the match, moreover, and the tougher the opposition, the more likely he was to succeed: the mark of a batsman of class.

In 1843 the Gentlemen followed up their triumph of the year before with an even more shattering victory, winning by an innings and 20 runs; and again Mynn played a leading part. The Players batted first, and despite a great innings of 73 by Wenman were all out for 137; Mynn took five wickets and C. G. Taylor, better known as a batsman than as a bowler, four. The Gentlemen then proceeded to make light of the excellent bowling of the Players, whose team included Lilly-white, Redgate and Hillyer. After the first wicket had fallen cheaply the two Mynns put on 57 for the second before Walter was out for 20. Then Alfred and Felix added another 30; but Felix, who was a notoriously bad runner, wrought Mynn's downfall. Alfred 'made a start for a run, but Felix did not leave his ground, and Mr Mynn in trying to recover himself slipped down, and was run out, after scoring 47 by some very splendid hitting.'

Now came the best batting of the innings. Felix was out for 22, but Taylor, a fine stylist, scored a beautiful 89. 'So splendid was his hitting,' said *Bell's Life*, 'that he kept the company in a complete state of rapturous excitement during the whole of his innings.' Bathurst, going in last, scored 28, and the innings closed for 256; after which the Players were disposed of for 99. Only Pilch, who scored 43, put up much resistance. Mynn, Bathurst and Taylor took three wickets each.

There were two notable incidents in this match. Taylor was out 'hat knocked on wicket', and in the first innings of the Players the Gentlemen's wicket-keeper, T. A. Anson, brought off a memorable piece of stumping, taking the ball with his left hand from one of Mynn's fastest shooters and putting down G. Butler's wicket.

In the following two years the professionals had their revenge. In 1844, however, it was only by 38 runs. The game was evenly contested, but in the fourth innings the Gentlemen, who had been two runs behind on the first innings, found the task of getting 144 runs against Lillywhite and Hillyer too much for them. Mynn took seven wickets for 70 runs in the Players' first innings (the analysis was for the first time given in the modern manner except for maiden overs) and three for 66 in the second. For the Players Hillyer had ten wickets in the two innings and Lillywhite nine.

The 1845 match was dominated by Lillywhite, now fifty-three years old, who took twelve wickets for 96 runs. Pilch made 44 in the Players' first innings of 127, and the Gentlemen were all out for 94, only Felix, who made 43, being able to cope with 'Lilly'. The Players then made 149, Mynn taking five for 64, and left the Gentlemen 183 to get to win. Most of them were again at sea against Lillywhite, but Mynn and Taylor made a great effort, Mynn scoring 55 and Taylor 28 out of a total of 115.

An extra match in 1845 was played at Brighton to provide a benefit for George Brown, but the old cricketer who had done so much for Sussex was out of luck; after the Players had scored 119 for three wickets the match was ruined by rain.

The next year saw one of the most exciting finishes in the whole series of Gentlemen *v.* Players matches. Both sides were very strong, the only notable absentee being Fuller Pilch, who was beginning to feel his years. On the Players' side two great cricketers, representing the old and the new Nottinghamshire, were seen for the first time. The first was William Clarke, now forty-seven years of age, who, astonishingly to relate, had never played in this match before. The second, George Parr, was twenty-seven years younger. He was making his name in the north as an aggressive batsman; soon he was to be the best bat in England and the acknowledged successor of Pilch.

The Players won the toss, and a large crowd, among whom *Bell's Life* 'noticed nearly every nobleman and gentleman who is a patron of, or participator in the game', saw them struggle for runs against Mynn and Bathurst, both at their best. These two bowled unchanged through the innings, and only Joseph Guy, who scored 25, was at all at his ease. Parr, on this his first appearance, was bowled by Bathurst for 0. The innings closed for 85, Mynn taking seven wickets for 37 runs and Bathurst three for 48. Walter Mynn caught two batsmen at long-stop from his brother's bowling.

The Gentlemen topped the Players' score by 20. R. P. Long made 34, C. G. Taylor 23 and Alfred Mynn 13; Clarke and Hillyer, both bowling finely, took all the wickets between them. The Players then scored 145, Guy again playing well for 31; Bathurst this time was the most successful bowler, taking five for 64 as against Mynn's three for 65. The other two batsmen were run out.

This left the Gentlemen 126 to get to win, and with Lillywhite and Hillyer bowling finely they had a hard fight. Mynn, Felix and Robert Grimston failed, but Taylor played one of his best innings, making 44 before being stumped by Tom Box off Hillyer. The most memorable performance, however, was by Arthur Haygarth, who lives in cricket history as the compiler of *Scores and Biographies*. Haygarth was one of the slowest scorers in the history of the game; 'Old Everlasting' Walker was a dynamo by comparison. On this occasion he went in first and was seventh out after batting more than four hours for 26. But he had done his work in wearing the bowling down, and the professionals must have been immensely relieved when, like Taylor, he was brilliantly stumped by Box off Hillyer.

The score was now 110, and it was anybody's match. Long, who had batted so well in the first innings, scored a lucky four through the slips; a few singles were scored, and then W. P. Pickering was bowled by Lillywhite – two wickets to fall and seven runs to get. Long and E. Napper brought the score to 124, and then Napper was leg-before-wicket to Hillyer.

With one run needed to tie and two to win Walter Mynn came to the wicket. He had opened the first innings, and why he now went in last there is no knowing; but in those days there was much more juggling with the batting order than in later ages. At any rate there could have been no better man for such a crisis. Walter was not a great batsman, but he was as solid a cricketer and a man as his brother; no crisis could upset him. He faced Hillyer amid tremendous excitement, and scored a single through the slips to the accompaniment of cheers from all over the ground. This gave him the bowling, and with the match a tie he faced the cunning of 'Lilly'. He played two balls, and then Lilly moved Guy, who had been fielding rather deep at point, close in to the bat. He was evidently trying to entice Mynn to cock up a defensive stroke, but for once the old bowler was out-manoeuvred; Walter lifted the third ball just over Guy's head to where he had been standing before, the batsmen ran a single, and the match was won by one wicket.

'We must leave it to our readers,' said *Bell's Life*, 'to picture to themselves how intense must have been the excitement as the game was drawing to its close; indeed we do not recollect anything approaching to it.' Hillyer took six wickets for 40 and Lillywhite three for 40.

The Players won by 147 runs in 1847, the Gentlemen being routed by the two veterans, Lillywhite and Clarke. They were all out for 79 and 48; Lillywhite's figures were six for 18 and five for 18, and Clarke's four for 26 and five for 28.

In the Gentlemen's side in this match there appeared for the first time one of the few bowlers who can be said with tolerable certainty to have been even faster than Alfred Mynn. This was Harvey Fellows, who was now twenty-two years old. He and his

Eton contemporary, the Rev. Walter Marcon, who played much less cricket, were unanimously acclaimed as the fastest bowlers who had ever been seen, and at the end of the century many of the older generation were prepared to swear that Fellows and Marcon had been faster than was Kortright. It is interesting to note that in the position of the arm both these bowlers reverted to the earlier tradition. Haygarth wrote of Marcon: 'The delivery was nearly underhand'. And of Fellows: 'The delivery was low – so much so, indeed, that by some it was called underhand, which, however, was quite a mistake.' This tends to bear out Pycroft's contention that the old under hand style was capable of greater speed than any other.

In this match Harvey Fellows took only three wickets, and Alfred Mynn only two; Alfred's 18 was the highest score in the Gentlemen's second innings of 48.

There followed two more amateur victories. The 1848 match was a remarkable one. It began with the Gentlemen being dismissed by Clarke and Hillyer for 31, their lowest score in the series. Mynn failed to score, and when the Players batted he took only one wicket. Harvey Fellows however, bowling at tremendous speed, took five, all bowled, and the Players were all out for 79.

In the Gentlemen's second innings the tables were turned, and it was the two fast bowlers whose batting came to the rescue of their side. Mynn came in when four wickets had fallen for 31, and at the end of the first day's play the score was 57 for five, with Mynn not out 24. He attacked the bowling from the moment he went to the wicket.

The next day the weather was bad, and there were frequent interruptions of the play. In the intervals between rainstorms three more wickets fell, and at 90 for eight the Gentlemen seemed to have little chance. But at this point Fellows joined Mynn, and the pair made a great stand, putting on 59 before Mynn was caught at long-stop by young William Pilch, Fuller's nephew, for 66. The Gentlemen's final score was 152, and Mynn and Fellows (who made 37 not out) were each presented with a ball by the M.C.C.

The Players were left 105 to get to win, and the odds were

still in their favour; but Alfred Mynn brought off one of his finest bowling performances. He was over forty now and very heavy; and he must have been tired after his great innings. But he bowled almost as well as he had ever done, and with help from R. T. King, the greatest point fielder of his time, who caught three brilliant catches, he took eight wickets. Unfortunately the full analysis has not survived. The Players were all out for 77, the amateurs winning by 27 runs.

This was Alfred's last great triumph for the Gentlemen. He was a useful member of the side for a few years more, but the initiative passed into other hands. In 1849, when Pilch and Lillywhite made their last appearances, the latter at the age of fifty-seven, the Gentlemen won by an innings and 40 runs; the bowling of Bathurst and Fellows was mainly responsible, and old Lilly, after being hit by Fellows in the first innings, refused to bat in the second.

The result was reversed the next year, when the Players won by an innings and 48, George Parr playing a great innings of 65 not out; Mynn failed to get a wicket, but brought off a very fine catch in the slips, off his old partner Sir Frederick Bathurst, to get rid of D. Day. In 1851 there were two matches, both at Lord's, and the Players won both by an innings. The Players were now well on top once more, and their ascendancy coincided with the decline in Alfred Mynn's play; in the two matches of 1851 he made a total of 19 runs and took a total of four wickets.

In 1852 he appeared for the last time. Before the match *Bell's Life* announced that 'Mr Mynn, having been reduced about two stone in weight lately, is expected to render more essential service to his side in consequence'. We are not told how much he weighed before this reduction, nor how he achieved it. A slimming diet was not a thing he believed in, and Richard Daft, who began playing with him at about this time, estimated that he weighed twenty-three or twenty-four stone. One is inclined to be sceptical about the *Bell's Life* statement, but if he had really got his weight down his self-denial was in vain; he made 15 and 5 and took one wicket. The Players won by five wickets.

After twenty years, during which he had borne the brunt

of the amateur counter-attack, his association with the Gentlemen's team was at an end.

It would be tedious to go into details of all the other representative matches in which Alfred Mynn played during this middle and greatest period of his career; but some mention of the most interesting ones must be made. For many years he played in almost every important match for which he was qualified. As his fame and his popularity grew he was more and more in demand; he was an immense draw to the crowds, and, as was said in his obituary notice in the *Kent Herald*, 'he was always ready to oblige, regardless of personal inconvenience or expense, and was also ever ready to mix with and instruct the humblest aspirants on the village green'.

It is a curious fact that after his injury in 1836 Mynn did not play again at Lord's until July 23, 1839. Then he was in the England team which beat a combined team of Nottingham and Sussex by an innings and a run. Mynn made 25, making a stand with Felix, who scored 36, and causing some amusement by making a hit which knocked over a spectator's beer; but the match (as also this particular hit) is interesting only as showing that boundaries had now been introduced at Lord's and that the players were not at all clear as to how they operated. The *Sporting Magazine* commented:

> Mr Alfred Mynn, being in with another very excellent bat, who on that occasion played in more than one sense with his usual *felicity*, lost two runs by the latter gentleman's supposing four to be *allowed* for a hit down to the *house* (which was not the case), and thus delaying to start till too late to secure more than half the number from a very bad hit, which floored a pot of beer on a table, and created much merriment, driving the crowd hither and thither like a shell in the midst of a military throng.

A new match was instituted at Lord's in 1840. Three leading fast bowlers were selected as the nucleus of one side, and three slow bowlers of the other; the teams were then filled up by the M.C.C., to make up two strong representative sides. The slow bowlers won by 33 runs, and Mynn, though he bowled well, did nothing remarkable. But when the match was repeated in

1841 he gave one of his best displays. He, Redgate and the amateur C. G. Whittaker were the chosen fast bowlers; Lillywhite, Bayley and Cobbett were the slow. The slow bowlers won again, by 60 runs, but the play on both sides was particularly fine and Mynn took seven wickets in the first innings and five in the second. He also made top score, 36, in the first innings, taking part in an excellent partnership with Pilch.

These two Kent cricketers were associated in a bigger stand in one of the leading matches of 1842. The Trent Bridge ground at Nottingham had been opened in 1838, succeeding the old Forest ground. The early matches played there were not of great importance, but William Clarke was ambitious for his county, and in 1842 he threw out a challenge to the M.C.C. to bring an England team to play Nottinghamshire. For some reason the challenge was not accepted, but Fuller Pilch stepped into the breach and announced that he would bring an England side to the north. The team he chose was fully representative, including Mynn, Lillywhite, Hillyer, Wenman, Box, Ponsonby and Dorrinton, and the match opened at Trent Bridge on August 22.

England won the toss and scored 228. Clarke bowled admirably, taking seven wickets, but he was mastered by Mynn and Pilch, who scored 61 and 60 respectively. Both batted, acording to *Bell's Life*, 'in a style the most superb possible, and while they beat the best balls down, they punished most severely the wide ones'.

Notts made 122, Mynn taking three wickets but not bowling at his best, and followed on. In their second innings Alfred was at the top of his form, and took six wickets. The Nottinghamshire score was 110, and England won by ten wickets.

It may have been before this match that Alfred Mynn made a hit which greatly impressed Dean Hole, a Nottinghamshire clergyman with a great enthusiasm for cricket. In his recollections of Trent Bridge the Dean wrote:

I saw Alfred Mynn, with his tall figure and handsome face, hit a ball which he could not resist, in practice before the match (the biggest hit I ever saw, or shall see!), over the booths, over the Bingham road, and some distance into a field of potatoes on the opposite side thereof; and we stood gazing as it rose, as rustics gaze at a rocket, and then relieved our oppression of astonishment with that universal note of admiration, 'Oh!'

A match in 1843, Marylebone Club and Ground *v.* England at Lord's, was memorable for a great innings by Felix, who scored 105 for England 'by some of the finest hitting ever exhibited'. England won by ten wickets; Mynn scored 21 and took seven wickets in the two innings.

His most impressive batting performance this year was in a minor match late in the season. On September 25 and 26 he turned out as a given man for the West Surrey Club against Islington Albion on the club's Wandsworth Road ground. Hillyer and Dorrinton were given men for Islington, who were all out for 45 in their first innings. West Surrey then made 126, of which Mynn scored 73, hitting the ball four times out of the ground. West Surrey won by an innings and 38 runs.

Many years later a correspondent in the *Sporting Life* recalled this innings:

I never saw anything so extraordinary as Mr Mynn's play on that occasion; he absolutely hit the ball out of the grounds in all the four directions. One hit sent it (the ball) over the Wandsworth-road, into the Brewhouse Meadow. Another hit sent it flying over the houses on the upper side of the ground; another hit sent the ball through the window of a house in Spring-place, considerable merriment being caused by the old woman refusing to give up the leather until her broken glass was paid for, and the fourth hit sent the ball over the boundary hedge on the north side.

The next two years produced no match that need be mentioned, but they saw a change in the Laws for which Mynn was partially and indirectly responsible. He had long ago shed his wildness in bowling, but his imitators, trying to bowl faster than their physique would allow, were still hurling down balls that went in any direction except to the wicket. William Denison, the Surrey cricketer and cricket writer, had for years been leading an agitation for a stricter law on wide balls to curb these dangerous young men. His appeal for a stricter definition of wides failed, but in 1845 it was enacted that if the bowler delivered a wide or a no-ball 'the striker shall be allowed as many runs as he can get, and he shall not be put out except by running out'. Previously only the one penalty run to the side was allowed.

The following season was an important one, for not only were the two famous single-wicket matches played between Mynn and Felix, and William Clarke's All England Eleven inaugurated, but special tributes were paid to two of the greatest cricketers of the day, Felix and Clarke. The match in honour of Felix was not described as a benefit, but it is probable that he profited financially from it. Alfred Mynn certainly did from a similar match played in the following year. Mynn and Felix were recognised as exceptions to normal custom. They were immensely popular, and their impecuniosity was notorious. It may be added that it was stretching a point to call them amateurs at all, for it was well known that both received financial assistance to enable them to devote their time to cricket.

The Felix match was played at Lord's on June 1, 2 and 3, 1846. The two captains, Felix and Pilch, chose their sides, and most of England's best cricketers played. Felix of course had Mynn, his closest friend, in his team; and others were Clarke, C. G. Taylor, Box, Dean and Parr. Pilch had Lillywhite, Hillyer, Haygarth, Dorrinton and E. G. Wenman. Wenman had virtually retired from important cricket, but he returned to the field for this match in compliment to Felix.

Pilch's side won by 34 runs, in spite of a brilliant innings of 59 by Parr; Pilch was the leading batsman for his own team, making a fine 31 not out in the second innings. Felix's side were all out for 47 in their first innings. Neither Felix himself, who was loudly cheered when he went in to bat, nor Mynn played any great part. Felix made 6 and 10 and Mynn 0 and 1, and Mynn took three wickets in the first innings and two in the second.

The most notable feature of the match was the visit to Lord's of Prince Albert (not yet Prince Consort). He rode on to the ground, 'attended by some of the élite of the land', and was invited into the pavilion; there he was shown bats, balls, stumps and all the implements of the game, which were evidently unfamiliar to him. Some years later Felix described the scene in Lillywhite's *Guide to Cricketers*, and related how the Prince, on viewing gloves and pads and being told why they were needed, said in wonderment at the customs of the English: 'And all this for pleasure?' In spite of this comment Prince Albert was apparently favourably impressed; for two years later it was reported that 'it is the intention of her gracious Majesty and her royal consort to have the Prince of Wales initiated in the "arts and mysteries" of the healthful and manly pastime of cricket'. The Prince of Wales, the future King Edward VII, was then seven years old.

The course of Clarke's benefit match did not run so smoothly. It was played at Southwell, Nottinghamshire on August 27 and 28, and was described as 'Six Gentlemen of England and Five Players *v.* Five Gentlemen of the Southwell Club and Five Players of Nottinghamshire, with Mr A. Mynn'. Mynn had been staying with George Parr at Radcliffe, and the two of them, with one or two others of the Notts team, decided to row most of the way to Southwell. Mynn and Parr were both convivial characters, and perhaps their rowing made them thirstier than usual; at any rate they arrived on the ground well after the start of the game, to face a furious Clarke. He had won the toss, but several wickets had fallen, and Mynn was commanded to go in to bat at once. He was promptly bowled first ball by Martingell, which did not help matters. Parr played brilliantly and saved the side from collapse by scoring 51, but Clarke was not mollified and more high words passed between them, ending in Parr walking off the ground and taking no further part in the match. It was impossible to quarrel with Mynn, and after Clarke's side had been disposed of for 108 Alfred took eight England wickets. The other batsmen were run out, but the England total came to 249, and the match was left drawn when the home side had scored 39 for six, of which Mynn made 20.

It was all rather a fiasco, but one hopes that the irascible Clarke had a profitable benefit. On this point history is silent.

Shortly before this there was another match in which Mynn

took eight wickets in an innings. He was playing as a given man for the North against the M.C.C. at Leicester, and he got four wickets in the first innings and eight in the second, though the M.C.C. won by 58 runs. Later in the season he took eleven wickets for the Gentlemen of England against Cambridge Town, a match with an exciting finish, Cambridge winning by one wicket. Mynn was in fine bowling form this year.

Yet a year or two later we hear suggestions that he was past his best. In a long letter to *Bell's Life* published on July 30, 1848, a correspondent signing himself 'A Member of a Metropolitan Cricket Club' complained that the elevens representing England and other important sides were of poor quality owing to the inclusion of too many veterans; he particularly instanced the fielding, 'perhaps the most important part in the game'. The correspondent wrote:

> The gentlemen who select the elevens for the great matches seem to forget that, except in some very rare instances (Lilly, for example, who is indeed a phenomenon), age must, will, and does tell, and youth must be served in cricket as in other matters, of which you know somewhat. Now, perhaps I shall make a good many cricketers laugh, and many more stare, when I say that, were I to select an All England Eleven to beat any other Eleven in the world, I would not have either Pilch, Mynn, or Felix, and for this very reason – they are all three stale men. Great indeed have they been in their day – none greater in my somewhat limited recollection – but their time has gone by, and they can well afford to live upon their reputation without intercepting with the long shadows of their sunset other rising suns. . . .

This letter led to hot controversy in the columns of the paper. Correspondents rushed to the defence of the 'three stale men', and one of them, over the signature 'Egomet', put his feelings into verse:

> Three cheers for the 'stale men', they'll never say die
>   Whilst a bat or a ball they can wield;
> In truth we *shall* laugh, aye, and stare, if you cry
>   That they ne'er should be seen in the field.

Our Alfred the Great is *full* great as of yore,
 Aye, and *Fuller*, deny it who will?
Though Felix's *infelix* oftimes in the score,
 Yet, 'in', Felix can show you some skill.

Then talk not again of the deeds they have done,
 But speak rather of those they will dare;
For backward their 'sunset's long shadows' will run
 Till unseen in their noon's brilliant glare.

Three cheers for the 'stale men', no 'freshmen', we say,
 E'er again such a trio will be;
Nine cheers will much better their merits display,
 For they are themselves three times three.

Another correspondent, 'A Man of Kent', pertinently
pointed out that 'Mynn, Felix and Pilch obtained a larger
score than *any other three* engaged in the most important match
of the season, "Gentlemen *v.* Players", at Lord's last week.'

Of course there was no doubt that 'A Member of a Metropolitan Cricket Club' was at least partially right. Mynn, the
youngest of the trio, had passed the forty mark, and his weight
was enormous; the correspondent was not the only person to
suggest that his fielding was not what it had been.

He had indeed reached the veteran stage, and from this
time onwards he did less and less bowling. But there was still
plenty of cricket in him, and he was still capable of turning a
side's defeat into victory. In 1850 a match was played at Lord's,
for Caldecourt's benefit, between the 'Old' and the 'Young',
the dividing age being thirty-six. The Young just won by 11
runs, but the Old scored 237 in the fourth innings, the highest
in the match, and the top score was 69 by Alfred Mynn. One
veteran, G. Rogers, was absent on the last day; otherwise the
Old might well have won. Mynn and Dakin, who scored 56,
made a fine fighting stand; *Bell's Life* recorded that 'Dakin
sent the ball into the beer cellar, and marked six for it, and Mr
Mynn sent it the other way under the spirit shop, and also
scored six'. Mynn, the paper said, hit the ball in every direction
and set the field at defiance.

These years saw the beginning of the keeping of cricketers'
averages. The first were published in *Bell's Life* in 1840,

compiled and contributed by Nathaniel Pilch, Fuller's eldest brother; the figures took account of all matches reported in the paper. In 1841 the compiler was the second Pilch brother, William; in the following years other contributors sent in their versions, and there was much argument between them on each other's accuracy. In 1846 *Bell's Life* first issued their own tables, which from then onwards became much fuller and more in line with modern practice.

Whether any averages were kept before 1840 is doubtful. Nathaniel Pilch, who survived both his younger brothers, said that William was the first man he had heard of who ever kept an average. But Nathaniel was then a very old man, and he may have forgotten his own earlier effort.

Nathaniel Pilch's figures of 1840 were for batting only; they gave the number of innings, average with number of runs over, and total runs. Mynn came sixteenth in the list with figures of 26 innings, average 7–15, and 197 runs. Felix headed the list with 310 runs and average 23–11, and Pilch was second with 567 runs and average 18–27.

In 1841 William Pilch put Mynn sixth in the list, with 401 runs and average 14–23; Fuller Pilch was at the top with 642 and 22–26. In 1842, when the figures were compiled anonymously, Mynn's figures were 373 runs and average 17, and he came fourth below Felix, Taylor and Pilch. In 1843 he scored 325 runs with an average of $15\frac{1}{2}$, and came fifth.

In this year bowlers were included for the first time. They were given three columns; number of innings, total wickets, and average. The average was the average not of runs per wicket, but of wickets per innings; the number of wickets now probably, as certainly some years later when more details were given, included catches made by the player as well as off his bowling. Mynn headed the list, with figures of 23 innings, 68 wickets, and average 3. Hillyer, ranked third, had the same number of wickets but in 29 innings, average $2\frac{1}{2}$. In between came Clarke with 10 innings, 25 wickets, and average $2\frac{1}{2}$. This list included all 'principal matches'; a rival list, for all matches reported in *Bell's Life*, gave Mynn 86 wickets against Lillywhite's and Hillyer's 75 each.

In 1844 Mynn was credited with 316 runs and 81 wickets

and again headed the bowling figures, and in 1845 with 182 runs and 47 wickets. Hillyer had now overtaken Mynn, and had 116 wickets this year.

These figures are unreliable and incomplete. (According to another compiler Mynn took 143 wickets in 1844). But from 1846 onwards, compiled by the *Bell's Life* staff, they can be accepted with less reserve. They included all matches the paper had reported, and gave most of the details that are now given, though not quite in the present-day manner. In 1846, one of his best seasons, Mynn made 567 runs, only Felix exceeding him with 577, and had an average of 14–21. He took 151 wickets, but Hillyer had 303 and Lillywhite 237. In 1847, though his batting average was two runs lower, his total figures were even better: 701 runs and 171 wickets. Only Felix (905 runs) and Pilch (810) were above him in batting, and Hillyer (298) and Lillywhite (261) in bowling. In 1848, the year of the 'stale men', he made 494 runs and took 111 wickets.

In 1849 *Bell's Life* gave Mynn 687 runs and 72 wickets, but according to the *Cricketer's Manual* for that year his figures were 674 and 146; the discrepancy in the bowling figures is hard to account for. After that he declined. In 1850 his batting and bowling totals were 479 and 52; in 1850 he made 414 runs, but for the first time was not included in the bowling figures. Nor was he ever again.

CHAPTER IV

THE GREAT KENT ELEVEN

*

When the great old Kent Eleven, full of pluck and hope, began
The grand battle with All England, single-handed, man to man,
How the hop-men watched their hero, massive, muscular, and tall,
As he mingled with the players, like a king amongst them all;
'Till to some old Kent enthusiasts it would almost seem a sin
To doubt their County's triumph when led on by Alfred Mynn.

But whatever his triumphs for the Gentlemen and in other representative matches it is in Kent cricket that the name of Alfred Mynn shines with the greatest lustre. He was a Kent man through and through, and his heart to the end was in his native county; he played in the county side for a quarter of a century, and Mr H. S. Altham, writing in 1926, called him the 'greatest of Kent cricketers'.

The glorious triumphs of the eleven for which he played are part of cricket history. Surrey, Nottinghamshire, and above all Yorkshire, have had their eras of supremacy, but Mr Altham has recorded his view that, 'taking into consideration the changed conditions and increased development of the game, one is still tempted to suggest that no finer county eleven has ever taken the field than that which represented Kent, in the 1830s and 1840s. And the stalwarts of the team, the five-fold rock on which its success was built, were the 'five mighty cricketers' acclaimed by W. J. Prowse. 'Felix, Wenman, Hillyer, Fuller Pilch, and Alfred Mynn' – the names have not yet lost their power to thrill. For not only could they, at their greatest, be justly rated the five best cricketers in England, but each one of them was a man of the highest character, and their comradeship was as the comradeship of King Arthur's Knights. In the words of Pilch the Kent eleven was 'an eleven of brothers, who knew one another, and never knew what jealousy was'.

Mynn and Felix first appeared for Kent in the same match in 1834, when the county put up a side after a lapse of five years. But the great days began in the following year when Fuller Pilch, the young Norfolk tailor and the best bat in England, was induced for a salary of £100 a year to come and live at Town Malling (West Malling) and take over the management of the ground. From then on he was the prime architect of his adopted county's success. Although for a season or two he continued to play for Norfolk and for the North he soon became a thorough Kentishman. As he himself said, 'as soon as any man had been twelve months amongst the cherry orchards and hop-gardens and the pretty Kentish girls, he couldn't help becoming Kent to the backbone'.

Pilch managed Kent cricket off the field as Wenman did on it. He was responsible for the ground, and his care and supervision put Town Malling, and later Canterbury, among the best grounds in the country. He was the principal selector of teams, and was ever on the look-out for budding talent. Many amateurs owed their success to his early help, and he encouraged aggressive play. 'We players,' he used to say, 'must show the public the game, and cannot go in and hit her; but I like a young gentleman who is active as a cat in the field, and as mischievous as a ship's monkey when he is in – who doesn't care for anybody, and who will hit her all over the shop.'

Pilch's play has already been described; for years he was the mainstay of Kent batting, and nobody in England could compare with him. In his whole career he made ten centuries, a most exceptional number at that time. As a man he was simple and unassuming, with a dry humour that made him the best of company. When the centre of Kent cricket moved to Canterbury he became the landlord of the Saracen's Head, which was thenceforward the favoured haunt of all his cricketing friends; he never married, and his sister helped him to run it. He is said to have been a silent man, but he was loquacious enough when Fred Gale visited him in the back parlour of the Saracen's Head and prompted him to talk of the old Kent eleven. To those recollections, faithfully recorded by 'the Old Buffer', we owe much of our knowledge of the great days of Kent.

As staunch a character was Edward Gower (or Ned) Wenman, who like Mynn was Kentish to the backbone. He was born at Benenden and lived there all his life; and he is not forgotten at the Bull Inn in that village to-day. The Wenmans were a great cricket family; altogether seven of them played for Kent at some time or other, though of the rest only John Gude Wenman, Ned's cousin born within a week of him, attained much distinction. The family made Benenden one of the best cricket clubs in Kent, and in the early 1830s before the county revival the team took on some of the strongest sides in England.

Wenman was big and strong, standing over six feet in height and weighing fifteen stone. He was an excellent bat, a hard hitter who could also defend, a sound back player with a brilliant cut. But he was most famous as a wicket-keeper. He was perhaps the first wicket-keeper who can really be called great, Tom Box of Sussex being a few years younger. Wenman stood up close to the wicket, even to bowlers of Mynn's pace, and being brilliant with his left hand took more balls on the leg than any wicket-keeper before him. At the same time he did not attempt to take them all. 'What's the good of Mr Walter Mynn for long-stop,' Pilch recorded him as saying, 'if I am to do all his work and knock my hands to pieces? No; let him do his work, and I will do mine.'

Wenman played for Kent for nearly thirty years, and he was the regular captain of the side. As such he bore a great reputation. Felix has left his tribute; in a letter to Fred Gale he wrote: 'Many and many a match have we played *sub silentio*, when we were under the superior generalship of Wenman. He had only to look, and we moved, like the stars obeying the dictates of a great centre.'

When Wenman was not available Pilch led the side; it is a commentary on the difference between that period and later times that neither of the great amateurs, Mynn and Felix, is ever recorded to have done so. Prowse certainly speaks of Kent being 'led on by Alfred Mynn', but this presumably refers to his being in the forefront of the battle rather than in command. There is, curiously enough, a single apparent reference to Walter Mynn captaining the Kent side. In the Sussex match at Brighton in 1836, reports *Bell's Life*, 'Lanaway having thrown up a halfcrown for W. Mynn to cry to he called a woman, and having won, Mynn chose to go in first'. This was the first Kent match after Alfred Mynn's injury at Leicester.

As a man E. G. Wenman was one of the most highly respected professional cricketers of his day. After paying tribute to Mynn and Felix in his *Oxford Memories* the Rev. James Pycroft wrote: '. . . if, as to moral qualities, I add to them the names of Cobbett and Wenman, I should name two of the first players of my day, who as Nature's gentlemen have left the most pleasing recollection on all who ever played with them.'

William Hillyer, who learned his cricket at Town Malling, was the youngest of the five, six years younger than Alfred Mynn. For years he and Alfred were Kent's opening bowlers; ' "Mynn and Hillyer!" ' wrote the Rev. E. V. Bligh. 'What terrors that phrase inspired to the elevens of All England and Sussex, and of one or two other counties which in the "forties" alone played cricket.' After a few years Hillyer's bag of wickets grew much bigger than Mynn's, and he was probably the better bowler, though he was not so much feared by batsmen. He bowled fast-medium with a big break from leg, and according to William Caffyn 'his ball had a decided curl in the air'. Caffyn also says that he had a remarkably easy delivery, but Gale in a letter to *Cricket* described his run-up to the wicket as a series of shuffles.

Hillyer, a man of medium height, was one of the best slip fielders in the country and a sound though unattractive bat, a reliable man in a crisis. He was a good-natured, popular cricketer, whose nickname was 'Topper'. Bligh describes him 'as I first remember him – in his top-hat and braces; with his none the less curling and crafty ball; his sharp twinkling brown eyes and peculiar hair-pull, or ear-rub, when he all but bowled a man. . . .'

There remains Felix, the brilliant, versatile, volatile, lovable Felix, Alfred Mynn's greatest friend. He was one of the most popular men who ever set foot on a cricket field, and he was the life and soul of the Kent eleven. His real name, as already mentioned, was Nicholas Wanostrocht; his Flemish great-uncle had come to England in the late eighteenth century and founded a school called the Alfred House Academy at Camberwell. This school descended to his nephew and in due course to that nephew's son, young Nicholas, then nineteen years old. Felix is said to have been a good teacher, and one may be sure that he won the affection of his boys, but like Mynn he put cricket before business and the school did not prosper under him. At least he coached his pupils on the field; at one time when their number was dwindling and when somebody commented that he had allowed the school to decline he replied: 'True, but if I have only eleven boys they shall play any other eleven boys in England.'

It was in deference to the parents of his pupils that Wanostrocht called himself 'Felix' when he played cricket. The game still implied gambling to the public mind, and for a headmaster to be closely identified with it was not the best advertisement for his school. In 1832 Felix moved the school to Blackheath, and it was after that that he began to play for Kent.

He was without question the most brilliant amateur batsman of the day. He matured rather late (he was born in 1804), but once established he had no rival in batting but Fuller Pilch. He was left-handed, with a beautiful style, and though a small man he had a cut that rattled through the field. Caffyn, in his *Seventy-One Not Out*, says that he was 'one of the very finest exponents of this stroke ever seen', and adds that not even W.G. could excel him. Pilch said it was a wonderful sight to see him bat. 'He knew the whole science of the game,' he added, 'and had a hand and eye such as no one e'er beat him at; and when he saw the ball was pretty safe to keep outside the off-stump, it was a beautiful thing to see him throw his right foot forward – for, as you remember, he was left-handed – and do a little bit of tip-toeing, with his bat over his shoulder, and if he did get the ball full, and it missed the watches, you heard her hit the palings on the off-side almost as soon as she left his bat.'

In defence Felix was a sound forward player. He was also an accurate left-handed underhand bowler, and though he was seldom called upon to do much bowling, he proved his quality in single wicket against Mynn.

But his talents were far from being confined to cricket; he was author, inventor, painter and musician. *Felix on the Bat*, published in 1845, is an admirable guide to the technique of cricket in his time, filled with his own quaint humour. His cricket inventions were numerous; tubular batting gloves were one, and another was the 'Catapulta', a bowling machine with variations of pace and length which had great popularity in cricket practice.

His water-colours are of considerable merit. He painted portraits of many of his cricket friends, as well as of himself, and his pictures of Mynn and others are the best likenesses of them that survive. As to music, he could, said Fuller Pilch, 'make music on anything, from a church organ to a pair of tongs'; he was much in demand with his violin on convivial evenings after matches, and for years he conducted the band at the Canterbury Festival.

Felix, says William Glover in his *Reminiscences of Half a Century*, was 'the Yorick of the cricket field'. He was for ever clowning, and he loved to take a rise out of old Lillywhite, a thing few others dared to do. When playing against him he would come jauntily to the wicket and waste a little time picking up a bit of paper or straw while the old man grew impatient; he would then pretend to notice him for the first time. 'Good morning, Mr Lillywhite,' he would say. 'Hulloa! a cricket match on to-day, eh? and you a-bowling? Well, let's have an innings'. Old Lilly did not care for jesting on sacred subjects, and he would growl in reply: 'You go and mind your batting, *Muster* Felix, and I will mind my bowling.'

Another story of Mynn and Felix is told by Arthur Haygarth. The following incident, he says, took place in a match at Lord's about 1846:

A. Mynn, who was bowling, delivered a ball off which a catch was given to N. Felix, who was standing 'point'. Now Felix was a jocose, amusing fellow, who even during the process of the match would play antics. On missing that catch he immediately fell to the ground, held his head down, tucked up his knees, and folded his arms round his knees, in fact, made himself as much into a ball as possible. Mynn

(I recollect the occasion as if it had been yesterday) walked up to him, took hold of him by the collar of the flannel jacket, and in a jocose manner also held him up, with one arm extended at full length for a second or so. Now Felix, though rather short, weighed, I should guess, about 11 st. . . . This anecdote will prove Mynn's great strength. I saw it myself, when looking on from the Pavilion at Lord's.

Felix and Mynn, the effervescent Fleming and the solid Kentish yeoman, were as different as two men could be, alike only in their good nature; but temperamentally they found themselves completely in tune. 'From the first moment of our introduction,' wrote Felix after Mynn's death, 'we chimed in together, and every time we met only cemented our Friendship.' Pycroft summed them up in a phrase that has often been quoted. Their amiability and good nature, he wrote, were 'perfect sunshine in the cricket-field'.

These were the great players of the Kent eleven when Mynn began to play for his county; but there were others who deserve mention. There was Tom Adams, a vigorous hitter and a great outfield. There was William Dorrinton, one of a family of cricketers, another fine hitter and reserve wicket-keeper. A little later there was William Martingell, a fast bowler from Surrey, brought into the team by Pilch. And there was Walter Mynn, unspectacular but reliable, always ready to hold the fort in a crisis, and the best long-stop in England. When Alfred first bowled in important cricket, according to Pilch, no man in England but Walter would long-stop for him.

There was something very admirable about Walter Mynn. Throughout his whole career he was overshadowed by his younger brother; yet not the slightest suggestion of envy or jealousy on his part has been recorded. The two brothers were constantly in each other's company, both on and off the field, and nothing seems ever to have ruffled their companionship.

Before the great Kent revival the home county matches were played mainly at Chislehurst. This was the ground of the West Kent Club, dominated by the Normans: a family which, though it can boast no player of world class, has perhaps produced more cricketers of good quality than any other family in England. George and Henry Norman appeared occasionally for Kent at this time, but the best of the West Kent members were Herbert Jenner and Charles Harenc. Jenner, who had captained Cambridge in the first University Match in 1827 and was to survive into the twentieth century, was one of the best amateur cricketers of the day; he could bat, bowl and field, and as a wicket-keeper some considered him better than Wenman or Box. Harenc was for a few seasons a bowler of real class; Lillywhite proclaimed him the best in England after himself.

On Pilch's arrival the county headquarters shifted to Town Malling, and Gale, in *Echoes from Old Cricket Fields*, has left an unforgettable description of the cricket scene in those far-away days which must be given in full. He writes:

Now, in imagination, you must come with me to a grand match at Town Malling, the description of which town, if put on paper, would so strongly resemble Muggleton in 'Pickwick', that I have an idea that the real scene of the match between Muggleton and Dingley Dell may have been drawn from Town Malling.

It is five o'clock in the morning, and after a restless night, from anxiety and excitement, we are off in a trap of some kind for a twenty miles' drive to the match; and, as we leave Rochester and get into the Malling road, we find no dearth of company, and the road is much like a Derby-day at an early hour, as the old hands know very well that if they mean to get any stabling they must be early. Nor are the pedestrians less numerous than the riders. We pass many a poor fellow on the tramp, who has started over-night, perhaps to be on the ground in time to see the first over, and to witness with his own eyes the feats of the mighty men of whom he has heard so much.

And what a sight it is in the town! All the inns are full of customers; and though it is only nine o'clock in the morning the horses are obliged to be stabled outside, with a canvas awning over them. And then, what a babel of voices we hear, interspersed with the north country dialect; as in an all-

England match, the north countrymen who played, had their followers, just as the Kentish yeomen assembled to support their eleven. Let us go to the ground, for it is ten o'clock, and the match will begin at eleven to the moment, and we must get a seat in a hop-waggon early, or stand in the sun all day. Here come a lot of players with a crowd of friends following them, in the hopes of seeing a little practice before the match begins. Those two tall men are Alfred Mynn and Wenman, and the short man who has already begun to chaff Lillywhite is Mr Felix. Fuller Pilch and Joseph Guy of Nottingham, who are rivals for the honour of being the best batsman in England, are walking side by side; and you can tell Pilch by his hands being crossed behind his back and a slight stoop in his gait. The man with a bit of straw in his mouth, who is criticising the wicket and suggesting a 'little more roller', is Tom Adams, one of the finest long fields ever seen; and the good-looking fellow with black ringlets is Hawkins, the barber, the celebrated Sussex point; and Mr Charles Taylor – the only man who would run in and drive Alfred Mynn's bowling – is easily recognisable by his tall white hat, in which he always played.

Such was the festive scene when England played Kent. And England v. Kent, which was now to be a leading feature of the cricket season, was the first match in which Alfred Mynn appeared for his county, though in this case the game was at Lord's.

It took place on July 7 and 8, 1834; and this was not only the first match Kent had played as a county for five years, but the first England v. Kent match on level terms that had been played since the eighteenth century. It heralded the golden age of Kent cricket.

Alfred Mynn, Wenman, Felix, Harenc and Jenner played for Kent; Pilch, Lillywhite, Cobbett, Box and Marsden for England. After Mynn's death a correspondent wrote to the *Sporting Life* giving a story of how Mynn came to make his first appearance for his county. Kent, he said, were found to be one man short, and William Ward, walking round the ground, 'observed a young man bowling with great energy and considerable precision'. He asked his name and was told that he was 'a Mr Mynn, from Kent'; whereupon Ward arranged for him to be included in the Kent side.

Nobody contradicted this story, but it is plainly nonsense. In the first place Mynn had for some years been a prominent cricketer in Kent; in the second he had played for the Gentlemen for the past two years, and both times William Ward had been a member of the same team. In such manner are legends born.

The match was not particularly interesting. Kent were all out for 21 in the first innings, the batsmen being badly at sea against Lillywhite. England made 61, only Marsden, with 18, attaining double figures. Mynn bowled only one opponent, but his victim was an illustrious one; of Pilch, said *Bell's Life*, 'one of Mr Mynn's ripping balls has prevented us saying much: Pilch had only gained two, when he was unfortunate not to be enabled to put a stopper upon a ball which *insinuated* itself into his wicket.' Kent made 72 in their second innings, and the 33 needed were knocked off by England for the loss of two wickets.

A return match was played in the following month at Chislehurst, and this time England won by nine wickets. But in the following year, at Chislehurst, Kent turned the tables, winning by an innings and 45 runs. Haygarth in *Scores and Biographies* detracted from the credit of the achievement by remarking that 'this can scarcely be termed a victory for Kent, as England had such a great 'tail' to their eleven, neither J. Broadbridge, Marsden, F. Pilch, Beagley, or Redgate playing'. But William Ward, Ponsonby, Lillywhite and Box were in the England side, and the fact remains that Kent won easily on level terms. Alfred Mynn and Hillyer apparently bowled unchanged throughout England's two innings of 57 and 106, Mynn bowling seven batsmen and Hillyer five. Alfred made 16 out of Kent's 208, the top scores being Mills's 40 and Walter Mynn's 35.

The 1836 match was drawn, and there was no further fixture till 1839. Mynn of course played no cricket in 1837 and not much in 1838, and Pycroft implies that this was the reason why the match was not played; but this seems hardly likely. Pilch had now joined Kent, and it would be a poor compliment to the county to suggest that they were capable of taking on England only when their great all-rounder was available.

He played in a number of other matches for Kent in these early years, but in general showed only moderate form. His best performance in the county was for Leeds against Hadlow in an unfinished match at Leeds on July 27, 1838. Out of Leeds's first-innings score of 108 Mynn, going in second wicket, made 59 not out, the next highest individual score being 12; and when Hadlow had been dismissed for 85, Mynn bowling four men, he again made top score in the second, 23 out of 94. 'The splendid batting of Mr A. Mynn,' wrote the *Maidstone Journal*, 'who after scoring 82 runs from his bat left the Hadlow club 117 to get in their second innings was greatly admired. When night spread her sable veil over the horizon, the cricketers retired to the Park Gate inn, where every accommodation was afforded by the worthy host.'

Another game in which he did well this year was Benenden *v.* Town Malling at Malling, in which he played as a given man for the visitors. This was also drawn, but Mynn made 39 not out out of Benenden's 87 and then took five Town Malling wickets; Town Malling made 122 entirely through the batting of Pilch, who made 58. The match was abandoned after Benenden had scored 105 for seven in the second innings. In spite of his success with the bat *Bell's Life* administered a gentle rebuke to Mynn. He had recently played his single-wicket matches against Dearman* and the paper wrote: 'Mynn seems to have damaged his hitting a little by his single wicket playing; giving more chances to the field than a first-rate player is allowed to give. It is to be hoped he will be satisfied with the renown pretty generally accorded to him of being the best single wicket player in England, and will give up that sort of play and regain his celebrity as a batsman at double wicket.'

The England *v.* Kent match of 1839 was one of the classic encounters of the 'middle ages'. It was played at Town Malling for the benefit of Fuller Pilch on August 19, 20 and 21. The best possible teams had been chosen, and Lord Frederick

* See Chapter V.

Beauclerk was the manager for the England team. It would seem that he also captained it, for it is recorded that, when the Kent batsmen were doing well, he 'frequently went up to the wicket to speak to the bowlers, whom his lordship changed several times'. The handling of a team in the field by some-body who was not himself playing cannot have been a frequent occurrence even in the more elastic conditions of those days; but Lord Frederick was an exception to all rules.

Kent won the toss and made 145, Pilch and Wenman playing admirably against some excellent bowling by Lillywhite, Cobbett and Redgate. 'Whether the balls came fast or slow,' wrote the *Maidstone Journal*, 'creeping grounders or regular flings, Pilch and Wenman knew exactly how to take them and frequently elicited the admiration of the company by the style in which they played.' Pilch was at last finely caught by Frederick Ponsonby in the outfield.

England replied with 130. Ponsonby was run out, and all the rest of the wickets fell to Alfred Mynn and Hillyer; Mynn was bowling at his best, taking seven wickets for 50, but for a long time Guy and the Hon. E. H. Grimston defied all his efforts.

It was in Kent's second innings that Sam Redgate performed his greatest feat, bowling what Mr Altham has described as 'perhaps the most famous over in all "mediaeval" history'. Stearman and Clifford opened the innings, and for nearly an hour no wicket fell; the score was 30, and Stearman, who was playing particularly well, had made 15. Then Redgate was brought on for Cobbett, and in his first over he completely changed the situation. His first ball bowled Stearman. Alfred Mynn followed, and suffered the same fate from the second. Pilch was the next man in, and the third ball whistled past his off stump; according to one account it actually shaved it. His respite was short; the fourth ball shattered his wicket.

In a single four-ball over Redgate had disposed of three fine batsmen two of them among the best in England. He and Lillywhite went on bowling in fine form, and Kent were all out for 64, leaving England 80 to get to win. In their bid for victory it was again Redgate who took the limelight. The rest of the side could do little against Mynn and Hillyer, but Redgate attacked them boldly, hitting five threes and then lifting a ball over the booth for four. Meanwhile wickets were falling, and three runs were needed when Lillywhite, now forty-seven years old, joined Redgate. The crowd watched in breathless excitement, and it is said that a gentleman present offered Hillyer five pounds if he bowled Lillywhite in his next over; presumably, like Lord Frederick, he went out to the wicket to make the offer.

Hillyer's first ball just missed the wicket. The second hit it; a tremendous shout went up, and Kent had won by two runs.

This match was one of the earliest games in which a rudimentary form of bowling analysis was recorded. The score as given in *Scores and Biographies* is reproduced opposite.

Redgate's triumph, alas, marked the beginning of his decline. Pycroft recorded that after each wicket in his famous over he drank a glass of brandy, presumably brought out to him by some over-enthusiastic supporter. No less an authority than M. André Simon has expressed the view that wine and cricket do not mix, and the same may be said of the distilled product of the grape. Alfred Mynn throve on beer, but Redgate had not Mynn's stability of character, and he chose the wrong tipple. The brandy was his undoing; nor were there lacking, so Pycroft tells us, certain jealous rivals ready to encourage his thirst so that his bowling would suffer. We may be quite certain that Mynn was not one of them; but poor Redgate's bowling did deteriorate very rapidly. A few years later he was a back number, and he died destitute at the age of forty.

Large sums of money changed hands at this match. During the great over the odds fluctuated as each wicket fell; one England backer was reported to have lost £1,500 on the result, and another £500.

Pilch had an excellent benefit; yet Kent nearly lost him. After the match he revealed that he had received an offer from Sussex which was so good that he felt unable to refuse it. But this could not be allowed. The Kent supporters rallied round, Pilch was assured that he would not suffer financially by remaining in Kent, and no more was heard of the matter.

Kent were a fine side this year. They played two matches

KENT	1st Inn.	2nd Inn.
W. Hillyer, st Box, b Lillywhite	9	b Lillywhite ... 0
W. Stearman, c Guy, b Lillywhite	12	b. Redgate ... 15
W. Mynn, Esq., c Cobbett, b Lillywhite	10	c and b Lillywhite ... 1
A. Mynn, Esq., b Lillywhite	11	b Redgate ... 0
F. Pilch, c Ponsonby, b Lillywhite	35	b Redgate ... 0
E. G. Wenman, c Box, b Lillywhite	37	b Lillywhite ... 8
C. G. Whittaker, Esq., b Cobbett	1	not out ... 0
R. Mills, c Box, b Cobbett	9	b Lillywhite ... 12
W. Dorrinton, b Lillywhite	0	b Redgate ... 0
W. Clifford, not out	0	lbw, b Lillywhite ... 18
T. Adams, c and b Cobbett	10	b Redgate ... 6
Byes 3, wides 4, noes 4	11	Byes 2, wides 2 ... 4
	145	64

Bowlers	Balls	Runs	M.O.	No-balls	Bowlers	Balls	Runs	M.O.	Wide
Lillywhite	176 for	57	20	0	Lillywhite	84 for	33	11	0
Cobbett	114 ,,	50	12	1	Cobbett	20 ,,	9	1	0
Redgate	76 ,,	24	8	3	Redgate	62 ,,	22	6	2
Taylor	8 ,,	9	0	0					
Garratt	8 ,,	5	0	0					

ENGLAND	1st Inn.	2nd Inn.
W. Garratt, b A. Mynn	5	c Dorrinton, b Hillyer ... 3
J. Guy, c Wenman, b A. Mynn	30	run out ... 10
Hon. E. H. Grimston, c Wenman, b A. Mynn	46	c Wenman, b Hillyer ... 0
T. Sewell, c Hillyer, b A. Mynn	4	b A. Mynn ... 1
J. Cobbett, c Hillyer, b A. Mynn	10	b A. Mynn ... 5
G. Jarvis, b Hillyer	9	b A. Mynn ... 7
T. Box, c Wenman, b Hillyer	3	c Stearman, b Hillyer ... 12
C. G. Taylor, Esq., c Hillyer, b A. Mynn	1	b Hillyer ... 3
Hon. F. Ponsonby, run out	1	run out ... 2
S. Redgate, b A. Mynn	5	not out ... 20
W. Lillywhite, not out	0	b Hillyer ... 0
Byes 12, wides 4	16	Byes 12, wides 2 ... 14
	130	77

Bowlers	Balls	Runs	M.O.	Bowlers	Balls	Runs	M.O.	Wides
A. Mynn	147 for	50	16	A. Mynn	108 for	37	11	2
Hillyer	72 for	30	6	Hillyer	106 for	40	9	0
Whittaker	28 ,,	12	3					
Mills	32 ,,	17	0					
Adams	76 ,,	21	10					

against Sussex, winning the first by two wickets and the second by three. Mynn bowled well in both, and in the first, at Brighton, he made 26 and 27.

In the following year Kent played Nottinghamshire for the first time, at Town Malling in June, and were beaten by ten wickets. This was a bad setback in view of Kent's reputation at this time; but neither Felix, Clifford nor Adams was playing. Guy played the leading part in the Notts victory with a beautiful 73 not out. Kent collapsed in their first innings and never recovered, though Pilch made 63 in the second. Alfred Mynn made 14 and 11, but took only two wickets.

Three Kent *v.* England matches were played this year. The first was at Lord's on July 6 and 7, and England won by 76 runs. Mynn took four wickets in each innings, and in Kent's first he was top scorer with 24. He and Adams, who made 14, joined in some vigorous hitting; Adams drove a ball on to the top of the tennis court, and Mynn answered him with a leg hit to the billiard rooms, striking the framework of the window and breaking five panes of glass.

Ned Wenman was ill and unable to play, and an anecdote from Felix about his absence shows that the less reputable aspect of betting was still not unknown.

'This,' said Felix to Pycroft, 'was uncertain to the last; and then, I am sorry to say, I saw a certain noble lord, and another who should have had a nobler spirit, walk down to the gate at Lord's and obtain the earliest information and then remark, "As Wenman is not playing, and that makes all the difference too, we can now afford to back England. We need say nothing of what we know of Kent's loss".'

'I have lived always a poor man,' added Felix, 'but I never condescended to such tricks as that.'

Kent had their revenge at Town Malling in August, winning by three wickets. Mynn and Hillyer bowled unchanged through the two England innings, Hillyer taking twelve wickets and Mynn seven.

It was in this match that Robert William Keate, nephew of the famous Eton headmaster and a future Governor of Natal, went in first for England and was bowled by Alfred Mynn for nought in both innings. When he had last come up against

Mynn he had also been bowled for nought, and soon afterwards he was beaten at single wicket by G. L. Langdon. This
series of disasters Benjamin Aislabie was inspired to commemorate in the following verse, in which 'b Mynn o' should
be pronounced 'beemino':

b Mynn o – b Mynn o – b Mynn o – Keate
Tried with his bat jolly Langdon to beat!
In vain, for with Langdon can never compete –
b Mynn o – b Mynn o – b Mynn o – Keate!

The third match was played at Bromley in September, and
England won by 139 runs. Kent had hardly a representative
team; neither Felix, Wenman, Dorrinton, Adams nor Stearman was playing. Alfred Mynn, moreover, was apparently
having trouble with his old leg injury and was unable to bowl
in the second innings. But the county side could hardly be
excused for collapsing for 23 and 30. Pilch made 8 and 9,
and the next highest individual score in either innings was 4.

A new era dawned for Kent in 1841, for in this year it was
decided that the county should play England at Canterbury;
and it was as a result of this match that the Canterbury Week
was born.

The origins of the most famous of all cricket festivals go back
to the formation of the Beverley Cricket Club in 1835. This
club had its ground in St Stephen's Field, on the estate of the
Baker family on the outskirts of Canterbury; and the leading
spirits were the Rev. John Baker and his brother William de
Chair Baker. Its matches were social occasions, and the hospitality of the Bakers was famous throughout Kent. The club's
chief rival was the Chilston Club, and in this annual match
great names soon began to appear. In 1839 Felix played for
Beverley and Alfred Mynn for Chilston.

The growing reputation of the Beverley Club, which in
1840 moved to a new ground near the Cavalry Barracks in
Sturry Road, induced the Kent promoters to borrow this
field for the great match which took place on August 10, 11
and 12, 1841. Kent had won at Lord's by 70 runs, but the
Canterbury game saw the result reversed. Pilch batted excel-

lently and Alfred Mynn took eleven wickets, but England won by 74 runs. The occasion was not free from unpleasantness. C. G. Taylor played for England, and the *Kent Herald* found it necessary to administer a mild rebuke to him for not conforming to the spirit of Kent cricket, referring to 'the young scion of nobility, whom *en passant*, we could have wished to see mingling a little more with the party he came to visit, and at least dining with them'. But much more serious was the rumour that arose among Kent supporters who lost money that the county side had sold the match. How this extraordinary idea of a return to the bad old days could have gained currency is difficult to understand, but feeling certainly ran high. It was even said that Alfred Mynn was hissed in Maidstone market when he next appeared there: an experience which must have been unique in the life of the idol of Kent. The *Kent Herald*'s cricket writer, however, effectively scotched the rumour in a strong denunciation of its instigators:

To any knowing the parties thus accused, and possessing either principle or honour, this rumour will seem preposterous, but as there may be some prone to censure without giving themselves time to reflect, it may be well to say a few words. Who is the man that would be bold enough to attempt to purchase the honour of eleven Kentish cricketers, numbering (without being invidious to others) the names of Baker, Mynn, Pilch, Wenman, and Dorrington? Such a man would no more dare to show his face on a cricket field again than the men who could be so basely bought. This villainous report emanated from some sordid 'snob', who had missed winning his sixpence by the match, and thus vomited forth his frothy poison, and what at first was an idle tale became a serious speculation. If such a thing were possible, would it be done so barefacedly? Would five good men have gone out without a run when a hundred runs were wanting? Perish such a thought with him who dares to think it. Did anyone hear that England's eleven was sold when the men of Kent put them out at Lord's Ground on the 26th and 27th of July last for 31 and 41 runs? Surely no more need be said. I have furnished a fair statement of the game as nearly as I could judge it, and I feel as a man of Kent ought to feel in giving the lie to this scandalous tale, and sign myself

A Scorer

This was not the best augury for the future of Kent cricket at Canterbury; yet it was from this very match that the idea of the great week came. John Baker, Frederick Ponsonby and Charles Taylor, in conversation during the game, began to work out plans for developing the present occasion into a more elaborate programme, in which cricket during the day would be combined with social entertainment in the evenings. Ponsonby, then a Cambridge undergraduate, was a keen amateur actor and had formed a university dramatic society. It was now suggested that he should get his Cambridge friends to come to Canterbury in the following year and give performances in the cricket week.

The three young men were true enthusiasts, and they did not allow their ideas to evaporate in idle talk. The Beverley Club took up the matter, and by May 1842 everything was arranged. The week was to be in August; two matches were fixed, Kent v. England and Gentlemen of Kent v. Gentlemen of England. Ponsonby and his friends, assisted by professional actresses from London, were to give performances at the theatre in Orange Street and there were to be a county fancy dress ball and a city ball at Barnes's Rooms, while a band was to play on the ground during the dinner interval at the matches.

All turned out as planned, and the first Canterbury Week was a triumphant success. As regards England v. Kent the outcome was a repetition of the previous season, for Kent won at Lord's (by 50 runs) and England at Canterbury. In the Lord's match Mynn again took eleven wickets; Taylor played splendidly for England in both innings, making 19 in the second with one hand after a ball from Alfred had broken one of his fingers.

The great week started with the return match on Monday, August 1. There was a crowd of 3,000 on the ground, which was flanked by marquees and booths as has been the custom ever since. The band of the 4th Dragoons were placed near the ladies' pavilion.

The match was as interesting as the occasion warranted. Kent won the toss, and opened with Walter Mynn and Adams to the bowling of Lillywhite and Dean. The pair raised the score to 21, a sound foundation, before Adams was caught for 12. Hillyer was stumped by Box at 37 and then Fuller Pilch came in. He was at the top of his form, but with two more added Walter Mynn was caught at the wicket for 21. Now Felix joined Pilch, and the two great batsmen made a glorious stand; in the words of *Bell's Life* they 'commenced such a style of hitting and fine play that we never on any previous occasion had the felicity of witnessing'. They put on 154 runs, and it was not till well on in the evening that Felix mishit a ball from Good that rose suddenly, and was caught at the wicket for 74. Pilch and Alfred Mynn then played out time, when the Kent score was 237 for four wickets, with Pilch not out 98.

Next morning Pilch was out at once, caught by Dean off Lillywhite without adding to his score. Thenceforth only Alfred Mynn (27) and Dorrinton (15) offered any resistance, and Kent were all out for 278. This might well be regarded as a winning score, but England made a vigorous reply and by the close had scored 122 for two, with Barker and Guy batting. These two batted equally well next morning, Guy making 80 and Barker 58, and the final England score was 266. Hillyer took six wickets and Mynn two. By now the wicket was badly cut up, and in Kent's second innings Lillywhite and Dean were almost unplayable. E. Bayley made 17 not out, but nobody else reached double figures and the county were all out for 44; Lillywhite took six wickets and Dean four. England then knocked off the 57 runs required for the loss of one wicket.

In the second half of the week the Gentlemen of Kent avenged the county's defeat, winning by 173 runs. Alfred had a good match; he made 24 and 39 and took four wickets in the first innings and six in the second. Felix made 48 and 61 out of the home side's 185 and 254.

The revels went with a swing. Four well-known actresses – the beautiful Mrs Nisbett, Miss Williams, Miss Mordaunt and Miss Engeham – appeared with the amateur actors who in a few years were to become known as the Old Stagers; the amateur band was conducted by Felix. Before the first performance Tom Taylor the dramatist,* who for years was the life and soul of the Old Stagers, came on in cricket clothes and addressed the cricketers in the audience in a prologue written by himself:

> *Cricket*'s the only thing I know a bit about;
> Ten years my shins and knuckles have been hit about!
> But, hello! Who are those I see down there?
> Pilch, Lillywhite, and Fenner – I declare!
> How are ye all? Where men like *you* assemble,
> It's not a little that shall make me tremble.
> While I stand here as champion of cricket
> *You* mind your fielding – *I'll* keep up my wicket.
> You will stand by me, never mind your County;
> Cricketers are all brothers; such I count ye.
> Your cricketer no cogging practice knows,
> No trick to favour friends or cripple foes;
> His motto still is 'May the best man win'.
> Let Sussex boast her *Taylor*, Kent her *Mynn*,
> Your Cricketer, right English to the core,
> Still loves the man best he has licked before.

The plays given were Sheridan's *The Rivals* and Colman's *The Poor Gentleman*, and the amateurs, without the assistance of actresses, also performed 'the Operatic Extravaganza entitled *Othello Travestie*! Being the most excruciating Comic-Operatic Tragedy that was ever tragedized by any Comical and Pastoral Company of Tragical Tragedians'. The list of characters conveys the flavour of this burlesque:

> Othello (an independent Nigger, but a thought too jealous)
> .... Hon. F. Ponsonby
> Iago (from the Emerald Isle) .... Hon. Spencer Ponsonby
> Brabantio (a *leetle* hasty) .... G. Bentinck, Esq.
> Cassio (a man of no note, except for liquor)   Captain Baker

* Author of *Still Waters Run Deep, A Sheep in Wolf's Clothing, Our American Cousin*, etc.

Roderigo (a silly youth, but partial to Mrs Othello)
.... Captain P. Munday
Duke of Venice (partial to beer and tobacco, like many other
dukes) .... J. Loraine Baldwin, Esq.
Ludovico (a decidedly respectable gentleman) G. Ellison, Esq.
First Policeman (not given to unnecessary interference)
.... T. Anson, Esq.
Second Policeman (very like his comrade) Hon. R. Grimston
Ladies:
Desdemona (a *striking* beauty) .... Charles G. Taylor, Esq.
Emilia (her attendant) .... M. G. Bruce, Esq.

On the Saturday the assembled cricketing gentry of Kent
decided to take a further step. A meeting was held at the
Fountain Hotel, under the chairmanship of Mr William Deedes,
the Kent M.P., and a resolution was taken 'to establish, upon
a more extensive scale, a Kent Cricket Club'. The Town Malling club was wound up, the Beverley ceased to exist as such,
and arrangements were made for Fuller Pilch to transfer his
residence to Canterbury and take charge of the Beverley
ground.

A couple of other matches played in 1842 must be noticed.
Kent beat Sussex at Town Malling in July by six wickets. The
victory was largely due to Mynn, who took five wickets in
each innings, bowling very fast, and made 51 in the first; he
took part in a fine partnership with Pilch, who scored 67.

In September Kent beat England by an innings and 10
runs in a third (but not truly representative) match played
at Bromley. It was a low-scoring game, England being dismissed for 64 and 30. Mynn took six wickets in the first innings
and five in the second.

The year 1843 was a fine one for Kent, though there were
two early setbacks. Neither was discreditable. Sussex won a
close match at Brighton in June by 20 runs, and a week later
the Gentlemen of England beat the Gentlemen of Kent at
Lord's by three wickets. Sussex had not won this match since
1836, and they had lost to Kent ten times in succession, so this
victory was an encouraging fillip; apart from old Lilly they
were a young side, full of promise. Kent had their revenge at

Canterbury (not in the Week), winning by 116 runs; Mynn took eleven wickets.

From this point in the season Kent were invincible. They met England at Lord's in July and beat them by three wickets. Alfred Mynn bowled magnificently, taking four wickets in the first innings and eight in the second. Six of these eight were bowled, and it was mainly due to him that England, who had led by 16 on the first innings, were all out for 63.

The match was remembered for a remarkable catch in England's second innings by Dorrinton. He was fielding long-stop, and Good, a left-handed batsman, tried to sweep a ball from Hillyer round to leg. He mishit it, and the ball sailed high over long-stop's head. Dorrinton started off at full speed towards the pavilion, and as the ball was travelling fast away from him he hurled himself forward and took it a couple of feet from the ground. An immediate collection was made for him among the M.C.C. members, and he was called to the pavilion to receive a donation of several pounds.

In the Canterbury Week Kent beat England by nine wickets. In this match the bowling analysis was recorded, and in England's first innings of 82 Mynn took five wickets for 45 runs; it would appear that extras were included in the 'runs' total. Kent replied with 152, Pilch making a beautiful 57 not out and Alfred Mynn 21, and England were then dismissed for 93. Alfred's figures were four for 49.

The Gentlemen of Kent beat the Gentlemen of England by 31 runs in the second match of the week. In this game Alfred put up one of the best bowling performances of his career, taking fifteen wickets. In the first innings he took eight for 37 and in the second seven for 36; again these totals included extras, of which there were totals of 22 and 11. No fewer than twelve of his fifteen victims were bowled.

Finally there was again a third Kent v. England match, this time at Jempsted Park, near Benenden, the seat of Mr T. L. Hodges. It was for the benefit of E. G. Wenman, in whose honour a dinner was held. Hodges, a prominent Kent cricket supporter, presided and proposed 'success to the noble game of cricket', adding that he could not do so without coupling with it the name of Edward Wenman, to whose benefit they were indebted to the present honourable and vast assemblage who came far and near to do honour to the integrity of a cricketer he felt pleased to respect.

Kent won by 99 runs. Alfred Mynn took five for 28 and six for 11. Eleven wickets in a match was a figure he achieved with remarkable regularity.

He was still playing from time to time in minor matches in the county, and two in which he appeared this year are worthy of note. The first, at Swingate, is of interest for the unusually dominating role played by Walter Mynn. The two brothers were playing for Oxney against Beverley, and in Beverley's first innings of 88 Alfred took six wickets and Walter three. Then Oxney made 152, and of these Walter scored 66. The game was left unfinished after Beverley had lost six wickets for 10. The two brothers took three wickets each. Walter hardly ever bowled in important matches, and nothing is known about his style of bowling.

Walter was in good form this year, and he was the most successful batsman in the second of these matches, Married v. Single of Bearsted on the village green. Walter, who was a widower, made 34 out of 106 for the Single, and Alfred 0 out of the married total of 70. But the most interesting member of the Married team was 'Wm. Mynn', who made 11 not out and bowled one and caught one according to the *Maidstone Gazette*; caught two according to the *Maidstone Journal*.

Was this Walter and Alfred's eldest brother? We cannot be sure; he was fifty-one years old in 1843, and established in business as a hop merchant in Southwark. There is no other record of his doings in the cricket field; and he had a son who was also William, and who may possibly have been visiting his uncles. But William Mynn, in a letter which will be quoted later, referred to himself as 'an old cricketer', and it would seem most likely that it was he who played at Bearsted; for a veteran he did not do badly.

At the close of this match, the *Maidstone Journal* records, 'an abundant supply of necessary comforts was provided by Mr Godding, of the White Horse Inn, whither the players, accompanied by a large portion of the spectators, repaired to partake, after which, merry songs and appropriate toasts closed the

Alfred Mynn, by Felix

Walter Mynn, by Felix

Alfred Mynn, by Bromley

Felix—Self-portrait

William Ward

William Clarke, by Felix, 1848

Harvey Fellows

Portraits
of
ALFRED MYNN, ESQ.ᵉ and N. FELIX, ESQ.ᵉ
taken just previous to their playing the return
Single Wicket Match,
FOR THE
CHAMPIONSHIP of ENGLAND,
at
BROMLEY, KENT.
Sepᵗ 29ᵗʰ 1846

Mynn and Felix, by C. Cousens, 1846

The All England XI, 1847—Guy, Parr, Martingell, A. Mynn Esq., W. Denison Esq., Dean, Clarke, Felix, O. C. Pell Esq., Hillyer, Lillywhite, Dorrinton, Pilch, Sewell

Sussex v. Kent at Brighton, engraving by W. H. Mason (for key, see page 214) Lillywhite is about to bowl to Pilch, with Box behind the wicket. Alfred Mynn is in flannels in the right foreground with his arm on his brother Walter's shoulder. In the left foreground, leaning on his bat, is Felix.

Alfred Mynn—the only surviving photograph

Admission

TO THE TESTIMONIAL IN HONOR OF

A. MYNN, Esq.

AT LORDS, JULY 26th & 27th, 1847,

Patronized by

THE MARYLEBONE CLUB.

A. Mynn,

Match—Between Two Select ELEVENS of all England.

Signed Ticket for the Alfred Mynn Testimonial Match at Lords, 1847

Alfred Mynn's Tombstone in Thurnham Churchyard, Kent

harmony and pleasures of the evening'. It may be confidently assumed, without straining the evidence, that the three Mynns were well to the fore in this part of the proceedings.

The 1844 matches were of less interest, though Alfred was in good form with bat and ball. In the Sussex and the England games honours were even, in each case Kent winning one match and losing the other. The Gentlemen of England beat the Gentlemen of Kent at Lord's, but the Canterbury match was left drawn.

The 1845 season was an unfortunate one for Alfred. It was not his form that was the trouble; he played well enough when he was able to turn out. But he was sadly harassed by financial tribulations.

This is an aspect of his career which has hitherto remained obscure. Now it is possible, at least so far as this particular year is concerned, to trace some details of what actually happened.

A number of writers have suggested that Mynn had frequent spells of imprisonment for debt; it was a fate that not infrequently befell more eminent persons than him in the first half of the nineteenth century. But so far as cricket historians are concerned I have been able to trace the assertion to no earlier date than 1914; in *Lord's and the M.C.C.* by Lord Harris and F. S. Ashley-Cooper, published in that year to commemorate the centenary of the present Lord's ground, it is stated that 'Mynn was often imprisoned for debt and bailed out by his supporters on the eve of a great match'.

'Often' may well be an exaggeration, and one might be inclined to suspect that Ashley-Cooper was guilty of a little embroidery. For when, seven years earlier, he had interviewed Edward Hodges, the question of Mynn's financial position had been discussed. Ashley-Cooper then recorded Hodges as saying that things did not prosper with Alfred, but that he had some generous friends in the brothers Banks and Walker and 'Lord Cavendish' (presumably the Hon. Frederick Cavendish, a keen cricket supporter). Hodges went on:

The last named used to follow him from place to place in order to see him perform, and was always eulogising his play. Once, just before the commencement of an important match, I saw him liquidate a debt for Mynn, and so prevent his arrest, for which a warrant was about to be served.

This is a very different thing from saying that he actually saw the inside of a prison; but whether or not such an experience was a frequent occurrence in Mynn's career it certainly did happen on more than one occasion in 1845.

Alfred was absent from the field in the earlier part of the season. In May and early June Bearsted played Gravesend twice. Alfred was always ready to turn out for his own village if not required for a more important match, yet only the name of Walter Mynn appears in the score sheet. 'Circumstances and urgent engagements,' says the *Maidstone Journal*, prevented Alfred from playing. Later in June the M.C.C. played the Western Counties at Lord's, and according to *Scores and Biographies* 'Adams, happening to be on the ground, was taken as a given man for the West, instead of A. Mynn, Esq., who was unable to come as was intended'.

The next match in which he might have been expected to play was Kent v. Nottinghamshire at Canterbury at the end of June; again Walter was playing, but not Alfred. And it was the same in two matches in the following week: Gentlemen of England v. Gentlemen of Kent at Lord's and Sussex v. Kent at Brighton. So far as the spectators were concerned he was clearly expected to play in both these last-named matches, as in both cases *Bell's Life* recorded that the betting on Kent slumped when it was learned that he was not to appear.

When at last he did play it was as a given man for East Sussex against Chalvington at Mountford. This minor match was played on July 11 and 12, and there is no contemporary comment on his re-appearance. But in his next match, England v. Kent at Lord's, we come across the first hint of what the 'urgent engagements' that had kept him away must have been.

The match started on Monday, July 14, and by the end of the day each side had concluded an innings: England 114, Kent 82. Alfred took five wickets and made Kent's top score of 18; he was evidently available for the whole day. But next morning he was absent. 'England,' records *Bell's Life*, 'on

commencing their second innings, sent in Barker and Martingell, the bowlers being Hillyer and Adams, in the absence of
Mr A. Mynn.' In the afternoon, however, he reappeared,
and the same paper relates:

> The appearance of Mr Mynn upon the ground was the
> signal for the commencement of loud and long-continued
> clapping of hands, in demonstration of their gladness at his
> return amongst them, and as it would appear as a mark of
> condemnation at the course of conduct which had been
> observed towards him by the person who was the real cause
> of his absence in the morning.

Obviously he had been in trouble, and the reason for it had
apparently spread around the ground. One would at first sight
be tempted to think that this might have been the incident
mentioned by Hodges; but *Bell's Life* gives a list of the more
distinguished noblemen present, and Frederick Cavendish's
name is not included. Also, as will appear, the debt was not
liquidated.

But a month later there is more definite evidence. *Bell's Life*
had been discreet to the point of obscurity; but some provincial
papers had no such inhibitions. Alfred played regularly during
the rest of July and the first half of August, evidently unmolested.
But a crisis came with the return Western Counties *v.* M.C.C.
match on the Lansdown ground at Bath on Tuesday and
Wednesday, August 19 and 20. Mynn, Pilch and Box were
playing as given men for the West, whose victory by an innings
and 94 runs was mainly due to Pilch scoring 117. Mynn took
eleven M.C.C. wickets, but his triumph was followed by
ignominious calamity. The account of the game in the *Bath
Chronicle* of August 21 ends as follows:

> At the conclusion of the game, a somewhat strange cir-
> cumstance created a considerable degree of excitement. A
> Sheriff's Officer, accompanied by W. P. Hall, Mayor's
> Officer, appeared on the Down with a very ominous piece of
> paper, in the shape of a warrant, for taking the person of
> Mr Mynn, or obtaining from him about 130*l.*, owing by
> him to some creditor in London. The parties arrived on the

ground at about one o'clock, but it was arranged that
Mr Mynn should not be disturbed till the conclusion of the
game, but that then he should surrender himself. When the
last wicket was drawn the players returned to their cottage,
Mr Mynn being followed closely by the Officers, who kept
their man in view. However, Mr Mynn got into the cottage,
and a number of his friends placed themselves in the door-
way, and effectively prevented the Officers from entering.
The upshot of the matter was that one of Mr Mynn's friends
undertook to pay the money, or to deliver Mr Mynn to the
Sheriff's Officer last night. We have not heard which course
was taken. The Sheriff's Officer says that he shall take proceedings against those who resisted him in the execution of
his duty.

The friend in question was not as reliable as Frederick Cavendish; two days later the *Bristol Mirror*, repeating the story as
told in the *Bath Chronicle*, added that 'the money not being
paid, Mr Mynn was safely lodged in Wilton gaol on Thursday'.
It was not till September 15 that Alfred played again – for
Gentlemen *v.* Players at Brighton.

The veil is lifted by a document preserved among the Kent
County Council archives, and by a few meagre references in the
press. The document is a statement of the affairs of Alfred
Mynn, dated August 29, 1845, and it reveals that in this year he
not only was in and out of prison a number of times but also
went bankrupt.

The examination with which the statement is connected was
held at Exeter. The Exeter division of the bankruptcy court
covered a large area of the west country, and it was at Wilton
that Mynn passed his last spell of imprisonment. But it appears
that he had previously been twice in Maidstone Gaol and once
in 'the Queens Prison in the County of Surrey'. This explains
his absences from the cricket field in the early part of the
season.

The account of his vicissitudes appears over Alfred's own
signature. He states that he was 'in no way of business' during
the period in question and that from February to May he was
staying at the Nag's Head inn in Southwark. But from May 26

to July 7 he was in prison. In July, apparently, he decided that his only hope of liberty lay in declaring himself insolvent, and he was heard on his petition at Maidstone before Mr. Commissioner Harris, who granted him his discharge.

Whatever the price he was now a free man, though not for long. Only one creditor had been named: John Wyatt of Stoke House, Alverstoke, Hampshire, who acted through his solicitor, Frederick Dolman of Carey Street. The sum mentioned was £127 12s., which agrees with the sum of about £130 which was said to be owing to a creditor in London at the time of the Bath arrest. But it appears that before the August proceedings Alfred was advanced a further £100 by Dolman to repay a loan from his brother John. The fact that he borrowed from the very man who was hounding him suggests that Wyatt was a money-lender, and Alfred was now perhaps able to convince Wyatt's solicitor that he could offer good security. Against the money-lender theory is the Hampshire address, which seems to make it unlikely. But in the absence of more evidence further speculation is futile.

By the arrangement of July 7 Alfred gave Dolman a warrant of attorney (his brother Walter standing as guarantor) to pay the money by instalments of £15, the first payable on July 25. But the money was not forthcoming. Alfred's brother-in-law George Powell had made himself responsible for it, but he fell ill and the time expired without payment being made. Powell later offered to produce the money, but Dolman refused to accept it unless a further £2 19s. was added for costs. This Powell refused to do, suggesting that this sum should stand over until the next instalment was due.

There the evidence of the statement of affairs ends, but obviously the wrangle between Powell and Dolman prevented a satisfactory settlement, and Mynn was arrested once more at Bath on August 20. Nine days later he signed his statement of affairs, and on September 9 he appeared in the bankruptcy court at Exeter. *Woolmer's Exeter and Plymouth Gazette* reported that 'nothing material was elicited by the examination', but that 'in answer to a question, the insolvent stated that he did not get anything by playing cricket'; a statement which does not altogether carry conviction.

A little light on what he did get out of cricket is cast by the statement of affairs. Mynn states that in July and August he received six sums of £5 and one of £6 for playing in matches. This does not seem very much, but he must have made a bit of a profit; his travelling expenses from Canterbury to Tunbridge Wells for a match are given as 12s., and for journeys to Gravesend and Rochester as £1 10s. 6d. 'Other travelling and tavern expenses' during the whole period came to 'about £10'.

But £5 a match was hardly enough to keep him going, and how the two Mynns were existing at this time is a mystery. Pycroft, writing a few years after Alfred's death, said that he was 'by vocation . . . a hop-merchant'; but there is no record of his being in the hop business till the last few years of his life, when he was playing only occasional cricket. Moreover he told the bankruptcy court that he was in no way of business in 1845. That he received generous help from his rich friends and patrons is undoubted, but he surely cannot have lived entirely on their bounty and the small sums he received for match expenses.

Be that as it may, the court at Exeter accepted his explanation of why the first £15 had not been paid, and Alfred was given his interim discharge. Once more he was at liberty, and so far as is known he had no more spells of imprisonment. Nor is anything further known of the action threatened by the sheriff's officer. Doubtless Powell and other friends now rallied round and saw him through till the debt was paid. It is pleasant to read that the functionary who set him free at Exeter was a Mr. Commissioner Bere.

The incident at Lord's on July 15 remains unexplained. It can hardly have been Dolman who molested him, for the first instalment of the debt was not yet due. It looks as though there must have been another creditor, who was perhaps paid off by one of Mynn's patrons.

To return to the Kent matches of 1845, the county lost the England match at Lord's by 80 runs; Alfred, perhaps unsettled by his experience in the morning, took only one wicket. A few days later the county lost to Nottinghamshire by eight wickets at Trent Bridge. This game aroused exceptional interest in the North. Notts, and William Clarke in particular, were intensely ambitious to beat the great Kent eleven, and Clarke in later years used to say that July 17, 1845, was the happiest day of his life: the day he bowled Felix and Mynn without a run between them.

Stories are told regarding both these scalps that fell to Clarke. Felix was in his most impish mood. He had made 54 in the Canterbury match, and when he advanced jovially to the wicket shouts were heard from the crowd of 'Now for some sport' and 'Here comes Clarke's master'. Clarke was nettled, and his temper was not improved when Felix, who loved baiting pompous and peppery bowlers, coolly took guard four yards in front of the wicket and waited for the first ball with his bat slung contemptuously over his shoulder. But it was Clarke who laughed last. Felix played a few balls, but then the old bowler suddenly sent down a fast over-pitched one, and Felix, jumping hurriedly back, knocked his own wicket down.

But it was Mynn's wicket that gave Clarke the greatest joy. Since 1836 Alfred had enjoyed an enormous reputation in the North, and Clarke seems to have had quite a fixation about him. Dean Hole tells the story:

William Clark [*sic*] was absorbed by one anxious ambition, to bowl him, or get him caught. He walked about the ground before the play began, and murmured at intervals to a friend of mine, who reported the interview, 'If I can only get *him* – if I can only get *him*!' The ground was cleared; Mynn and his colleague went to the wickets, and the umpire called 'Play'. Then Clark bowled, and Mynn seemed to prepare to hit, but changed his mind, and quietly blocked the ball halfway between wicket and crease. Clark bowled again with a similar result, but the ball was stopped much nearer the wicket. A third ball came, but the batsman went back so far that as the ball fell from his bat, *a bail fell also!* For two seconds there was a profound silence; there might have been nobody, where many thousands were. We Notts men were mute with amazement, dumb with a joy which hardly dare believe itself. The 'Lambs' could not utter a bleat. They they roared like lions! They left their seats, and, not satisfied with shouting, they danced and capered on the sward!

It may be remarked that on the score sheet these two batsmen, who seem to have fallen into exactly the same trap, are both down as 'b Clarke'. But 'hit wicket' at that time was not always recorded as such.

It was indeed a poor season for Kent. The England match at Canterbury was lost by 31 runs, in spite of some good bowling by Mynn and Hillyer; the second match of the Week was left drawn. In the England match Mynn made 36, and that was his highest score of the year for the county. Kent's lack of success produced the following poem from a writer signing himself *Cantiensis*:

> Ah! Suffer not ingloriously to pine –
> Glory well earned – laurels no longer thine
> To grace another brow. Yet may we see
> Restored to Kent the palm of victory,
> By nobler feats than those which first obtained
> Her name adorned – her bright renown regained.
> Assume new vigour, and defeats forget
> That now are past; think not thy sun is set.
> 'Tis but a mere eclipse that darkens now
> Its shining orb; still, Kent, upon thy brow
> May it be seen to shine with fairer ray
> Than yet has graced thy most illustrious day;
> And may success, to each new effort lent,
> With honour re-adorn the name of Kent.

The decline was indeed only temporary; yet the writing was on the wall. The five mighty cricketers were not getting any younger, and though there were a few young men coming on they were not of the calibre of their elders. Actually two new recruits joined the eleven this year. One was Martingell, who as already recorded was brought from Surrey by Pilch. The other was Edwin Martin, a hard hitter and brilliant field, who was a useful member of the team for the next six years or so. He is chiefly remembered for a strange story of his later years told by Pycroft.

He once kept a cricketer's shop at Oxford, and there he secured the friendship of a wealthy collegian, who set him up in a farm at Leominster; after which Martin's history is one of those remarkable ones which every now and then tend to show that fact may be stranger than fiction.

Martin had kept on his Oxford shop while attempting to attend to his farm on the borders of Wales. Finding the two incompatible, he sold his stock, and with several hundred pounds of the proceeds in his pocket, he one morning left home on a favourite horse. This was in the year 1849, and from that day to 1869 – twenty years – nothing more was ever heard of him. But in November of that year a man fell from his horse and was killed, at Barcombe, near Lewes; and Martin's relatives were astounded by the news that he whom they had long lamented as probably robbed and murdered had lived unknown so many years, and might then be seen a corpse at the Royal Oak Inn of Barcombe. His papers had disclosed the address of his friends.

Pycroft was often inaccurate, and his story will not hold water. Not only was Martin playing for Kent up to 1851, but in 1858 he played in the Veterans match at the Oval. But one wonders what the basis for this curious tale was, and whether it had any foundation in fact.

Kent had quite a good season in 1846, though Mynn played comparatively little part in their success. The England match at Lord's in July was most exciting. Kent batted first and made 91; Alfred Mynn and Martin were joint top scorers with 21. Mynn and Hillyer dismissed England for 71, Mynn taking five wickets and Hillyer four. Only C. G. Taylor, with 16, put up much resistance. Kent went in again with a lead of 20, but Lilly-white was in devastating form and took seven wickets, the county being all out for 66. Fuller Pilch made 27, and Alfred Mynn again batted well for 17, but nobody else scored more than 4.

This left England 87 to get to win, and at the close of the second day they had made 52 for five. On the final morning Mynn and Hillyer made them fight for every run, but Taylor played magnificently. Three more wickets fell while the score crept up, and then, with one run needed to tie, Taylor was caught off Hillyer for 43. Sewell joined Dean, hit the ball for two, and won the game for England by one wicket. Mynn took four wickets and Hillyer three, and such bowling as theirs, said *Bell's Life*, 'has not been witnessed since the match, some years since, with ten gentlemen with Lillywhite and Broadbridge against eleven players, when the players was put out for 24 the first innings, and 37 the second'.

Making his first appearance at Lord's in this match was William Pilch the younger, son of Nathaniel and nephew of Fuller. He had played for Kent before, but only now became a regular member of the team. He was a sound bat, though not in the class of his uncle.

Mynn was in good form with bat and ball, but a few weeks later he met with a minor disaster. He and Tom Box played as given men for Essex against Gravesend at Gravesend, and during the home team's second innings the two of them (Mynn was presumably in the slips and Box of course behind the wicket) both ran for a catch and crashed into one another. Mynn was not a good man to collide with, but we are not told what injuries Box received; he played for Sussex in their next match, but then had to drop out of cricket for a fortnight. Mynn hurt his knee, evidently once more aggravating the old injury. He did not play again for three weeks, and missed the Canterbury Festival. In spite of his absence Kent avenged their defeat at Lord's by beating England by an innings and 3 runs, Hillyer and Martingell bowling unchanged throughout the two innings. The *Kentish Gazette*, while applauding Kent's victory, lamented the absence of 'the first player of the day, Mr Alfred Mynn, unique type of a Kentish cricketer, noble specimen of a Kentish yeoman'.

There were two great events in 1847. One was the opening of the St Lawrence ground at Canterbury, which from that day to this has been the setting for the greatest of cricket festivals. Pilch was at work on the pitch in the early months of the year; the Week opened on August 2, and the *Kentish Gazette* thus described the scene:

In our last we described the new ground of the Kent club. It is situated an easy distance for the pedestrian from the heart of the city, and abuts upon the Old Dover Road, the ancient Roman Watling Street. The area is a park-like plot adjoining to, and part of the original pleasure grounds of St Lawrence House, the seat of the ancient Kentish family of the Rookes, renowned for their attachment to royalty, and consequent persecutions in Charles II's time. Marquees and pavilions, and refreshment booths, erected in different parts of the ground, forming a ring fence, the Union Jack and Royal Standard gaily floating in the breeze, gave a picturesque effect to the *tout ensemble*, and the appearance on those days when the company was most numerous it is impossible to adequately paint. The view produced an indescribable impression. Brilliant galaxies of Kent's famed beauties promenading or reclining in their carriages, the well-dressed beau, the moustached militaire, the commanding figures and noble mien of the representatives of Kent's ancient houses, the honest bluff countenances of the more staidly attired yeomen – all combined to perfect a scene only to be witnessed in merry England, and in which Kent is unsurpassed by any other county in the kingdom.

Kent celebrated the occasion by beating England by three wickets. Hillyer took twelve wickets, and Felix made seven catches at point. This, however, was the third such fixture this year. Kent had previously won the usual Lord's match in June by 95 runs, and an extra contest, the most important of 1847, had taken place at Lord's on July 26 and 27. It was played in honour of Alfred Mynn.

Felix had been given a testimonial match the year before, and now it was Mynn's turn. It was no secret that he was to benefit financially; one object was said to be to compensate him for the expenses he had incurred after his Leicester injury. That was eleven years before, but possibly the surgeons' bills were still unpaid; in any event he had certainly got into debt and had gone bankrupt two years before. But the main purpose of the match was to show the pride and affection in which the great cricketer was held in Kent and throughout the country. Players and followers delighted to do him honour, and the response to the proposal was magnificent.

The first announcement of the plan was made on June 22, when the *Maidstone Journal* revealed that James Dark had offered the use of Lord's ground for a match in honour of Mynn. It was soon decided that only a Kent *v.* England match would be worthy of the occasion, and to make the arrangements a high-powered committee was appointed, consisting of Colonel Liddell, Robert Grimston, Frederick Cavendish, Frederick Ponsonby, Charles Harenc, A. M. Hoare, Felix and S. W. Ward. William Mynn arranged to sell tickets and receive subscriptions at his premises in the Borough.

Announcing the formation of the committee, the *Maidstone Journal* said that 'the Marylebone Club have adopted this plan to show the great esteem in which Mr A. Mynn is held as a gentleman and as a cricketer, and there is no doubt but all cricketers, as well as the admirers of England's national game, will nobly respond to the call of their great leader at Lord's'.

It is not stated how much Mynn made out of the match, but it must have been enough to relieve him of financial embarrassments for some time to come. Most of the great players of the day took the field, including Wenman, who now seldom played; only Lillywhite and George Parr, among those of the first rank, were absent. According to *Bell's Life* 'one of the largest assemblages ever witnessed congregated at Lord's, . . . not less than 5,000 of the friends and supporters of Mr. Mynn rallying round to do him honour'. And the central figure rose nobly to the occasion.

England won the toss, and scored 82. Clarke, rather surprisingly going in first, made 32 and Hoare 13. The rest were at sea against Mynn, who bowled as fast as he had ever done in his younger days. All his seven wickets were clean bowled.

Kent sent in Adams and William Pilch, but the earlier wickets fell cheaply. Wenman received a great ovation, but was beautifully caught by Haygarth, and five wickets were down for 45 when Mynn joined his old comrade Fuller Pilch. He was cheered all the way to the wicket, and he soon set about the bowling. He quickly lost Pilch, and only Martin gave him much support after that; but it was Mynn who did the scoring. Every hit was cheered, particularly two big ones for five each; the score had been taken to 97 when Hillyer, the last man, came in, and the two great bowlers then added 18 for the last wicket. Mynn was at last stumped by Box off Clarke, having made 48 out of 70 added while he was at the wicket.

England opened their second innings with Haygarth and Dean, and scored 11 without loss before close of play. Next day they were all out for 94; this time it was Hillyer who did most of the damage, but Mynn brought off two fine catches in the slips off his partner. Kent were left with 62 to get to win, and when three wickets had fallen for 57 Mynn came in just in time to make the winning hit. Once again he received the united cheers of the great crowd assembled to do him honour.

The full score of this memorable match was as follows:

ENGLAND	*1st Inn.*		*2nd Inn.*
J. Dean, b Mynn	3	– b Hillyer	9
W. Clarke, run out	32	– c Dorrinton, b Hillyer	2
A. Haygarth, Esq., run out	5	– lbw, b Hillyer	13
A. M. Hoare, Esq., run out	13	– c Mynn, b Hillyer	6
J. Guy, b Mynn	5	– c Wenman, b Mynn	6
T. Box, b Mynn	6	– c Bayley, b Mynn	3
O. C. Pell, Esq., not out	4	– b Martingell	10
R. T. King, Esq., b Mynn	0	– c Mynn, b Hillyer	13
D. Day, c Dorrinton, b Hillyer	0	– b Mynn	1
H. W. Fellows, Esq., b Mynn	3	– run out	6
G. Yonge, Esq., b Mynn	0	– not out	10
Byes 10, wide 1	11	Byes 9, wides 4, noes 2	15
	82		94

KENT	*1st Inn.*		*2nd Inn.*
T. Adams, c King, b Clarke	19	– run out	18
W. Pilch, b Clarke	0	– b Fellows	4
W. Martingell, b Clarke	0	– not out	19
N. Felix, Esq., run out	2	– b Day	14
F. Pilch, b Fellows	12		
E. G. Wenman, c Haygarth, b Clarke	9		
A. Mynn, Esq., st Box, b Clarke	48	– not out	2
W. Dorrinton, b Fellows	0		
E. Martin, b Yonge	12		
L. H. Bayley, Esq., run out	0		
W. Hillyer, not out	5		
Byes 8, wides 0	8	Byes 4, wide 1	5
	115		62

One more Kent incident in 1847 may be mentioned, though its significance was in the future. This was the appearance for the county, against Surrey at Preston Hall, near Aylesford, of a tall, gangling youth of eighteen named Edgar Willsher. He lived at Bearsted, where his promise as a fast left-handed bowler and free-hitting batsman had attracted the attention of Alfred Mynn. In this match he went in last, was bowled for nought in both innings, and took no wickets. He did not play for Kent again till 1850. But in the years to come, when the story of Mynn and Hillyer had faded, he was to develop into one of the best bowlers who ever played for Kent.

Kent continued to hold their own against All England till the end of the decade. In 1848 they had quite a good season, and Alfred Mynn was in splendid form. For the Gentlemen of Kent against the Gentlemen of Surrey at the Oval he made one of his highest scores, 72 in the second innings. He also took three wickets in the Surrey first innings and six in the second; but the home side won by one wicket.

It seemed this year as though the county had been rejuvenated by new blood of a high order. A young bowler named Edmund Hinkly, from Benenden, who had played once or twice for the eleven before, sprang into sensational form in the England match at Lord's. He was a fast left-hander with an easy delivery and a break from leg. In this match England made 120 in their first innings, but Hinkly took six wickets, Hillyer getting the other four. Kent replied with 90, and then Hinkly proceeded to take all ten wickets in the England second innings of 74, five of them bowled. Unfortunately Kent then collapsed for 49, and England won by 55 runs.

It was a great performance on the part of the young bowler, particularly as Kent's regular pair, Mynn and Hillyer, were both playing; it was rare for Mynn to fail to get a wicket in either innings. But Hinkly was only a nine days' wonder. His health broke down early, and though he had a couple of brilliant seasons he soon ceased to be a force in Kent cricket.

Kent had their revenge at Canterbury. The first day's play was completely washed out by rain, but in two days Kent won by ten wickets. In this match Hinkly had no success, if indeed he was called upon to bowl. Mynn took a characteristic eleven wickets, Hillyer five and Martingell three.

Alfred Mynn and William Pilch hit off the five runs Kent needed for victory, and Haygarth records that when Mynn made the winning hit George Parr pocketed the ball and ran off with it. This led to a ruling that at the end of a match the ball should be deemed to be the property of the umpire. It is good to know that this conduct was nipped in the bud, like the ridiculous custom of scrambling for stumps that after the 1939 war reduced the final stages of test matches to a farce.

Kent sustained a sad loss after the season was over in the death of William Dorrinton. He caught a chill while playing for the All England Eleven in the North of England, and died in November at the age of thirty-nine.

In 1849 the county played Yorkshire for the first time, beating them by 66 runs at Sheffield at the end of May. There was no return match, and the counties did not meet again till 1862. Yorkshire's great days had not yet come.

The Sussex match at Brighton in July was a great triumph for Alfred Mynn, for in the first innings, at the age of forty-two, he made 92, the highest innings he ever played for his county. He had a great partnership with Adams, who scored 78; they were together for four hours. Perhaps Mynn was tired by this long innings, for he took only two wickets in the match; Kent won by 116 runs. Curiously enough it was at Brighton that Alfred had made exactly the same score for the M.C.C. in 1836; he only once exceeded it.

Kent also won, by 18 runs, the return game at Tunbridge Wells: a match that was graced by the presence of the Duchess of Kent, Queen Victoria's mother, who 'appeared to take great interest in the play, and was welcomed with heartfelt cheers by the large assemblage'. In this match Hinkly took eleven Sussex wickets.

He had another triumph when Kent met England at Canterbury. The county had lost the Lord's match, but they won at home by 206 runs. England were dismissed in their first innings for 48, and Hinkly took eight wickets. Kent's second innings came to 227, and the highlight was a stand between the two old friends Mynn and Felix. 'Right and left they sent the ball,' reported the *Canterbury Journal*, 'giving life to every part of the field.' Mynn made 54 and Felix 47.

There was nothing wrong with Kent's play in this match. But in fact it was the last victory they were destined to win in this great series of matches against All England. In the following year indeed they came near to winning again, losing by only 15 runs at Canterbury. They were set to get 169 runs in the last innings, and Fuller Pilch with 51 and Wenman, making one of his now rare appearances, with 29 made a great effort. But the bowling of Harvey Fellows turned the scale; he took seven wickets, all bowled.

The second match of the Week, Gentlemen of Kent *v.* Gentlemen of England, was most exciting. The Gentlemen of England scored 153, Spencer Ponsonby making 67; and the home side were all out for 95. Then the visitors made 106, and Mynn, producing something like his old pace, took six wickets. Only John Walker, the young Cambridge and Southgate cricketer, played him with confidence.

This left the Kent amateurs 165 to get to win: a big task. Harvey Fellows bowled at his fastest, and at the end of the second day the side had lost six wickets for 40. But next morning Felix and the Hon. E. V. Bligh, Lord Darnley's brother, pulled the game round. Felix made 36 before he was run out, but nine wickets were down for 151 when C. V. Oxenden joined Bligh. Very slowly they knocked off the runs (or rather Bligh did, for Oxenden did not score), and at one point six maiden overs were bowled in succession. Then Bligh hit a three to the leg, and the match was won.

Bligh made 44 not out. Recalling the match in later years he wrote: 'I well remember these two things chiefly, one, the wrath of Felix because (he said) I ran him out – Felix was a terribly bad runner for all his excellencies; the other, a narrow escape which I had from being *pancaked* by Alfred Mynn, who came out from the tent to hoist me in, and then nearly tumbled over me'.

In the corresponding match at Lord's in 1851 the Gentlemen of Kent won by an innings and 25 runs. Once again Mynn and Felix were associated in a glorious stand, Mynn making 85 and Felix 75. Alfred followed this up by taking six wickets in the England second innings of 64.

But in spite of these feats by the amateurs of the county the glory of the great Kent eleven was fading. In 1852 England beat them by an innings at Canterbury, and from then on the decline was rapid. People began to say that it was absurd to go on playing on level terms, and there were murmurings too against the management of Kent cricket. It was said that the so-called Kent County Club was really only a Canterbury Club; that it was dictatorially run by William de Chair Baker; that there was no attempt to find good new players, and that the teams were not representative of the county in general.

But the real truth was that the great players were getting old, and there were no new ones of quality to take their place. Hinkly had been a disappointment, and Willsher had not yet fulfilled his early promise. Mynn was a shadow of the bowler he had once been, and after 1851 he bowled less and less. Hillyer, though six years younger, was not in the best of health, and he too began to fall away. The batting was still sound, but again this depended on the veterans, and none of them could hope to continue much longer.

Fuller Pilch was under no illusions as to what had happened. 'The fact was we all grew old together,' he told Gale at the Saracen's Head in after days, 'and I often think some of us played a year or two too long; but then, the truth was, though I say it, the public liked the names of Mynn and Felix and Wenman and Hillyer, Adams, Dorrinton, Martingell – ay, and of Fuller Pilch too. And I think we kept the candle burning a little too long, till railways drew people away to take their pleasure somewhere else, and everyone was so busy that they didn't care for making a country holiday unless there was a lot of fiddling and dancing, and play-acting, and what not. They didn't come to hear a good old English song as they did then, so it has all drifted into committee cricket now, and our old backers are under the turf instead of on it.'

Great days were to come again in the history of Kent cricket; but never quite so great as in the time of the five mighty cricketers.

It remains to deal with Alfred Mynn's performances on the stage. It is hard to visualise him as an actor, but for years on end he took part in the Old Stagers productions. Certainly he played no big parts, and he seldom got a mention in the lengthy notices printed in the Kent papers. But his huge size and genial personality made him a favourite with the audience, and in the comic pieces that were a feature of Canterbury Week he was the willing butt of the wags of the company. Sir Edward Chandos Leigh, author of *Bar, Bat and Bit*, relates that Tom Taylor was very fond of introducing Alfred in different characters at the Old Stagers suppers. 'I remember Taylor,' he adds, 'making him strip almost naked, and showing him off in a lecture on the Farnese Hercules, amidst shouts of laughter.'

He probably appeared first on the Canterbury stage in 1847. There is no mention of him in that year, but when in 1848 he played a sentinel in *Charles XII* it was announced that this was his second appearance for the Old Stagers. In 1849 he was in the cast of a 'musical burletta' entitled *The Beulah Spa!*; his part was that of William, 'third waiter at the Beulah Spa, and a general favourite'. He also played in a farce, *X.Y.Z.*, as 'Mr Bill (a person with no real existence)'.

From then on he seems to have appeared regularly. In 1850 he was again a waiter in *Pleasant Dreams!*, and in 1851 a 'gent' in *Hearts are Trumps* and 'Recruit Strong i' th' arm' in *Deaf as a Post*. There is no mention of him in 1852, but in 1853 he was noticed by the *Kentish Gazette*:

> It is only justice to the 'Grand German Water Drinker' to compliment the management upon the admirable selection of gentlemen to fill these important roles, amongst whom Mr Mynn stood out in bold relief, imbibing no less than 12 tumblers in the miraculously short time of as many half minutes; doubtless (as described in the bills) an unrivalled feat.

One does not normally associate Mynn with water-drinking, but no doubt he was ready to devote his capacity for liquid to the most uncongenial tasks in the cause of art.

Again this year he appeared as a 'visitor to the baths'

146

in Tom Taylor's *A Trip to Kissengen*: and in 1854 he was 'Mirza Hadji Baba (Chief Keeper of the Monkeys)' in the same author's *Barefaced Impostors*. In another performance of the same piece later in the week the cast was switched round, and Alfred played 'Abu Stoutansstrong (Keeper of the Pasha's Penguins)'. *Barefaced Imposters* was evidently a success, as it was revived in 1857, Mynn again playing Abu Stoutansstrong. Thereafter he was among the actors every season until the year of his death, though it is not recorded what parts he played.

CHAPTER V

CHAMPION OF ENGLAND

*

Though Sir Frederick and 'the Veteran' bowled straight, and sure, and well;
Though Box behind the wicket only Lockyer can excel;
Though Jemmy Dean as long-stop would but seldom grant a bye;
Though no novices in batting were George Parr and Joseph Guy;
Said the fine old Kentish farmers, with a fine old Kentish grin,
'Why, there ain't a man among 'em as can match our Alfred Mynn!'

It has been said that only two cricketers have been honoured with the title 'The Champion' – Alfred Mynn and W. G. Grace. The assertion needs qualification. W.G. was the greatest figure in the history of cricket, the champion of champions, and whatever great players may arise in the future, however far his individual deeds may be surpassed, nobody can ever rob him of his pre-eminence. He stands, and will always stand, alone.

Mynn is in a different category. Prowse alluded to him as 'our Champion', and the word crops up not infrequently in contemporary press reports of his doings; but, loosely used, it was applied to many other cricketers both before and after his time, even to Richard Newland as long ago as 1744. There was, however, one sense in which Alfred Mynn was genuinely champion of England and was known as such. This was in single wicket. The title was quite unofficial, but was accorded to him after 1838 by general consent; nobody else ever bore it before or after.

Single wicket* as it used to be played has long disappeared from cricket; and though one is tempted to reflect how good it would be to see two great cricketers pitted against each other, man to man, it is not a cause for regret. On modern wickets, even with one or two fielders given, a single bowler

* See Note on Single Wicket, page 215

would be hopelessly handicapped and the batsman, particularly if of the Hutton type, might well never get out.

Even in the great days of single wicket one cannot but feel that many of the matches must have been excruciatingly dull. One reads of games going on for a full day or more with perhaps a dozen runs scored, and of a batsman playing well for hours without scoring at all. Yet these games aroused immense enthusiasm, and were more fully reported than many of the great matches. This was partly the result of betting; individual encounters gave more scope for gambling than games between elevens. Yet there were some matches which deserved all the support they got, and among these were a number in which Alfred Mynn took part.

There were good reasons, of course, for the slow scoring, and as single wicket is such a distant memory it may be as well to append the Laws as they were in force for this kind of cricket in Mynn's time:

When there shall be less than five players on a side, bounds shall be placed, twenty-two yards each, in a line from the off and leg stump.

The ball must be hit before the bounds to entitle the striker to a run, which run cannot be obtained unless he touch the bowling stump with his bat, or some part of his person; returning to the popping-crease as at double wicket, according to the 22nd law.

When the striker shall hit the ball, one of his feet must be on the ground, and behind the popping-crease; otherwise the umpire shall call 'No Hit'.

When there shall be less than five players on a side, no byes nor overthrows shall be allowed. The fieldsman must return the ball so that it shall cross the play between the wicket and the bowling stump, or between the wicket and the bounds. The striker may run till the ball shall be so returned.

After the striker shall have run one notch, if he start again he must touch the bowling stump, and turn before the ball shall cross the play to entitle him to another.

The striker shall be entitled to three notches for lost ball, and the same number for ball stopped with bat, with reference to the 29th and 44th laws at double cricket.

When there shall be more than four players on a side, there shall be no bounds. All hits, byes, and overthrows shall then be allowed.

The bowler is subject to the same laws as at double cricket.

Not more than one minute shall be allowed between each ball.

The word 'notch' for a run, of course, dates back to the days when scores were recorded by cutting notches on a stick.

The provisions for sides of less than five players apply to nearly all matches recorded. There were seldom more than three on a side, and the most important games were between single players. In these matches, the Laws show, the batsman was heavily handicapped. He could score only in front of the wicket, he was not allowed to run out to hit the ball, and he must run twice the length of the pitch to score. Obviously the ideal single-wicket player was a man who was at once a hard forward hitter and a fast bowler. The Laws might have been framed for the particular benefit of Alfred Mynn.

The first single-wicket match which Mynn is recorded to have played was against T. Hills of Malling, who after defeating T. Marshall of Sevenoaks was regarded as the champion of Kent. The game was played in Leeds Park on August 22, 1832; no fielders were given. Hills made 24 and then bowled Mynn for 7. In the second innings, however, Hills was bowled for 0, and Mynn knocked off the 18 runs needed for victory. For some reason it was ruled that wides should not count in this match. This was bad luck for Hills, for Mynn, at twenty-five, was still in his wild bowling stage, and Hills complained afterwards that Alfred had bowled at least fifty wides, which might well have given him the match. Hills, an underhand bowler, delivered no wides.

A return match was played at Town Malling on September 4. This time the result was more decisive. Hills again batted first and was bowled for 2. Mynn made 32 before being run out, and then caught and bowled his opponent for 9, winning by an innings and 21 runs. Hills had no more complaints to make.

Sometimes if a match finished early a single-wicket game

would be got up between some of those who had been playing. Thus after the Kent *v.* England match at Chislehurst in 1834 three members of each side took each other on: Mynn, Wenman and Mills for Kent; Pilch, Marsden and Lillywhite for England. Mynn made 5, Wenman 0 and Mills 3, making the Kent total 8; England replied with 16 (Pilch 10, Marsden 1, Lillywhite 0, extras 5). Lillywhite took all three Kent wickets; Mynn bowled Pilch and Marsden, and Lillywhite was run out. There was time for no more, and England were declared the winners on the first innings.

A fortnight later, at the end of Leeds Park *v.* M.C.C. at Leeds, the same three Kent players took on Cobbett, Marsden and Dark. Again only one innings was played, but even so the game was not finished. The three England players scored 21; Wenman was then bowled by Cobbett for 0, Mynn caught by him for 4, and Mills was not out 5 when time was called.

More interest attached to a challenge match played in the following year between two pairs of cricketers, H. Hall and Cobbett against Mynn and a fellow amateur, A. Jackson. Hall was the proprietor of the Camberwell ground, where the match was played, but it was Cobbett and Mynn who drew the spectators. Cobbett, medium in pace, was one of the best bowlers in England, and a sound bat as well.

Hall and Cobbett batted first. They received 46 balls between them and mustered a total of three: two scored by Cobbett and one wide. Both batsmen were bowled by Mynn. Mynn then scored 5, Jackson 0, and with two wides and a no-ball the total came to eight. In the second innings Hall and Cobbett got seven (Hall 4, Cobbett 1), both again bowled by Mynn. Jackson collected another nought, and Mynn made the three runs needed for victory.

It does not sound a very thrilling match; but the *Sporting Magazine* reported that it 'proved a great treat to the amateurs of this noble and enterprising game, the bowling, hitting, and fielding being all first-rate'.

The game finishing early, another was played with A. Rich substituted for Jackson. Mynn and Rich made 3, Hall and Cobbett 5; but there was rather better scoring in the second innings. Mynn made 13 and Rich 14; with two no-balls the total was 29. The match was left drawn when Hall had made five not out.

Mynn played in two more single-wicket matches this season. The first was at Reigate, when he, Hall and Heath, representing the Camberwell Clarence Club, were beaten on the first innings by three of Reigate – Killick, Allworth and Kent. Mynn made 15 of his side's 29, but Kent topped his score, making 17 to bring the Reigate total to 30 after his colleagues had made one between them. There were 12 wides.

The second game was once more on Hall's ground, though Hall himself was not playing. The sides were Mynn and Marsden on the one hand and Redgate and Good on the other. This should have been a good match, but it was ruined by injuries. Mynn had hurt his left hand and had to bat one-handed, and Redgate, who batted first, received a bad blow on the knee from Mynn and was unable to bowl. This robbed the game of interest; Redgate and Good made 6 and 28; Mynn and Marsden 14 and 10. Good made the best score, 20 in the second innings; but Mynn made a courageous reply, getting 9 with his one hand.

Alfred Mynn's name is found in no more single-wicket matches till 1838. But in that year he played his two famous matches with Dearman of Sheffield.

A series of events led up to these games, and Mynn was not originally involved. It all started with Marsden, also of Sheffield, throwing out a challenge to 'F. Pilch or any other man in England' to play two matches, home and home, at single wicket. This challenge was first issued in 1830, but it was not till 1833 that Pilch accepted. Then he overwhelmed his opponent. He was not a great bowler, though he usually managed to get wickets when he did bowl; but his batting was far too good for Marsden, who however was well suited to single wicket, as he was a fast underhand bowler and a hard left-handed hitter. But at Norwich, Pilch's home ground, Marsden made only seven runs in his two innings, and Pilch, with 73 and four extras, won by an innings and 70 runs. The return match at Hyde Park, Sheffield, was equally devastating. Pilch made 78 in his first innings and 100 in his second, and won by 127 runs.

By these games Pilch established himself as being without a rival at single wicket except Alfred Mynn. There was much talk of a coming match between the two, and on May 31, 1835, *Bell's Life* reported that a match had been arranged. Three weeks later the following letter appeared in the paper:

Camberwell, June 16th, 1835.

Sir – Having been much annoyed by numerous letters and inquiries in consequence of a reported match of single wicket, for 100 guineas, between Mr Fuller Pilch and myself, you will perhaps oblige me by inserting this letter, as the only means of checking any further annoyance to me. I am open to Mr Fuller Pilch, or any other player in England, from 20*l.* to 50*l.* a side, for a single wicket match at cricket, between this and the 31st of August, provided it is played at Lord's or the Camberwell Ground. If, therefore, Mr Pilch feels inclined to accept the challenge, time, place, and amount of stake, may be easily arranged, by applying to Mr Hall, at his Cricket-ground, Camberwell.

I am, Sir, obediently yours,

A. MYNN.

At first sight this letter would appear to be the only surviving literary effort from Mynn's pen, though its pompous and petulant tone seems most uncharacteristic. But Alfred, it seems, had nothing to do with it. On July 12 the following paragraph was printed in *Bell's Life*:

We have authority for saying that the challenge, in our paper of the 21st ult., from A. Mynn to Fuller Pilch, was without the consent of the former. The fact is, that within the last three months there was a private offer, on the part of a friend of Mynn's, to back him against F. Pilch; granting the latter the privilege of naming his own sum, time, and place, but the friends of Pilch declined the invitation.

Who was guilty of this forgery? We shall never know, for the matter does not seem to have been pursued; presumably it was somebody who had a financial interest in a meeting between the two cricketers, and wanted to force the issue. But

153

Mynn and Pilch never did play each other, and it is clear that Pilch had no intention of taking part in such a game. Years later he said that he never liked playing against Alfred, because the two of them were 'like brothers'. But this hardly seems an adequate reason. It would appear that Pilch was not keen on single wicket; his two games against Marsden were the only important ones he ever played.

But meanwhile James Dearman was ambitious to prove himself a champion. Two months after Marsden's discomfiture at Pilch's hands Dearman had defeated Thomas Heath at Sheffield by 105 runs, scoring 107 in his first innings. He now felt he could succeed where his fellow Yorkshireman had failed.

The challenge was not made till 1838, and it came as usual through the columns of *Bell's Life*. On May 13 the paper announced that Dearman would be backed against any man in England for £100. Acceptance was prompt; on May 27 the following answer appeared:

Sir – In answer to Mr Dearman's challenge in your paper to-day to play at single-wicket with any man in England, I beg leave to accept that challenge, and I hereby offer to make the match: to play home and home for £100 each match, and to toss for the choice of the place of playing the third or conquering match for a similar sum should each party win one of the two matches. I wish to avoid advertising my name, and will therefore merely add that I live within 35 miles of London, and am Sir, yours respectfully,

A CRICKETER.

Bell's Life added: 'Should Dearman agree to the above, we will furnish him with the means of ascertaining who the Cricketer is, and where the match can be made.'

We learn from Denison that the southern cricketer's backer was Mr Selby of Town Malling, and the cricketer was apparently Fuller Pilch. On June 3 *Bell's Life* reported that Mr G. Hardesty of Sheffield was ready to make the match on Dearman's behalf, and soon afterwards it was announced that the contest would be between Dearman and Pilch. On July 8, however, a further announcement was made:

Pilch had withdrawn from the match, and Alfred Mynn would play instead. It was reported that there had been a misunderstanding about the stakes, Pilch insisting on £200 a side; but when discussing the game with Gale some thirty years later Pilch simply said that he 'chose to name a man, and named Alfred Mynn'. Once again, it appears, Pilch was not anxious to play a single-wicket match.

The first match was played at Town Malling on August 20, 1838; Caldecourt and Good were the umpires. Mynn took the game with the utmost seriousness, and had actually gone into training for it. When he was dressing to play he called Pilch into his bedroom. Pilch found him standing without his shirt on, and Alfred asked him anxiously: 'Fuller, do I look fit to play to-day?' 'Why, he looked fit to carry a church and a whole congregation round the town,' was Fuller's comment later.

Gale, it is interesting to note, states that this was the only match he ever saw that was actually played for money. One frequently reads of matches being made for £100, £500 or occasionally £1,000 a side, but according to another writer this merely meant that the backers had guaranteed the money in the event of loss. W. W. Read says that the usual stake for a single-wicket match was a tripe supper or a boiled leg of mutton with turnips.

Dearman and his friends had arrived the day before; Selby lent his carriage for Mynn to go and meet them at Rochester, and they were entertained with the greatest hospitality at Selby's house at Malling. Interest throughout Kent was enormous, and when the match started there were 5,000 spectators on the ground. The physical contrast between the players was marked, for Dearman, though strong and sturdy, was only five feet two inches tall; they were promptly nicknamed David and Goliath.

Goliath won the toss and went in to bat. Gale watched the match and remembered the Kentish hero batting in a close-fitting jersey bound with red ribbon, a red belt round his waist, and a straw hat with a broad red ribbon. His stalwart form and immense power and reach, wrote Denison, seemed to set at defiance the fine bowling of his antagonist, and he appeared to

155

place the ball pretty well as he pleased. He was in for about half an hour, receiving 82 balls and making 58 hits, off which he scored 33 runs, before Dearman caught him. One wide made his total 34.

The issue was put beyond all doubt when Dearman went in. The little Yorkshireman seemed utterly confounded by the pace of Alfred's bowling, and in eight minutes' batting he touched only one ball out of nine, off which he scored two runs. There was one wide, and Dearman's score stood at three when a 'ripper' from Mynn took the top of his middle stump and split it halfway down.

This was more than the northerners had bargained for. At the beginning of the game the betting had been even, but now it was five to one on Mynn, and when Alfred, batting with consummate ease, reached 50 in his second innings, it rose to twenty to one. Gale records that Mynn scored largely by cover-point hits, 'though he lifted two balls apparently into some adjoining county'. He had made 88 when at last Dearman bowled him. He had made 119 hits off 178 balls, and again there was one wide, making his total for the two innings 123.

Against such play Dearman had no chance, but he managed to gather eight runs in his second innings. He was a good off-side hitter, and Gale thought that Alfred out of sheer kindness of heart gave him a few off balls to score off. But it was nearly six o'clock, and a shout arose from the Kentish yeomen: 'Time's short, Alfred! Finish him off!' Alfred obliged. With the 18th ball down came another 'ripper', and up went the stumps.

'I have a vision in my mind,' wrote Gale thirty-three years later, 'of a middle stump flying up in the air and spinning like a wheel, and perhaps if anyone will go and look for it on the Town Malling ground, it will be found spinning still.'

Dearman had been overwhelmed. But he had shown spirit and pluck, and Denison paid tribute to him in an immortal phrase. 'It is but justice to Dearman to say,' he wrote, 'that he delighted the spectators throughout by his unflinching bottom.'

An impromptu verse, said to have been written on the field by 'an old cricketer', was published in the *Maidstone Journal*:

York challeng'd *England* to a match of cricket,
The stake one hundred guineas – single wicket;
Kent takes the gage, the first game nobly wins,
And now against the *World* will back her *Mynns*.

After the great match a three-a-side game was started,
Dearman's backer Hardesty partnering Mynn and Dearman
against Pilch, Redgate and 'a gentleman on the ground'. But
it was not played out and earned no place in *Scores and Biographies*.

Dearman can have had little hope of reversing the result in
the return match, but the game of course had to be played.
Mynn travelled up to Sheffield the following week; Selby and
his wife went with him, and Selby acted as long-stop in the
match. What long-stop did, in view of the Laws of single-
wicket, had no bearing on the play, but he probably had quite
a tough assignment.

The game was played on the Hyde Park ground on August
27; again there was a crowd of 5,000 on the ground. Dearman
batted first, and after the first few balls he made one or two good
hits, seeming to have a better sight of the ball than at Town
Malling. But he made only two; a terrific ball from Mynn,
'almost at lightning speed', took off his bails. Mynn then hit his
bowling all over the field, till at last Dearman, who was normally a fast roundarm bowler, 'threw in a slow underhand
"poppy" and took down his off stump'. Mynn's score was
recorded as 89 balls, 46 hits, 46 runs; his feat, in single-wicket, of
scoring as many runs as he made hits was considered quite out of
the ordinary. But, as Haygarth commented in *Scores and Biographies*, 'Mr Mynn was always a tremendous punisher'.

Dearman made a brave effort in the second innings, surviving for 53 balls and making 8 before Mynn bowled him.
But the second match had been as one-sided as the first.
Dearman, who was helped by six wides in his two innings but
bowled twelve himself, was beaten by an innings and 36 runs.

If the game had little interest, the Sheffield trip was a social
success. Hardesty and Dearman were determined not to be
outdone in hospitality; the Selbys and Mynn were warmly
fêted, and they and their friends were invited to stay on for a

couple of days and play an impromptu match between two teams representing North and South. The South won by 196 runs; Mynn did little with bat or ball in the first innings, but he scored 40 and bowled eight northerners in the second. He dismissed Marsden, Dearman and Barker in one over, and his bowling was described as the best ever seen in Sheffield.

After the game dinner was served on the ground, and the cup was produced that had been presented to Marsden, some years previously, on the occasion of his playing an innings of 227. It was filled with sherry, and Marsden's health was drunk by all the company. 'The ceremony,' reported *Bell's Life*, 'was finished by giving him three times three, hearty cheers, with the true Kentish fire, which seemed to please the Sheffielders, Mr Mynn standing up and giving the signal.'

Alfred Mynn was now undisputed single-wicket champion of England, and it was eight years before anybody ventured to challenge him. During this time he is recorded as playing in only one single-wicket match. This was in 1829, at the conclusion of the Mitcham v. Town Malling match at Mitcham. Three Surrey men – Sewell, Good and Martingell (who came originally from Surrey and had been playing for Mitcham in this match) – took on the two Mynns and Hillyer. The Surrey three made 11 and the Kent men 10; there was no time for a second innings. Walter and Alfred made three runs each, and Alfred bowled all three of the opposition.

When the challenge for the championship at last came it was from Felix. It was arranged that the first match should be played at Lord's, and each player was to be allowed two fielders.

Felix might seem an odd contender for the title. He was a splendid bat, but not a great hitter in front of the wicket; and though he was a better bowler than was generally known (for he was seldom called upon in big cricket) his slow left-handed lobs were not at all suited to single wicket. Few people thought he had a chance against Mynn. He had, however, practised ardently for the match, bowling at a single stump and batting against his own invention the Catapulta.

Felix himself said afterwards that his pretensions to play against Mynn 'were not founded upon any chimerical belief that I should bowl his wicket down, but in the belief, that, having two fieldsmen, I should bowl him a ball at which I knew he could not resist the wielding of his mighty shoulders'. In the event he put up a much better show than either Hills or Dearman had done.

The match was played on June 18, 1846. Mynn originally chose as his fielders E. and W. Banks, the wealthy brothers who so often befriended him; it is probable that they were his backers on this occasion. W. Banks, however, dropped out before the game, and the second fielder on the day was E. Swan. C. G. Taylor and G. J. Boudier fielded for Felix.

There were about 3,000 spectators on the ground, and in the pavilion were most of the great cricket figures of the day; Lord Frederick Beauclerk was there, and so were Lord Charles Russell, Frederick Cavendish, Frederick Ponsonby, Robert and E. H. Grimston, Colonel Lowther, Sir Frederick Bathurst, William Deedes, Charles Harenc, Squire Osbaldeston and Arthur Haygarth. Also present was Mynn's old friend John Willes.

Felix went in first, and off the first ball made a beautiful cut behind the wicket; it was of course useless. He made several more good strokes, but was quite unable to score. In hitting the fifteenth ball he broke his bat, and this unsettled him. The next ball lowered his wicket.

Mynn did not do very much better. He drove Felix's second ball to the end of the ground, but scored only a single. He added four more singles, and then off the sixteenth ball he put up a catch as Felix had hoped he would; it was a hard hit back to the bowler, and Felix graphically described the incident in Lillywhite's *Guide to Cricketers* many years later:

I bowled him a ball 'well up', he hit at it with all his might, and it came like a shot from a cannon straight to my face. I had only time to put up my hand to save my life. Fortunately the ball lighted exactly in the centre of the palm of my hand; the force with which it travelled caused my fingers to close upon the ball, and the shouts of the assembled hundreds gave the catch all the appearance of design.

Mynn had stayed in exactly as long as Felix had, but he had

scored five to his opponent's nought; and this, as it turned out, was enough. Felix played better than ever in his second innings, 'affording a rich treat to the spectators by making fine cuts and leg hits, all behind the bounds.' The experience must have been heartbreaking for him; he made stroke after stroke that would have brought him runs at double wicket, but he could not score in front of the bounds. At last, after half an hour's batting, he scored a run; and then came the dinner interval.

After dinner the same pattern showed. Felix played Mynn's bowling with great skill, but the fielding was keen and he could not get the ball away in front of the wicket. He made two more runs, one by a splendid cut that got past Banks, and Mynn bowled one wide; but that was all. At last Mynn got through his guard.

Felix had resisted the great bowler for nearly three hours and played 247 balls, making 175 hits; but it was all in vain. His total score was 4, and Mynn won by an innings and a run.

The time was filled in by playing a three-a-side match between six highly distinguished cricketers – Mynn, Felix and Taylor on one side; Lillywhite, Parr and Dean on the other. Lilly skittled the amateurs out for 4 (Taylor 1, Mynn 2, Felix 0, wide 1), and then Parr made 3 before Mynn bowled him, and Lilly got 5; when he was bowled by Taylor stumps were drawn.

This game was memorable for the fact that Lillywhite bowled a wide. It was said to be the only wide he was ever seen to bowl at Lord's, and it was greeted with cries of 'Bravo Lilly!' from the pavilion.

A return match between Mynn and Felix was immediately arranged, and it was decided to play it at Bromley. It opened there on September 29, on the ground attached to the White Hart Hotel, the manager of which, Mr Pawley, had made excellent arrangements. Two sides of the ground were bounded by two long marquees, and the only thing that could have improved the occasion, commented *Bell's Life*, 'would have been that one of these monster marquees should have been entirely tenanted by the fair sex'.

The umpires were Caldecourt and Sewell. Press accounts are conflicting as to who the fielders were. The names mentioned are R. J. P. Broughton, C. H. Hoare and a certain

Mr Mailer or Marles. Hoare apparently fielded for both sides, but it is not clear how the others were divided.

Felix again won the toss, but soon after he started his innings a heavy rainstorm broke and play was held up for half an hour. This was to the benefit of Felix, for the soft ground hampered Mynn's fast bowling, but in spite of this it was Lord's over again. Felix played admirably, but could not get the ball away in front of the wicket. He stayed in for 65 balls, but scored only one run from the bat, which with two wides brought his total to three.

When Mynn went in Felix bowled very well and forced him to play for safety; but Mynn managed to collect four runs before being bowled by the 31st ball, which was a shooter.

At this point dinner was taken, and at four o'clock Felix began his second innings. He stayed in for the rest of the day, but without scoring a single run. Mynn had worn so deep a hole with his foot in the soft turf that he was frequently thrown off his balance; the result was that he bowled eight wides and one no-ball, and these extras constituted Felix's whole score after the delivery of 167 balls.

The game was resumed next morning. The ground was firmer now, and Mynn bowled no more wides. Nor did Felix have any better success; the score remained stationary until Mynn found the wicket with the twenty-fourth ball of the day. Mynn was left with nine runs to get to win, and these he knocked off without much difficulty in a quarter of an hour.

Once again a three-a-side match was got up to finish off the day; Mynn, Denison and Caldecourt playing Felix, Sewell and Hoare. It was again left unfinished.

The Mynn-Felix matches had been slow and low-scoring, but they were not entirely one-sided. As Mr G. D. Martineau has pointed out, Felix spent much longer at the wicket than Mynn; in the two matches he resisted the bowling for 518 balls. The fact remains that in this time he scored only four runs from the bat.

After the Felix match Mynn received a challenge from Hunt of Manchester, but he declined on the ground that the season was too far advanced. Hunt apparently thought better of his temerity, for the challenge was not repeated next season.

It was also suggested that George Picknell of Sussex should try for the championship title, but again nothing came of it.

Mynn never played another individual single-wicket match, and the title of champion remained his till he died. In his later years he played in occasional games between sides of three or four, but they are of little interest; nor did he particularly distinguish himself in them.

That he was a worthy champion cannot be doubted: probably the greatest single-wicket player who ever lived. He had played six matches man to man, and won them all decisively.

The story that W. G. Grace was presented with his pads as the only cricketer worthy to wear them is suspect. But one would like to believe it true. For they were both cricket champions. Mynn like Grace overshadowed all his contemporaries, as much in character as in physique and prowess.

CHAPTER VI

AUTUMN DAYS

*

And whatever was the issue of the frank and friendly fray
(Aye, and often has his bowling turned the fortune of the day!)
Still the Kentish men fought bravely, never losing hope nor heart,
Every man of the Eleven glad and proud to play his part;
And with five such mighty cricketers, 'twas but natural to win –
As Felix, Wenman, Hillyer, Fuller Pilch, and Alfred Mynn!

In 1846 William Clarke founded his Eleven of England, or the All England Eleven as it came more usually to be called. Whichever title is used the assumption savours of arrogance; for Clarke's was a purely private venture. He did not lack enemies, and when acrimony arose a few years later there were plenty of critics to point out that Clarke had no vestige of right to collect a band of cricketers of his own choosing and declare that they represented England.

There is no reason to suppose, however, that Clarke had any such thing in mind in the first place. His aim was to form a touring team, drawn from among top-class players in all parts of the country, and take it anywhere in Great Britain where cricket had taken root and where the local players were interested in benefiting from the presence of high-class performers.

As to the quality of the Eleven, it was a plain fact that few men played for Clarke in the early days who were not worthy of a place in an England team. The first match played was against twenty of Sheffield on the Hyde Park ground on August 31 and September 1 and 2, 1846, and the team consisted of two amateurs, Alfred Mynn and V. C. Smith, and nine professionals: W. Clarke, F. Pilch, J. Guy, W. Dorrinton, J. Dean, W. Hillyer, W. Martingell, T. Sewell and G. Butler. That was certainly a team that could hold its own with any in England. In the following year Felix, Lillywhite and George Parr joined the Eleven, Parr making a century in his first match; and Felix was appointed president of the club. The management, however, and the arrangement of matches remained exclusively in Clarke's hands. Clarke was secretary, and Mynn, Pilch and Hillyer were the other members of the committee.

It was of course a commercial venture. A handsome profit was made from gate-money, and out of this Clarke is said to have paid his professionals from £4 to £6 a week during the tours. It is highly probable that Mynn and Felix took part on much the same terms. Once again one feels that it was only by courtesy that they could be called amateurs.

Controversy soon raged, and continued for many years, on whether the formation of the Eleven was a good or a bad thing for cricket. At first the tours took place only at the end of the season; a little later at the beginning and the end. But as time went on the Eleven's doings encroached more and more on the season proper, and it was complained that other matches declined in interest because Clarke took the best players away from the teams to play in his games against odds. Again, even when the centre of the season was not touched, the system threatened many good second-class clubs which depended for their quality on the presence of high-class professionals as coaches during the off-periods. Now such coaches were hard to get.

These were valid objections, and there can be little doubt that on a short-term view the All England Eleven did do harm to the first-class cricket programme. But looking back from the vantage point of a later age we can see that in the long run far more good than ill came from the venture. For what Clarke did was to spread the knowledge of cricket through the land. He took his high-powered team to all corners of Britain, playing against teams of twenty-two, twenty, eighteen, sixteen or fourteen; and where cricket was in a rudimentary state his encouragement helped it to blossom. Many subsequently great cricketers might never have developed their play but for the All England tours, and these tours paved the way for the introduction of the county championship. The verdict of William

Caffyn, who a little later became one of the Eleven's most distinguished members, was that Clarke 'did more than anyone else to popularise our great national game'.

It should be added that the formation of the Eleven was made possible by the development of the railway. In the stage-coach days these regular tours could never have been carried out.

The matches played by the Eleven, taken as a whole, were not of great interest. The opposition was usually weak, and whatever the odds Clarke's team generally found little difficulty in winning. And from the point of view of the career of Alfred Mynn the games are of less interest still. He played regularly for a number of years, but he usually went in low down in the order and made few good scores; while there was such a wealth of professional bowling talent in the side that there was little demand for his services. Possibly, too, he was not over-keen on bowling fast at batsmen who were for the most part 'rabbits'.

At the same time his membership of the team was a sound commercial proposition both for him and for Clarke. For Mynn it provided a regular, if modest, source of income to bolster his always shaky financial position, while from Clarke's point of view the illustrious all-rounder, however little he actually did on the field of play, was the greatest draw the Eleven possessed. Wherever the side went Alfred Mynn was the centre of interest. In the words of Alfred Cochrane 'he was always surrounded by a gaping crowd, anxious to see him or to speak to him, or merely to bask in the glamour of his colossal presence'.

Only occasionally do we hear of him doing anything of note for the Eleven. In 1851 he was in good batting form. Against twenty-two of Stockton-on-Tees he hit a ball out of the ground in an innings of 19, and in the next match, against twenty-two of Northumberland at Newcastle, he played a fine hitting innings of 52, making a big stand with Clarke, who scored 72. Against twenty-two of Gainsborough he made 15 in a low-scoring match, making a stand with his brother Walter, who only very rarely turned out for the Eleven.

In the following year his best performance was against nineteen of Liverpool. He went in first with the promising young Surrey player Julius Caesar, and scored a brilliant 53 out of the Eleven's total of 113. A correspondent in *Bell's Life* expressed his pleasure at seeing 'jolly old A. Mynn going in first and getting 53 as of old'.

The early years of the All England Eleven are more interesting from the social angle than on the field. This was the first time a team had gone on tour as an entity, living together and sharing their pleasures as well as playing together. They were, for a time at least, a happy company, and a spirit of comradeship quickly developed. The team were made welcome wherever they went, and there was great junketing when they visited a small centre whose enthusiasm for cricket had not previously been rewarded with a sight of great players.

Richard Daft, soon to be the Eleven's finest batsman and one of the best of old cricket writers, gives an idea of the atmosphere of those days. In *A Cricketer's Yarns* he writes:

Certainly one never sees such holiday-making and high jinks as we used to in the old All England days, especially at those matches played in small county towns. The All England match was the topic of conversation months before the event took place. Special committees were formed to get up entertainment in the evening, and when the great day arrived the excitement was often intense. I was talking to a gentleman not long ago who told me that in order to see one of these matches he rose at four o'clock in the morning and walked a dozen miles or more to the place. Another old friend, a clergyman, now nearly eighty years of age, was telling me the other day of the first time he saw me play – at Loughborough. He was rector of a small country village in Leicestershire, situated about fifteen miles away from Loughborough, and as no carriages were to be had, he and some friends engaged a cart belonging to the village chimney-sweep and made the journey in this vehicle to the match and back.

The nobility too played their part in entertaining the cricketers. In 1847 the Eleven were in Yorkshire before playing their next match at Newcastle-on-Tyne. They had a week to spare, and Lord Milton, who had played against them at

Sheffield, invited them to spend it at Wentworth House near Rotherham, the seat of his father Earl Fitzwilliam, and play a match there. *Bell's Life* records:

A most joyous and a most English-like week it was; for, in the first place, whilst the hospitable board of the noble earl each day – it may almost be said each hour – groaned beneath every substantial delicacy of the season, so in the second was there so marked a personal attention on behalf of the members of the family towards them as was not merely extremely gratifying to all, but that at once convinced them they were welcome partakers of their lordships' munificence. Whilst the gentlemen of the Eleven were received and regaled in the drawing and the dining-rooms with the family, the professional players had one of the large halls in Wentworth House appropriated for their use. Beds, too, were also set apart for each of the Eleven, the umpires, and the scorers under the roof of this splendid mansion, by the direction of the noble viscount (Milton), and the Hons. G. and C. Fitzwilliam. . . . Throughout each day Earl Fitzwilliam, and the Honourable Ladies Fitzwilliam, Lady Milton, and a string of company, occupied chairs upon the lawn, whilst there were a considerable number of visitors who ranged themselves around the scene of action. The lawn is in the front of the house, which is 210 yards in length, and comprises between 14 and 15 acres of beautiful turf. This spot has been devoted by the noble earl to the purposes of cricket.

The 'gentlemen of the Eleven' were Mynn, Felix, O. C. Pell, T. Townley and E. Macawin, and one wonders how they reacted to all this lavish magnificence. One senses that Mynn at least might have been more at ease drinking beer with the professionals in the large hall. For the match, which was left unfinished, the members of the Eleven were split up among the teams captained by Lord Milton and his brother Charles Fitzwilliam. Mynn failed to score and took only one wicket; perhaps the hospitality was too much for him. He did, however, make two catches.

Four years later the Eleven were splendidly entertained when they visited Scotland. After they had been held to a draw by twenty-two of Glasgow a dinner was held in their honour, with the Earl of Eglinton in the chair; and here we find Mynn in the role of an after-dinner speaker. Called upon for a toast he proposed the health of Sir Thomas Moncrieffe, the Glasgow captain, and his team, saying that 'they had shown a great deal more terrible play than they (the Eleven) had antici- pated'. The toast was drunk with great applause, 'accompanied by several rounds of Kentish fire by Mr Mynn'.

For a couple of years Felix kept a scrap-book, which is still preserved in the pavilion at Lord's. Miscellaneous cuttings are pasted in, but the principal part consists of anecdotes in his own writing, ornamented with sketches and water-colours. The title-page is characteristic:

The
Doings of the Eleven
Being a true, full and particular
account of the Campaigns of 1851 and 1852
wherein will be found
an
Enigmatical
chart of the Gentlemen and Players thereto attached;
a
Geographical
account of the places wherein the cricketing battles were fought;
and a
Topographical
account of those very same battles – the whole
interspersed with anecdotes gleaned by the
way side
Incursions, Excursions, Accidents and Offences.
London
Published by Much Loss & Co – Read by Many Less & Co
Baily Brothers
Cornhill

Mynn figures in a number of Felix's stories. One concerns the occasion when the Eleven were returning to London and 'our Alfred the Great (so called from his gigantic stature)', wishing to spend a quiet afternoon in the country, left the train at Blissworth and instructed the porter to get his luggage out of the van. The porter looked at him, decided that the largest man must obviously have the largest luggage, and got out the biggest object he could find in the van. It was the ponderous printing press that Fred Lillywhite carted around when touring with the Eleven. The train was on the way out before Mynn discovered the mistake. 'No hurried expression of rage escaped the lips of the disappointed luggagee,' records Felix. 'A smile of utmost good nature played upon his manly features. . . . With the aid of telegraph and luggage van, in a few hours all troubles were adjusted. The printing press was sent on to London and the trunk containing the accoutrements of Alfred was sent back from London – and we thought the innocent matter worth recital.'

Felix's water-colour, captioned 'Alfred the Great at Blissworth', shows a vast Mynn waving the train out, oblivious of the porter in the background wheeling the printing press in his direction.

Much of the team's time was spent in playing practical jokes on one another. Most of these, it must be confessed, sound woefully unfunny, and sometimes cruel, as when Tom Box, who was proud of his long hair in the style of the age, was tricked into being cropped like a convict by colleagues who told the barber he was a harmless lunatic. But such jokes were the fashion of the time.

Alfred's name is not attached to any such malicious doings. He did, however, occasionally find himself in circumstances that sorely tried his good nature. Pycroft told the following story of him:

He was once going to a cricket match in a drag, which stopped at some public-house on the way. A brawny fellow came up to him and asked, 'Is your name Alfred Mynn?' On being assured that it was, the questioner said, 'I am going to give you a jolly good licking!' Mynn smiled. But the question was repeated till someone said, 'Take care, he is dangerous and in earnest!' Then followed a fight in the next field, for Mynn was a first-rate boxer. In a very short time he had knocked his opponent down three times. At the third he asked, 'Well, where is that licking?' The man replied, 'I'm not going to get up no more while you are there'. Not long afterwards Mynn received a present of wine from the man's father, who said that he was only too glad that somebody had at last been found to give his son the thrashing he so richly deserved.

Edward Hodges told a rather different story:

Alfred was a most kind-hearted man, and the last person in the world to hurt the feelings of anyone, but one day he was in the company of some friends and cricketers when a common fellow, wishing, I suppose, to show off his courage, began to banter Mynn and raise his temper. Alfred bore it patiently for some time, but at last, unable to stand it any longer, he quietly lifted up the window sash, walked over to the fellow without saying a word, caught him up by the scruff of the neck, and lifted him up and dropped him out of the window, which was about eight feet from the ground.

I am inclined to suspect that these two stories relate to the same incident, and that the first is an elaborated and garbled version of the second. One rings true; the other does not. I find it difficult to visualise Alfred Mynn going into a field and solemnly engaging in a stand-up fight with a man he could have slung over his shoulder with one hand; but that he should quietly and resignedly drop a troublesome bore out of the window is in line with all that we know of his character.

Alfred's popularity increased with the years. It is displayed by the number of affectionate nicknames applied to him. Many, of course, referred to his size. References to 'Alfred the Great', 'the Great Man of Kent' and 'the Kentish Giant' abound in the sporting press of those days. Lillywhite called him 'the Squire', and Daft 'the Don'. Lord Sondes of Lees Court, his early patron, is said to have first given him the latter name.

One nickname, which was widely applied to him in later ages, is suspect: this is 'the Lion of Kent'. *Bell's Life* said in its obituary of Mynn that he was given the name after his single-wicket victory over Hills, but I have been unable to find a single reference to him as 'the Lion of Kent' during his lifetime. The phrase occurs frequently in the columns of *Bell's Life* and other journals; but it is almost invariably applied to Fuller Pilch, though at least once to Wenman. 'Lion' was a term often then used to describe a great cricketer: George Parr was called 'the Lion of the North'. But Mynn's lionhood seems to be posthumous.

Many of the stories about Mynn relate to this period of the 1850s. As he grew older he became more and more of a 'character', developing those individual idiosyncracies that give the flavour of a man's personality. We hear much of his drinking habits. When in Nottinghamshire he usually stayed with George or Butler Parr. These two Notts cricketers were not related, but both lived at Radcliffe-on-Trent, and both became great friends of Mynn; Butler Parr was a brewer. Alfred Mynn's capacity for beer was a matter for awed admiration among his friends, but rather curiously he did not like to drink it out of large glasses: not for him the quart tankard. So Butler Parr used to have ready a large jug and two small glasses, and while his guest was disposing of one he himself filled the other for him; and so it went on till the jug was empty.

Caffyn tells us of his custom of taking a tankard of light bitter beer to bed with him to drink during the night; he also recalls how Alfred loved good living, and was as gargantuan an eater as he was a drinker. 'I have often,' he writes, 'seen him eat a hearty supper of cold pork and retire to bed almost directly afterwards.' This might perhaps account to some extent for his snoring, which was on the same heroic scale as everything else about him. Richard Daft, in *Kings of Cricket*, recounts an agonising experience:

I shall never forget once staying with him at the old 'Three Tuns' Hotel in the Borough in London. My bedroom was divided from his by a wooden partition only. I had not been long asleep before I was awoke by a noise which sounded like the roll of thunder. For a little time I could not for the life of me make out what it was, but all at once it struck me that it must be the old 'Don', as he was familiarly called, snoring. This I was not so much surprised at when I called to mind the tremendous supper he had eaten immediately before retiring to rest. I hammered at the partition, and after a considerable time succeeded in waking him. I could hear him turn over in bed, and in doing so he seemed to make the room shake. Now, thought I, I must try to go to sleep before he starts again; but I had no sooner begun to doze than the horrible noise commenced again, and this continued off and on during the whole of the night.

On another occasion, Caffyn relates, a hotel at Hungerford provided an old four-poster bed which was not equal to Alfred's weight. During the night it collapsed, alarming the whole house.

The thought of Mynn dancing is an awe-inspiring one; but William Glover, author of *Reminiscences of Half a Century*, records that at least once he took the floor. Glover writes:

I once enjoyed the felicity of 'catching out' the jovial Alfred the Great, of Kent, after one of his tremendous long field forward hits. In the evening his very serene Highness was regaled for a time with the delicious strains of string quartet music. I cannot clearly trace the train of events, but it is certain that a *dance* was suddenly proposed later on, and my statement will surprise many who have seen the giant, when I say that his Greatness actually joined in the merry whirl. I had seen Lablache positively revolving on the stage with the petite Sontag, and, therefore, nothing could be absolutely impossible in the dancing world.

In any case, the success of the 'revolutionary' leader was undoubted, and that infallible court of appeal, consisting of feminine judges, unanimously declared that the stupendous Alfred, like his high and mighty musical brother, was one of the 'lightest' trippers they ever had the pleasure of dancing with.

Who was the 'high and mighty musical brother'? So far as is known none of the Mynns had any musical talent: certainly not Walter. Probably Glover was referring to Alfred's 'brother cricketer', Felix.

The year 1851 must have been a sad one for Alfred, for death was busy with the Mynn family. In April John Mynn, the head of the family, died at Hellingly at the ripe age of eighty-eight, just a year after his wife; three months later died another John, the second of the four sons of William Mynn of Goudhurst. This younger John was fifty-seven; he died in Chelsea, but that is almost all that is known about him. Whether Alfred was ever in touch with his old uncle we do not know; and there is little to suggest that he was on closely intimate terms with his brother, though John apparently lent him money at the time of his financial crisis in 1845, But two other losses this year touched him much more closely.

On March 24 his second daughter, Mary Ann Emily Mynn, died at Thurnham; she was twenty years old, and according to the record at Somerset House she died of rheumatic pericarditis after an illness of seven days. 'Her loss will be as irreparable,' said her death notice in the *Maidstone Journal*, 'as her piety and virtues will be long remembered by all who knew her.'

Nine months later, four days before Christmas, her eighteen-year-old sister Eliza Susannah, Alfred's fourth daughter, died 'rather suddenly in London'. Eliza's death certificate reveals an otherwise unknown tragedy in the Mynn family; for she died from gangrene of the lungs in Bethlem Hospital, Southwark. And Bethlem was the successor, on a new site, of that 'Bedlam' that provided so constant a source of amusement to sordid-minded spectators in the eighteenth century. Poor Eliza Mynn was a lunatic.

The two girls lie in a single grave in Thurnham churchyard, a few feet from where their father was buried ten years later.

In 1852 Mynn played in a benefit match at Broadwater, near Godalming, for Caesar, Martingell and Caffyn. The All England Eleven played sixteen of Godalming and District, and the match was mainly memorable for the presence of William Beldham of Hambledon, the greatest batsman of the eighteenth century. He walked seven miles from his home at Farnham, and Caffyn recalls him, in his tall hat and 'beautifully clean smock-frock', talking to the players 'in the most intelligent manner' about the cricket of old times. Beldham was at this time eighty-six years old. Astonishing to relate, he was destined to outlive Alfred Mynn.

The harmony of the All England Eleven was rudely shattered this year. Several brilliant young cricketers had now joined the team. One was Tom Lockyer of Surrey, who was quickly making a name for himself as an even better wicket-keeper than Box or Wenman. Another was James Grundy, a fast roundarm bowler from Nottinghamshire. But the most important was John Wisden of Sussex. Wisden, who lives in cricket history as the founder of the *Cricketer's Almanack* which still bears his name, was a miniature dynamo. He was only five feet four inches in height and weighed seven stone, but he was a fast bowler with a beautiful action who in 1850, playing (rather curiously) for the North against the South at Lord's, had performed the remarkable feat of clean-bowling all ten batsmen in an innings. He was also an excellent bat.

These young players, as well as some of the older ones, found they could not get on with William Clarke. Clarke was dictatorial and cantankerous on the field and close-fisted off it; disputes arose about payment, and in the middle of the 1852 season Wisden and Dean took the initiative in breaking away and forming a new touring eleven of their own. They called it the United England Eleven, and the first match was played against twenty Gentlemen of Hampshire at Portsmouth in August. A week later a meeting was held at Sheffield, where the United eleven were playing, and a resolution was passed to the effect that none of its members 'shall at any time play in any match of cricket, for or against, wherein William Clarke may have the management or control (county matches excepted), in consequence of the treatment they have received from him at Newmarket and elsewhere.' The signatories were John Wisden, James Dean, Thomas Adams, Thomas Hunt, George Granger Brown, John Lillywhite, Thomas Nixon, George Picknell, Samuel Dakin, George Chatterton, Thomas Lockyer, James Grundy, Thomas Sherman and Henry Wright.

It need hardly be said that Alfred Mynn remained loyal to Clarke and to his old friends. His amiability was proof against any high-handed behaviour. Clarke of course was apoplectic with fury. Never again would he have any dealings with the men who had deserted him, and as long as he lived there was no hope of any *rapprochement* between the two elevens.

At the end of the year the battle flared up in the columns of *Bell's Life*. The campaign opened with a prodigiously long letter dated from Cambridge and signed 'A Lover of Cricket'. It was headed 'Notes on Cricket; or, Doings of the Past Season', and it ran to two full columns of small print. The heading belied the contents; after a few opening remarks of a general nature the writer launched out into a venomous attack on the All England Eleven in general and William Clarke in particular. He began with the old criticism of the title given to the team, and proceeded to deal with Clarke's management. Clarke, he said, had recently formed a committee, but only to forestall criticism; he still kept all the arrangements in his own hands. Fuller Pilch, said 'A Lover of Cricket', had refused to serve on the committee, 'not *exactly understanding* how affairs were managed', and George Parr was appointed in his place. Then he went on to the financial arrangements, becoming somewhat incoherent in the process:

Although there is *at present* this committee, they have nothing whatever to do with selecting players (they however do not do it) or the arrangements in any way. Thus if a match was wanted by a county club, Clarke must have been applied to, who (with perhaps but one or two exceptions) never matches for less than £66 (unless for a well known player, a playing matches at a very short distance), and in many places will get £70, and has, I believe, got £75. This is a bargain made by himself, and he *receives* and *pays* all (the latter not until some months have elapsed after the season is over), so that it can easily be imagined why such an eleven travel the country. Clarke receives the amount for 'first-rate players', and pays it partly to 'second-rate ones'. Thus, it may be said, he obtains money under an 'equivocal state of things'. His lowest sum, as I above stated, for a match is, in almost every case, £66. He pays as follows, as near as possible: – Felix, I will say, about £6, Parr £5, Martingell

175

£5, Box £5, Caffyn £4 10s., Caesar £4 10s., Guy £5 (doubtful if so much), Anderson £4, Bickley £5, Mynn £5, the Umpire £4, and the Scorer £1 10s. – total £54 10s. Clarke, therefore, to account for the £66, pockets for himself £11 10s. every match!! and, if he gets £70, the additional sum is added. . . .

The printer may have been responsible for the more garbled portions, but 'A Lover of Cricket' was clearly not a master of English. The passage's chief interest is in giving some idea, though probably not an accurate one, of the rates of pay; from the figures given it would hardly seem that Clarke was guilty of gross profiteering. In another passage the writer attacked individual members of the eleven. Mynn, he said, 'is useless now at any point of the game, in comparison to those we have to fill his place'.

Thereafter the slanging match waxed fast and furious. A correspondent signing himself 'Middle Off' replied vigorously in support of the All England Eleven. Felix, writing without rancour, defended the title, saying that it was assumed 'to distinguish themselves from others, and not with a view to pass themselves off as the best eleven cricketers of England'; he did not deal with the financial issue.

Clarke's own reply appears to have been first published in another paper, but it was reprinted by *Bell*. 'If I had taken the advice of my friends,' he began, 'and some of the leading members of the Marylebone Committee, I should not have answered this "Lover of Cricket"; but as the article in question is principally directed against me with a *leetle* colouring, I thought I had a duty to perform to myself and the public to expose the malicious fabrications of this impartial lover of cricket.'

Clarke went on to say that both his players and the secretaries of clubs were quite satisfied with his arrangements. He denied any rift with Fuller Pilch, and quoted a letter in which Fuller wrote: 'In reply to yours, I am not aware of ever drawing my name from your committee, and I am very sure I never told any one so. I had not read the long, sickly, childish prattle till after I received yours.'

On the question of pay Clarke said that his accuser was right as regards only three of the players he had named. Regarding his own profit he added, not unreasonably, that he orginated all the Eleven's matches, and his time in the winter was wholly devoted to making and arranging them. As to Alfred Mynn, 'nine times out of ten', said Clarke, 'I am written to to request him to come'.

Of 'A Lover of Cricket' he wrote: 'I know his name to be *not Sorrywether*, but something like it, a portly *barrister*, *noted* for his *old Dando qualifications* and his expensive professionals, old Dean and old Lilly, who cost about two penny postage stamps.'

Clarke clearly knew who his assailant was, but in spite of these allusive hints nobody since that time, so far as I am aware, has identified him. One can only conclude that he was some backer of the United England Eleven, probably of the name of Merrywether.

'A Lover of Cricket' wrote another long and rambling letter, in which he renewed his jeers at Mynn. Dean and Martingell wrote in his support, though not mentioning Mynn. The correspondence, continuing well into the new year, became increasingly unedifying.

Through all these wranglings Alfred Mynn, whose name had been bandied about as much as any, remained silent. It was not his custom to write to the press, and he was not the man to let himself be ruffled by attacks of such a nature. But he did not lack a champion. On January 16, 1853, *Bell* announced the closure of the correspondence, but in the next issue one more long letter was allowed. With the measured tread of an elder statesman William Mynn, hop merchant of Southwark, stepped into the fray.

For all the evidence that survives Walter and Alfred might almost have been illiterate; the eldest of the Mynns, however, showed that he was highly articulate on paper. Both in its dignity and in its moderation his letter was in marked contrast with the snapping and snarling that had gone before. It opened with an appeal for concord:

> Mr Editor: My name I trust will be a passport to the columns of *Bell's Life*, and my motive in addressing you I

hope favourably received. As an old cricketer, and of a family not unknown to cricketing fame, I feel greatly interested in all that concerns that noble and national game, and consequently great pain and regret at seeing the schism a 'Lover of Cricket' in *Bell's Life* has occasioned, among those whom I had fancied were as closely united as the Freemasons. From personal conversation with many, as well as from their letters, I see the chasm widening, and an ill feeling spreading, which if not speedily allayed, will be as injurious to them as to the noble science, of which they are some of the stars. To these ill feelings I appeal. Would it not be more consistent with their position as public men to call a little sober reflection to their aid, by which they may arrive at a truth, viz., that the public have nothing to do with their private quarrels, and whether it would not be better to drop their criminations and recriminations (alike discreditable to their heads and hearts), meet among disinterested friends, and by timely and mutual concessions adjust their real and imagined differences, than go on quarrelling, ridiculed by all reasonable and rational people?

William went on to deal with an allegation by Martingell that a subscription of a shilling each per match had been exacted from all the players as a fund to pay Clarke's expenses as secretary; he showed that the fund mentioned, of which Alfred Mynn was secretary and treasurer, had been provided by purely voluntary subscriptions for a benefit for Clarke. The eleven had first agreed to pay £1 each, and this was later altered to a shilling for each match played in 1851.

So far William's tone had been one of sweet reasonableness. But when he came to deal with the personal attack on his brother it took on a note of asperity:

Before concluding my letter, I appeal to the readers of *Bell's Life* whether I am not justified in noticing the uncalled for allusion to my brother, A. Mynn, by the 'Lover of Cricket'? Why does not this self-elected critic on the doings of cricket give us his name? It is unmanly to attack (perhaps) better men than himself, and withhold his name. Whether he be of aristocratic or plebeian origin matters not; he is no

Englishman if he refuses to let us know who and what he is. As to my brother, his character as a cricketer during the 23 years he has been before the public, is too well known to be injured, and to that public, if by my side, he would appeal. But as he requires no aid even from a brother to prove his honesty of purpose, I tell the 'Lover of Cricket' that he never will attempt to force himself before the public one day longer than he is welcomed, or feel he cannot sustain his character as one of the England Eleven.

Yours, etc.,

WM. MYNN.

No. 4, Counter-street, Borough, Jan. 17, 1853.

Possibly William protested a little too much. Alfred loved cricket far too much to give up just because some of his skill had left him, and perhaps he did go on a little too long. But the letter gives a pleasant picture of Mynn solidarity. And at any rate it cannot be said that the old cricketer had outstayed his welcome; enthusiasts all over the country were still clamouring for a sight of him.

There was plenty of cricket in him yet. He had grown enormously heavy, he was slow in the field, and he did comparatively little bowling; but in his late forties he could still hit the ball harder than most men half his age. In 1853 he went on playing regularly for the All England Eleven, but after that his appearances became less frequent, though he is found in the team as late as 1857. He still toured with the Eleven, and when he was not playing he often stood as umpire.

It was in that capacity that he acted when in June, 1854, the Eleven travelled to Bristol to play twenty-two of the West Gloucestershire Club, on a ground belonging to the Full Moon Hotel. The West Gloucestershire had been founded largely through the enthusiasm of a local physician, Dr Henry Mills Grace of Downend, who had high hopes of the cricketing ability of his five sons. In this match, which the All England team won comfortably by 149 runs, Dr Grace went in first for the home side, while his eldest son Henry made the only double-figure score (15) in their first innings. And watching the game with his mother was the doctor's fourth son, then six years old. His Christian names were William Gilbert.

This, so far as is known, was the only occasion on which the two cricket champions were present on the same cricket field at the same time. Neither was playing, and it is safe to assume that neither was conscious of the presence of the other.

In the 1853 Canterbury Week the declining prestige of Kent was cruelly emphasised. There had been much talk of the Kent *v.* England match being too one-sided, and now there was scarcely room for doubt. England scored 324, Caesar making 101 and Caffyn 55, and Kent were dismissed for 47 and 98. It was the last such match played on level terms during Mynn's lifetime. Thenceforward Kent received given men or else were combined with some other county.

In the second match of the week, however, Mynn had a personal triumph that showed he was by no means finished. England won by seven wickets, but Alfred made 33 and 33, top score in both innings. Harvey Fellows scored 61 not out for the visitors.

The following year, a month after the Bristol match, the All England Eleven visited Maidstone to play eighteen of the local club on the Mote Park ground. This time Mynn played for the home side, and in the first innings he scored 42; Maidstone won by eleven wickets. In his next match he did even better, scoring 11 and 54 for Kent against the M.C.C. at Lord's.

In the Canterbury Week of this year Fuller Pilch and Edward Gower Wenman appeared for Kent for the last time. Both were over fifty; Pilch had played his first match for the county in 1836, and Wenman as long ago as 1825.

Still Alfred went on. In July 1855 he played for the last time at Lord's, for the Gentlemen of Kent and Surrey against the Gentlemen of England, and a month later he helped Kent to beat Sussex at Brighton with a splendid first innings of 38. He and Adams, who made 24, 'sent the ball flying in all directions', and Mynn hit one ball from Dean out of the ground for six. In the second innings he again did well with 21.

During the next two years he played quite often, but intermittently. Every now and then he would attract attention with some big hitting, and occasionally he took wickets.

It was during these years that he became associated with the
Southgate Club, which had been founded by the Walker
brothers and was to develop in the next decade into the Middlesex County Cricket Club. The Walkers stood for all that was
best in cricket. They were brilliant players themselves; six of
the seven brothers played at some time or other for the Gentlemen against the players: a record not equalled even by the
Fosters. Moreover the only one who missed the honour (Alfred,
the second brother) must be accounted distinctly unlucky
to have done so: he was not noticeably below the family
standard.

But their performances in the field were far from being their
only service to cricket. A wealthy family of brewers, they were
among the last of the great patrons of the game, devoting their
money to the welfare of cricket and cricketers. Isaac Walker,
father of the seven, had died in 1850, and the head of the family
was now John, the eldest brother. His house at Southgate, then
well in the country, was called Arnos Grove, and here he
formed his club and entertained his cricketing friends. His
mother, who still lived in the house, was an old-fashioned lady
could not bear the smell of tobacco about the place. So John
Walker, attentive to her comfort, had a spacious annexe built
where he and his friends could enjoy their brandy and cigars.

Here the best cricketers in England regularly met. When the
club started, about 1847, the teams consisted of the Walkers
and their friends in the neighbourhood, but in 1855 Walter
Mynn, who had virtually retired from important matches,
began to play for them. From then onwards the club increased
in stature. The Walkers invited prominent cricketers to appear
as guest players, and within a few years it came to be considered
one of the greatest honours in the game to be asked to play at
Southgate. Like Hambledon before it this local club was soon
able to take on the strongest teams in England. Most of the
leading players of the day were to be found in its ranks. There
was one proviso: only the highest standards of conduct, on and
off the field, were acceptable.

In this distinguished circle the old Kentish yeoman was a
welcome and an honoured guest. Alfred Mynn first appeared
for Southgate in 1857, and in the few years remaining to him he

played a considerable proportion of his cricket on the lovely ground at Arnos Grove. John Walker, who became one of his greatest friends, was the most generous of men, and that he helped Alfred financially we know from Edward Hodges and others. The extent of his help cannot be ascertained; Walker benefactions were always shrouded in secrecy.

Mynn's friendship with the Walkers started some years before he played for their club, and the first game in which he played against Southgate was the result of his own initiative. As he gradually dropped out of the county side he took to playing for the Maidstone club, and in 1855 he invited John Walker to take his team there. The match was played at Mote Park on August 27 and 28; both Mynns played for Maidstone, and the five eldest Walkers (John, Alfred, Fred, Arthur and Teddy) for Southgate.

Maidstone batted first and made 100; the top scorers were W. Hammond and Alfred Mynn with 34 each. Southgate replied with 108, Fred Walker making 22 and John 20; Alfred Mynn took four wickets. In the second innings Maidstone made 122, but Alfred got only one. Southgate then scored 118 for six, winning an evenly contested match by four wickets, mainly owing to the batting of Fred Walker, who scored 43 not out. Hammond was run out in Maidstone's first innings, and all the other nineteen wickets were taken by Walkers.

The game had proved most enjoyable, and in the following year a return match was played at Southgate. Maidstone strengthened their team by bringing in Edgar Willsher, but Southgate won by an innings and 44 runs, scoring 182 to Maidstone's 51 and 87. For Southgate A. H. (Arthur) Walker made 40 and John 37, while again nearly all the wickets were taken by the brothers. For Maidstone Alfred Mynn made 20 and 21, and he made a hit that was long remembered at Southgate. V. E. (Teddy) Walker, who was to become the greatest cricketer of the family, was at this time nineteen years old; he had just left Harrow. With the confidence of youth he thought he could easily get Alfred's wicket, and tossed him a slow tempting ball with a view to a catch in the outfield. The veteran gave a mighty heave, and the ball sailed out of the ground and out of sight over the trees.

Teddy Walker in his old age loved to tell this story of his own discomfiture.

It was probably owing to the Walker connection that Alfred used to visit Harrow, where it is recorded that in his last years he often went down to the school ground to bowl to the boys. He was now dividing his time between Bearsted and London, for it appears that he was at last devoting himself to business. Little detail can be discovered, virtually the only source being the meagre entries in the London Post Office Directory. These show that the firm of William Mynn and Company, hop merchants, had been established since 1843 in Counter Street, Southwark; but in 1853 the name was changed to Mynn Brothers. In 1857 two firms are listed: William Mynn and Company, and Mynn Brothers and Company. In the following year 'Mynn Brothers' is changed to Walter Parker Mynn and Company, and in 1859 Walter's name disappears and is replaced by Alfred's.

Little can be deduced from these entries, but it is perhaps legitimate to surmise that William was the solid business man of the family, and that he assisted his younger brothers, when their cricketing days were ending, first by taking them into his own firm and then by helping them to set up on their own. Walter, who was married for the second time in 1849, had taken a house in Merrick Square, Southwark; Alfred's home seems always to have been at Thurnham, but probably the brothers used each other's houses as convenience dictated.

The cricket scene in the last years of Alfred Mynn's career was greatly changed from that he had known when he had first emerged from the village greens of Kent. The railway had transformed travel, and teams moved easily over the whole country. There were cricket clubs everywhere and inter-county matches flourished, though there was still no county championship. Boundaries were the rule, and roundarm bowling was general, but it was no longer such an object of dread to batsmen. The majority wore pads, and wickets had on the whole improved, though Lord's was a glaring exception. In the improvement of grounds William Lillywhite and his three sons played a large part. This enterprising family, who were also responsible for the first regular cricket annuals, formed themselves into a firm which advised and helped in the preparation and maintenance of cricket pitches throughout the country.

Among the great figures of Mynn's younger days many were dead and gone. William Ward died in 1849, and Lord Frederick Beauclerk in 1850. And in the latter year died also John Willes. No record survives of any contact in later life between Alfred and his old mentor, although as mentioned Willes saw his protégé beat Felix at single wicket. But the two must often have met in Kent, and one can be sure that Alfred, with his warm heart and grateful disposition, never forgot the man who had taught him to bowl.

Some of Mynn's contemporaries died young. Poor Sam Redgate was only forty at his death, destitute and a victim of the brandy bottle. James Cobbett, who died in 1842, was only thirty-eight. Dearman, Mynn's old single-wicket opponent, died at forty-seven in 1854.

The two great bowlers who had gone on playing so long died within just over two years of each other. Old William Lillywhite, sixty-one years old, was given a farewell benefit match in 1853. It was England against Sussex at Lord's; George Parr was a given man for Sussex, and also in the team were Lilly's two elder sons, James and John, and C. G. Taylor, who had not played for several years. In the England side were Clarke, Guy, Caffyn, Lockyer and Hillyer. Lilly opened the bowling, but after eleven overs he was taken ill and had to leave the field; in the special circumstances a substitute was allowed for the rest of the match, which England won by 197 runs.

This wonderful veteran survived for another year; then he died very suddenly. On the evening of August 20, 1854, his youngest son, Frederick Lillywhite, left him in apparently good health; but on the following morning he was taken ill and by the evening he was dead. He was buried in Highgate cemetery, and a monument was erected by the M.C.C. bearing the following inscription:

LILLYWHITE. Born June, 1792; died August 21st, 1854. A name to be remembered as long as THE NATIONAL GAME OF ENGLAND, by the practice

and tuition of which for years he earned an honest liveli-
hood. Rarely has man received more applause in his vocation. Few have administered to more happy hours. From
an humble station he achieved A WORLD-WIDE RE-
PUTATION, teaching, both by precept and example,
A SPORT in which the blessings of youthful strength and
spirits may be most innocently enjoyed, to the exercise
of the mind, the discipline of temper, and the general
improvement of the man. THIS MONUMENT testifies the
respect of the noblemen and gentlemen of the MARYLE-
BONE CRICKET CLUB, and of many private friends,
TO ONE WHO DID HIS DUTY in that state of life to
which it had pleased God to call him.

Almost exactly two years later, on August 25, 1856, William
Clarke died. He was fifty-seven, and had gone on playing almost
till the end. His death paved the way for a reconciliation
between the two elevens. In the following year George Parr,
who had taken on the All England secretaryship, approached
Wisden, and a match between the two teams was arranged in
aid of the newly instituted Cricketers' Fund. It was played at
Lord's in June 1857, and the All England Eleven won by five
wickets. Thenceforward the match between the two elevens
was played regularly and soon became the greatest event of the
cricket season, ousting Gentlemen *v.* Players from that position.
But by that time Alfred Mynn had ceased to play for All
England.

A new generation of cricketers was rising to fame. The great
counties now were Surrey and Nottinghamshire. Surrey had a
magnificent batting team. Julius Caesar was a fine, hard-hitting
forward player; William Caffyn an elegant stylist. H. H.
Stephenson was developing into one of the best batsmen in
England, and George Griffith, a left-hander whose head was
set so closely on his shoulders that he seemed to have no neck,
was a mighty hitter. There was also Lockyer, who was a good
bat as well as being the best wicket-keeper who had yet
appeared. The team moreover was reinforced by three brilliant
amateurs: the Rev. C. G. Lane, a powerful hitter and one of
the best cricketers ever to have emerged from Westminster

School; F. P. Miller, a sound bat and magnificent field, and F. Burbidge, a fine off-side hitter. The bowling was not so strong, but Caffyn was first-class at medium pace, while Caesar, Griffith and Stephenson were all good bowlers.

Notts had a more balanced side. Parr was still a great batsman, and there were others coming on; notable among them was Richard Daft, the finest stylist of the day, a batsman even more elegant than Joseph Guy. Among the bowlers James Grundy was fast and dangerous, while R. C. Tinley, who started as a fast bowler, took to slow lobs with which he had great success. But the most formidable was John Jackson, the best fast bowler of his epoch. A splendid figure of a man, he was six foot tall and fourteen stone in weight; if not so fast as Harvey Fellows, he was far more accurate, and like Alfred Mynn he had an easy action that enabled him to keep up his pace hour after hour.

A county that had a new lease of life at this time was Cambridgeshire, owing to the presence of three great cricketers. One was George Tarrant, the only bowler who after the Fellows era rivalled Jackson in speed. For a few overs his speed was terrific, but he was a smaller man than Jackson and he had not his stamina. Tarrant was an unreliable, cantankerous character who was not very popular.

But above all Cambridgeshire had two great batsmen, Thomas Hayward and Robert Carpenter, who by 1860 stood indisputably as the best in England, succeeding Parr as Parr had succeeded Pilch. They were a great contrast. Hayward, the son of old Dan and uncle of his later and famous namesake, was a delicate, nervous, neurotic man who would stand waiting for the ball with his bat anxiously twisting in his hands, held so loosely that it looked likely to be sent flying. But as soon as the ball was delivered he was suddenly transformed into a master; he had every stroke in the game and was the hardest man in England to get out.

Carpenter was the reverse – robust, upright and devoid of nerves, a strong forward hitter. Between the two there was little to choose, though Hayward on the whole had the more impressive record.

Of the other counties Sussex were still strong, with Wisden

186

as the star; while Middlesex, though they had as yet no club
and played few matches as a county, had a good potential
team with the Walker brothers and Tom Hearne, the first of the
great family of professionals.

And as the decade ended reports began to reach headquarters of a brilliant young amateur down in Gloucestershire. Edward Mills Grace, third son of the Downend doctor,
who set all rules at defiance and treated the best bowlers with
deplorably successful insolence.

Kent, sad to relate, had little share in the new talent. The
only bright spot was the form shown by Willsher, who was
becoming a very fine bowler indeed. And even his success had
its dark side, for his arm was so high that accusations were being
made of unfair delivery. A few years later he was to be the
centre of an overarm storm that rivalled the roundarm controversy of Alfred Mynn's early days.

Of the 'five mighty cricketers' Mynn alone now played in an
occasional match. Pilch and Wenman were in retirement,
and in 1857 the other two were both overtaken by failing
health. Felix suffered a stroke; Pycroft records that this took
place after he had been playing for Horsham against West
Grinstead, and he goes on to relate how the great cricketer
accepted his fate. Written in pencil in a book of scores containing the Horsham match, says Pycroft, was the following note
in Felix's handwriting:

Farewell! Farewell!
May 20th, 1857.
After this match I was most terribly admonished by
Almighty God, being struck down by paralysis when in the
enjoyment of good health.

N. FELIX

Pycroft is always unreliable as an historian, and there is no
record of Felix playing cricket after 1854. But it seems certain
that he had a stroke in 1857. He spent his last days at Brighton
and Wimborne, mostly in a bath-chair and finding solace in
drawing. A number of subscriptions were raised to support
him in his infirmity. Pycroft tells how he offered to take him to
watch cricket, but Felix could not be persuaded. 'No,' he

said, 'old recollections, and I fear old friends too, will crowd around; the gap is too wide, the fall is too great, it would upset me quite.'

Hillyer's illness was of a slower and more wasting kind. In June 1857 an anonymous letter in *Bell's Life* revealed that since the end of the previous season he had been suffering grievously from rheumatism; it was some time before it was known that what he in fact had was consumption. The writer suggested that Hillyer, whose 'character as an upright player is perfectly unimpeachable', was deserving of a benefit. The suggestion was quickly taken up, and the following month another correspondent proposed that the benefit should take the form of a match between an England team and a side composed of sixteen or eighteen veterans.

The proposal hung fire until the following year, but then the Surrey committee offered the use of the Oval for the match, on a date to be chosen by Hillyer. He selected August 5, 6 and 7, 1858, and arrangements went forward. Subscriptions were invited and a large and influential committee was formed which included Frederick Ponsonby, Arthur Haygarth, John Walker, Lord Darnley, W. de C. Baker, Alfred Mynn, Edmond Wilder, Herbert Jenner and Squire Osbaldeston. Most of the great players expressed their willingness to play on one side or the other. At one point it was suggested that Hillyer himself should play, but he was in no condition to do so. It is not even certain that he was present, though he must have struggled to Kennington if he found it physically possible.

The match was worthy of the occasion, though at the end of the second day it appeared that the veterans had little chance. Eighteen of them took the field; Alfred Mynn, now fifty-one, was one of them, but the oldest was Wenman, who at fifty-four once more emerged from his retirement for the sake of his old comrade. It had been hoped that Fuller Pilch might do so too, but he did not feel equal to it.

England batted first on Thursday, August 5. Frank Tinley took a few cheap wickets, but Parr and Stephenson made a big stand before Parr was caught at long-stop by Heath and Stephenson by Wenman at mid-off. Then Wisden played an excellent innings, and the England total reached 196.

This was too much for the Veterans, none of whom could muster 20. But Guy played as elegantly as he had ever done and was top scorer with 19. Mynn, going in at the fall of the ninth wicket, was bowled by Stephenson for 0, the third victim of a hat-trick. The Veterans had to follow on, 114 behind, and on Friday evening they had lost seven of their second innings wickets for 58, with Napper and Wenman batting.

But on Saturday the old gentlemen staged a gallant rally. Martingell, Tinley, Heath, Sampson and Sewell all made runs, but the partnership that caught the imagination was that between the two old warriors Ned Wenman and Alfred Mynn. Wenman played steadily, but Mynn struck powerful blows and brought back memories of the great days of twenty years before.

Wenman was the first to leave, caught by Parr off Jackson. As he passed his partner Mynn grasped his hand.

'Good-bye, my fellow cricketer,' he said, 'We have played many a happy match together, and our career is now over.'

The Veterans' innings closed for 169, which was enough to make a match of it and left England 51 to get to win. But Miller and Stephenson had little difficulty in knocking off the runs. Here are the scores, as recorded in *Scores and Biographies*:

ENGLAND

Age

28. Julius Caesar, c Mynn, b Tinley	1		
30. F. P. Miller Esq. c Box, b Tinley	6	not out	20
33. A. Haygarth Esq., c Heath, b Tinley	12		
30. W. Caffyn, c Box b Nixon	19		
32. G. Parr, c Heath, b Hodson	56		
25. H. H. Stephenson, c Wenman, b Martingell	37	not out	21
21. V. E. Walker Esq., b Martingell	7		
31. J. Wisden, not out	28	c Hodson, b Martingell	6
31. John Lillywhite, c and b Hall	10		
31. T. Lockyer, b Tinley	3		
25. J. Jackson, run out	1		
Bye 1, lb 7, wides 5, noes 3	16	Byes 3, lb 1, wides 0	4
	196		51

Bowlers	Balls	Runs	Wides	No-balls	Bowlers	Balls	Runs
Martingell	134	56	1	2	Martingell	20	16
Tinley	149	41	1	0	Tinley	20	15
Nixon	58	28	0	0	Nixon	16	5
Hodson	34	22	2	0	Dean	20	11
Dean	91	21	0	0			
Hall	34	12	0	1			

Eighteen Veterans

Age.

42. James Dean, c and b Stephenson........ 9   b Jackson 0
46. George Brockwell, run out.............. 0   c Caffyn, b Miller 7
50. John Heath, b Caffyn............... 2   st Lockyer, b Walker......15
42. John Hall, run out............ 2   b Stephenson 3
45. Henry Sampson, c and b Walker....12   b Walker...............15
43. Edwin Napper Esq., b Stephenson ...17   c Lillywhite, b Stephenson 13
45. Thomas Adams, c Caesar, b Caffyn..... 3   c Miller, b Walker 1
39. William Martingell, c Parr, b Caffyn 0   b Jackson 21
44. Joseph Guy, b Jackson 19   b Stephenson 0
49. Thomas Box, b Stephenson 0   b Jackson ... 5
51. Alfred Mynn, Esq., b Stephenson........ 0   b Walker............... 19
54. Edward Gower Wenman, b Stephenson 0   c Parr, b Jackson 12
52. Thomas Sewell, c Wisden, b Walker.... 2   b Walker.......... 12
34. James Chester, b Jackson 0   c Miller, b Wisden........... 2
39. Frank Tinley, c Wisden, b. Walker 5   run out 16
43. Edwin Martin, c Caffyn, b Walker 1   c Wisden, b Jackson........... 8
49. James Hodson, b Jackson 0   not out 0
43. Thomas Nixon, not out............ 7   b Jackson 1
Byes 1, lb 1, wides 0, no ball 1 3   Byes 10, lb 2, wide, 1, no ball 1 14

82   164

Bowlers	Balls	Runs	No-balls	Bowlers	Balls	Runs	Wides	No-balls
Caffyn	60	21	0	Caffyn	56	14	0	0
Wisden	36	8	0	Wisden	52	13	0	0
Walker	76	18	1	Walker	128	57	3	0
Stephenson	81	25	0	Stephenson	110	26	1	1
Jackson	16	7	0	Jackson	100	24	0	0
				Miller	48	16	0	0

The match brought in £400 for Hillyer, helping to bring some comfort to the few years remaining to him.

CHAPTER VII

KIND AND MANLY ALFRED MYNN

*

With his tall and stately presence, with his nobly moulded form,
His broad hand – 't was ever open! – his brave heart – 'twas ever warm! –
All were proud of him, all loved him! . . . As the changing seasons pass;
As our Champion lies a-sleeping underneath the Kentish grass;
Proudly, sadly we will name him – to forget him were a sin;
Lightly lie the turf upon thee, kind and manly Alfred Mynn!

When Alfred Mynn said good-bye to Ned Wenman on the pitch at the Oval he may well, in the emotion of the moment, have really believed that his career was at an end; but if so he deceived himself. He was too much in love with cricket to abandon it while anybody was willing to give him a game. And that would be as long as he was physically capable of handling a bat.

Actually he played again immediately after the veterans' match. John Walker took a Southgate team to Wimbledon to play the local club, and Alfred, apparently at short notice, joined the side. Southgate won by an innings and 62 runs, dismissing Wimbledon for 32 and 42. The five eldest Walker brothers played, and as usual they took nearly all the wickets between them, while Fred made the top score of 48. Mynn went in last and made 3 not out.

In 1859 he took a prominent part in the formation of a new Kent County Cricket Club. Dissatisfaction with the existing club had increased throughout the decade. The committee were said to be incompetent, and one correspondent in *Bell's Life*, signing himself 'Scrutator', proclaimed that 'hardly a single member of that body knows how to handle a bat'. The club, 'Scrutator' continued, existed only for the benefit of the Canterbury Week; and that festival was merely a social event without interest for cricketers.

'Scrutator' certainly exaggerated, and he was answered by a member of the Canterbury committee. But exasperation at the state of affairs was deep-rooted, and to a great extent certainly justified; Kent had fallen disastrously from its once proud position in the cricket world. William de Chair Baker was growing more dictatorial with the years, and though it was generally admitted that he had performed great services for Kent cricket it was felt that it was time for new management. Above all it was urged that Kent's cricket headquarters should be located at some place more central than Canterbury.

The club, moreover, was in financial difficulties. The team's lack of success had had its inevitable result in the falling off of support, and by 1858 the position was desperate. The initiative was then taken by Edward and Henry Bligh, brothers of the Earl of Darnley. At an impromptu meeting held after the Kent v. Sussex match at Tunbridge Wells they and a few others decided to take steps to form a new club, not in opposition to Canterbury but to represent the county as a whole.

Members of the Canterbury club next took up the matter. Some thirty of them attended a meeting at which it was resolved that a committee of practical cricketers should be formed, to be responsible for the selection of county teams. But this did not suit Baker. He called another meeting, at which it was said that only three members were present, and there the proceedings of the earlier assembly were declared null and void. Baker undertook the management of the club's affairs 'on condition that he should not be fettered by any committee whatever'.

As this sort of high-handed behaviour was one of the very points complained of, it was clear that there was no co-operation to be hoped for from Canterbury; the Blighs decided to go ahead with their plans. A meeting was convened by circular throughout the county and was held at the Mitre Hotel, Maidstone, on March 1, 1859. Lord Darnley presided, and among those present were Walter and Alfred Mynn; their names were recorded as seconding some of the resolutions passed. It was now decided to form an entirely new club, on the then novel principle that it should have no fixed ground but should be migratory, so as to give each district in turn a chance to see first-rate matches. Darnley was elected the first president, Lord North

N 193

and W. South Norton joint honorary secretaries, and the Rev. George Goldney honorary treasurer. The committee chosen consisted of Henry Bligh, Alfred Mynn, Captain Brenchley, F. H. Norman, Edward Leigh Pemberton, W. W. Knatchbull-Hugessen and Edward Gower Wenman.

Baker accepted the situation with a good grace, and sent a token donation to the new club.

It was important that an interesting game should be arranged to launch the club, and recourse was had to the ever generous John Walker. He agreed to raise a Middlesex team at his own expense, and the match was played at Southgate on June 16 and 17. The Middlesex team included, inevitably, John Walker and his next four brothers, and also John Wisden, Tom Hearne, John Lillywhite and George Wells. Alfred Mynn, F. H. Norman, W. S. Norton and Edgar Willsher played for Kent. The county side could not be called a strong one, though about the best Kent could raise at this time; and it was no surprise when Middlesex won by 78 runs. Mynn made 16 in the first innings. He hit one ball from Wisden on to the top of the highest tree on the ground; the newly established *Sporting Life* commented that he showed that 'there was plenty of hitting in him yet'.

The return, played at Canterbury on July 25 and 26, was the last match in which Alfred Mynn played for his county, twenty-five years after he had made his first appearance. He took one wicket, a rare occurrence now, for 22 runs; John Wisden was caught off his bowling by J. A. Pepys. Mynn also caught Arthur Walker off Hollands, but his batting was undistinguished. He was caught by Alfred Walker off Teddy for 0 in the first innings, and bowled by Wells for 6 in the second.

The result was an even bigger win for Middlesex than at Southgate, the margin being an innings and 58 runs. It was Teddy Walker, now twenty-two and perhaps the best all-rounder in England, who dominated the game. He made 71, and took five wickets for 37 in the first innings and three for 52 in the second.

This same year found Mynn acting in a military capacity. Aggressive gestures by Napoleon III had created alarm that the Emperor was planning to follow in his uncle's footsteps.

Threats of invasion were in the air; a wave of fierce patriotism swept England, and Volunteer Rifle Corps, forerunners of the Territorial Army, were formed up and down the country.

Kent, as the county most vulnerable to invasion, was in the van. In May a corps was formed at Maidstone, and soon afterwards, through the initiative of Mr Charles Wykeham Martin of Leeds Castle, a subsidiary unit, known as the Leeds and Hollingbourne Volunteers, was raised for the range of hills extending from Boxley to Charing. It was this unit, consisting mostly of farmers, that Alfred Mynn joined, though according to one account he was already a volunteer, having helped to form a corps of yeomanry many years before.

He was probably present at the climax of the volunteer movement, the grand parade of twenty-five thousand men before the Queen and the Prince Consort in Hyde Park on June 23, 1860. The Leeds and Hollingbourne contingent, fifty strong under the command of Lieutenant Blackett, mustered at the Star in Maidstone, where they joined their headquarters colleagues and marched to the station headed by their band. At London Bridge they were met by the Leeds commander, Major Wykeham Martin, who led them through London to the park.

The *Maidstone Journal* was enthusiastic about the turnout of the Leeds and Hollingbourne men, who averaged nearly six feet in height and 'were in a fair state of perfectness in their drill'. But one suspects the paper of partisan licence in going on to relate how the Prince Consort pointed out to the Queen 'the difference between the residue of the Maidstone men and the Dorking incapables, who so unfortunately were associated with them in the next batch that marched past'.

Mynn was almost certainly present on October 27, 1860, when Wykeham Martin invited all the members of the corps to a garden party at Leeds Castle, whose 'ivy-clad precincts', reported the *Maidstone Journal*, 'once again resounded with the measured tramp of armed men – not dependent vassals summoned by the feudal lord of the castle to engage in some vengeful foray, but loyal volunteers assembled to enjoy the munificent hospitality of its kind-hearted owner'.

The volunteers of 1859 never fired a shot in anger. Alfred

Mynn was the least bellicose of men; but he was as true-born an Englishman as ever lived, and one cannot doubt that he would have joyfully bashed the bayonets of any Frenchmen who dared to come arrayed to straighten out the crooked roads of England.

Still he could not tear himself away from the cricket field. His name appears in three score sheets in 1860: twice in local games for Bearsted and once for Gentlemen of Kent against Gentlemen of Surrey at Maidstone. In the three matches he made ten runs and took no wickets.

At the beginning of 1861 he had the melancholy duty of paying his last respects to his old friend William Hillyer, youngest of Kent's great cricket quintet and the first to die. Hillyer's death from consumption took place at Maidstone on January 8; he was buried at his native village of Leybourne, and was followed to the grave by Walter and Alfred Mynn and Edgar Willsher.

In May Alfred was present at the annual dinner of the Surrey County Cricket Club, and then, ten days later, he played cricket for the very last time. Suitably enough it was for Southgate, among his good friends the Walkers. The match was a twelve-a-side game on Sir Fowell Buxton's ground at Upton Park in Essex. Only one innings of each side was completed, but for such an occasion the score is worthy of record:

UPTON

J. H. Jewitt, Esq., c Waller, b A. H. Walker	9
G. Levick, Esq., c. V. E. Walker, b. A. Walker	0
T. Handley, b V. E. Walker	24
G. Helder, Esq., b A. H. Walker	6
H. A. Alexander, Esq., run out	16
Gurney Buxton, Esq., b A. Walker	25
G. Baker, b Mynn	10
H. English, Esq., not out	27
G. Banes, Esq., c and b J. Walker	3
Edward Buxton, Esq., c Waller, b J. Walker	2
W. Tyler, run out	0
E. Duncomb, b J. Walker	0
Byes 2, leg byes 2, wides 5	9

131

SOUTHGATE

J. Chalkly, Esq., b Baker	10
C. Waller, Esq., run out	10
E. W. Vyse, Esq., c Baker, b Banes	3
W. Earl, b Baker	0
F. Walker, Esq., c Banes, b Baker	26
V. E. Walker, Esq., run out	60
A. H. Walker, Esq., c. E. Buxton, b Levick	4
J. Walker, Esq., c Levick, b E. Buxton	21
J. Waller, Esq., not out	17
A. Walker, Esq., b E. Buxton	1
Alfred Mynn, Esq., c English, b E. Buxton	4
W. H. Miller, Esq., c E. Buxton, b Handley	12
Byes 12, leg byes 4, wides 10, noes 2	28
	196

At long last Alfred Mynn's cricket career was at an end, though he cannot have known it. But the Upton match was not quite the last occasion on which he was present on a cricket field. A few days later he is recorded as watching, with Pilch and Wenman, the match at Maidstone in which the Players of Kent beat the Gentlemen of Kent by an innings and 227 runs; the game was memorable for a great innings of 160 by George Bennett for the professionals. And at the beginning of August, again at Maidstone and this time with his brother Walter, he saw his county triumph by nine wickets over Surrey: a feat which must have gladdened his heart as the dawn of better times. Later that month he was at the Canterbury Festival, for his name appears as one of the 'principal characters' in the Old Stagers' productions.

In all these reports there is no hint of ill-health. Yet the end was near. As late as October 21 a member of the editorial staff of the *Sporting Life* saw him 'apparently as hale, hearty, and vigorous as ever'. A fortnight later he was dead.

The cause of his death was diabetes, which could be a ferocious killer in days before the development of insulin treatment. It must have attacked Mynn with terrifying suddenness. All that is known is that he died at Walter's house in Merrick Square either on Thursday, October 31, or on the morning of November 1 (his death certificate is here at variance with all the other contemporary accounts). Notice of death was given by Mary Ann Mynn, Walter's second wife. Walter himself was probably away from home; a passage in a letter from Felix seems to suggest that he was with him at Brighton at the time.

If Alfred Mynn's service with the Volunteers had had no great significance in the context of national security, it at least enabled his friends to pay their last tribute to him with a military funeral. On the Monday following his death the body was taken from Southwark to his house at Thurnham, and the funeral took place on Wednesday, November 6. Throughout the day the rain poured down in torrents; otherwise, wrote *Bell's Life*, 'the whole of the county of Kent within thirty miles would certainly have been there'. At Bearsted Green, where he had so often played, the Leeds and Hollingbourne Volunteers, fifty-five strong, were drawn up under their commander Major Wykeham Martin. From there the cortège proceeded past the White Horse, where the dead cricketer had been the centre of so many a convivial evening, on its way to Thurnham church. It was led by the firing party under Sergeant Roper; then came the Volunteers' band, playing the Dead March in Saul; then the hearse and the mourners' coaches; finally the rest of the Volunteers. Many of Mynn's friends and neighbours emerged from their houses and braved the rain to join the procession as it approached the little church tucked away on Thurnham Hill. The burial service was conducted by the Rev. B. Parkinson, after which the firing party took up their position and fired three volleys over the grave.

Mynn lies under the shade of a yew tree in a corner of Thurnham churchyard, next to the grave of his two daughters Mary and Eliza. In 1863 a graceful tombstone was erected with the following inscription:

BENEATH THIS STONE
ARE DEPOSITED THE REMAINS OF
ALFRED MYNN,
SON OF WILLIAM AND ANNE MYNN,
OF TWISDEN LODGE, GOUDHURST,
IN THE COUNTY OF KENT, WHERE HE WAS
BORN ON THE 19TH DAY OF JANUARY, 1807.

KIND AND MANLY ALFRED MYNN

HE DIED AT 22 MERRICK SQUARE, LONDON,
ON THE 1ST DAY OF NOVEMBER, 1861.
HIS KINDNESS OF HEART AND GENEROSITY OF
DISPOSITION DURING MANY YEARS OF PUBLIC
LIFE AS THE CHAMPION OF ENGLISH CRICKETERS
ENDEARED HIM TO A LARGE CIRCLE OF ADMIRING
FRIENDS. HIS WIDE SPREAD POPULARITY IS
ATTESTED BY THE CIRCUMSTANCE THAT
FOUR HUNDRED PERSONS HAVE UNITED TO
ERECT THIS TOMBSTONE, AND TO FOUND IN
HONOR OF A NAME SO CELEBRATED THE
MYNN MEMORIAL BENEVOLENT INSTITUTION
FOR KENTISH CRICKETERS.
A SUM OF £121 16S. 0 HAS ACCORDINGLY BEEN
INVESTED IN INDIA 5 PER CENT STOCK
FOR THE BENEFIT IN PERPETUITY OF THE
OBJECTS OF THE ABOVE NAMED CHARITY.

The Mynn Memorial Benevolent Institution owed its
formation in the first place to the initiative of Fred Gale,
devoted as always to Alfred's memory. In *Bell's Life* on November 24, 1861, there appeared a letter signed with his initials,
'F.G.', asking 'whether the death of one of the greatest cricketers
and one of the truest Englishmen who ever trod the green
sward is to be passed unnoticed by the cricketing world'.
He suggested that a committee of twelve should be formed
consisting of an even number of gentlemen and players: two
representatives each from the M.C.C., Kent, Sussex, Surrey,
Nottinghamshire and Hampshire. The letter continued:

The labours would be comparatively light, for I feel
convinced that when the committee was once formed they
would simply have to suggest through your columns the
easiest mode of securing the support of the cricket clubs of
England, and I believe that every cricket club in England
against which, or for which Mr Mynn has played, would
send its donation. Let us hope that after providing for the
erection of a monument which would mark the last resting-
place of the 'Lion of Kent' – which monument should be as
handsome and unpretending as the man to whose memory

199

it would be dedicated – a large surplus would remain in hand; and if the committee should be doubtful as to the mode of its application, I would suggest that the balance should be invested in the Cricketers' Fund, and be entered in the books as the 'Alfred Mynn Testimonial'; so that every cricketer who may hereafter want relief may know, that however great he himself may have been in *his* day, there lived before him one who was greater still. . . .

Gale was over-sanguine in his estimate of the response to such an appeal, but the main provisions of his suggestion were eventually adopted. In February the names of Edward Bligh, William de Chair Baker, W. S. Norton, Fuller Pilch, Wenman and Willsher were proposed for the committee, Bligh and Baker to act as trustees of the fund. In March the committee was formed and subscriptions invited. The final arrangements were made at a meeting held at the Mote Park ground, Maidstone, on August 29. It was resolved that a portion of the sum subscribed should be set aside for the provision of a tombstone; as regards the surplus a resolution was passed 'that the sum subscribed for the memorial be placed in the names of trustees for investment in some public securities to be hereafter approved. That the interest of the fund, if the same shall be at present not sufficient, be allowed to accumulate until the whole shall produce not less than £5 per annum. That the interest thus accruing be applied annually to the relief or maintenance of a retired Kentish cricketer. That the recipient of the interest be elected annually by the committee of the Kent County Club, or in case of emergency by the Marylebone Club. That personal respectability and good character be indispensable qualifications for the election of recipients.'

The deed as finally drawn up is dated May 25, 1863. The first trustees were Frederick Ponsonby, Edward Bligh, Walter Mynn, Frederick Norman, John Walker, Charles Whittaker and Edmond Wilder.

The total sum was disappointingly small, and after the initial impetus little interest seems to have been shown in the Memorial Institution. W. South Norton, who was connected with the Mynn family by marriage, telling the story of the fund in *The History of Kent County Cricket*, published forty-six years after Alfred's death, ended his account with the words:

> I see, almost every day in the papers, notices of legacies generously given to many charities, but I have not observed that much favour has been shown to the above, which is not widely known. I would respectfully urge charitable donors and testators to think of dear Alfred Mynn, and honour his memory by a contribution.

Not much more is recorded of the Mynn Memorial Institution, though among the cricketers who received grants in later years were Edward Henty, the wicket-keeper, and Walter Wright, the bowler. After the 1939 war all the Kent cricket charities were amalgamated.

Walter Mynn survived his brother by seventeen years, dying at Peckham on October 17, 1878. For a time he carried on the hop business in the Borough, but a few years after the death of William Mynn in 1864 the family name disappeared from Southwark. Of Walter's last years little is known. He did not lose his interest in cricket, for Lord Harris, who was born in 1851, remembered meeting Ned Wenman and Walter Mynn – 'large, silent men' – at a Canterbury Week. But Edward Hodges recorded that Walter 'did not make headway' after Alfred's death; when he last met him he was keeping a billiard-room off the Edgware Road.

That he left his widow in straitened circumstances is suggested by an incident in the Canterbury Week of 1880, two years after his death. An England eleven played thirteen of Kent, and five dozen copies of a portrait of Alfred Mynn were sold on the ground; the proceeds of the sale were given to Mrs Walter Mynn.

This may perhaps suggest also that Alfred's widow was adequately provided for; otherwise one would expect that she too would have benefited. For Sarah Mynn was still alive in 1880. She died of paralysis at Croydon on the following January 27, aged sixty-nine, as unobtrusively as she had lived. Apart from the mention of her marriage and her death and of the births of her children she might, so far as written records go, never have existed.

Has there ever been a cricketer so universally loved, both by those who knew him and by those who merely watched him play, as Alfred Mynn? Patsy Hendren perhaps, between the wars; I can think of no other. From his comrades in the field, the rich patrons who helped him in adversity, the cricket writers and sporting journalists, comes a unanimous chorus of affection, unjarred by a solitary note of disparagement. Before we finally take leave of him let us take a last look at what some of his contemporaries had to say of him.

'Dear, genial Alfred!' was the simple tribute of Edward Hodges, who knew him longer than most. 'A more delightful man never lived.'

Richard Daft, the most elegant batsman of the 1860s and one of the first and best writers of cricket reminiscences, recalled with gratitude the encouragement he received from Mynn when he first appeared in the field. 'The great cricketer,' he wrote in *Kings of Cricket*, 'did not live to see me through a great part of my career, though he did live to see me attain many successes in the cricket field, and paid me many kind compliments on my play.' And speaking of a picture of Mynn by Felix that had come his way he wrote: 'I must confess that when I saw the portrait I was quite startled for the moment, it was so natural and life-like. I have seen many portraits of Mynn in my life, but I have seen none so good as this one. In looking at it, it seems hard to me to believe that he whom it represents has been nearly thirty years in his grave.'

In another passage Daft briefly summed up his old friend and mentor: 'Mr Mynn was one of the kindest-hearted men I ever met, and was as gentle in his manner as he was strong in person. I have often felt glad that I was not born ten years later than I was, for in that case I should not have had the pleasure of knowing one of the most famous cricketers and good-hearted fellows of his own or any other generation.'

At least one glowing assessment of Alfred Mynn's character was published in his lifetime. William Denison, the Surrey cricketer, who often played with him, wrote in *Sketches of the Players*, published when Mynn was forty:

He is signalized too for possessing one of the most even

dispositions that man has ever been gifted with. Rarely has it occurred that his temper could be ruffled; and at cricket, his natural good humour has never been known to have been cast aside. His countenance bespeaks equanimity of temperament, and an inclination to pass through life without a single angry indication, or without offering offence to his fellow-man. Gratitude for a kindness displayed towards him is a leading feature in his character, and one of the greatest sources of delight to his mind is to give utterance to his thanks, for the attention paid to him by Mr Ward and others of the leading patrons some years since, when he was for several months placed on a bed of sickness, in consequence of the severity of a series of blows received in a match at Leicester, upon his right knee and leg during a long innings. . . .

V. E. Walker, than whom no cricketer was ever more highly respected, wrote: 'Mynn was stately and upright, and I think he was as fine a specimen of a thorough English yeoman as was ever seen, with a heart as big as a balloon.' And in a talk with A. W. Pullin ('Old Ebor') Walker said: 'He was the most magnificent specimen of an Englishman you could possibly see, and all that has been said and written about his kindliness of heart I can personally corroborate. When you had a grip of his paw you knew all about it.'

Somewhat similar words, used by a closer contemporary, were recorded by the same author in *Talks with Old English Cricketers*. Herbert Jenner-Fust (Herbert Jenner in his cricketing days) was the Cambridge captain in the first University match ever played, in 1827. He was a year older than Mynn, but he lived till 1904, dying at the age of ninety-eight. He said to 'Old Ebor': 'A very fine and manly fellow was Alfred Mynn, and all that has been said and written of his great qualities does his memory no more than justice. He was as large in heart as he was great in cricket. It is indeed hard to say what he was and what he was not. In his day he was tremendously popular.'

Lord Harris, the greatest figure in the history of Kent cricket, was only ten years old when Mynn died; but he recalled his father's enthusiasm. 'I now regret,' he wrote in *A Few Short*

Runs, 'that I never talked with my father about the play and the players of the period 1825-1840. He was quite a good player himself, and most anxious to help me at the game, but most reserved, and I was then more enthused with the present than the past. . . . The only thing in his cricket talk of the past that I can remember is his immense admiration for Alfred Mynn. That feeling seems to have been universal, for the Lion of Kent had evidently a most equable temper and lovable nature, and we naturally regret that we have not seen him and others of the great players of the past. . . . '

Notable among tributes to Alfred was that of the Rev. E. V. Bligh, brother of Lord Darnley and a member of one of the greatest of Kent cricket families, one of the leading figures in the formation of the new county club in 1859. In an article in the *Kent Magazine* in 1896 Bligh wrote:

Who that remembers good old Alfred Mynn – though he never *was* old – does not delight to think of the tall gigantic figure, the upright gait and broad shoulders, the splendid chest and fine proportions of this great Kentish man! . . . A more genial man there never was; natural as a child; large-hearted and good-natured; courteous to a degree both towards gentlemen and professionals; perfect in his demeanour; 'a good old Kentish Yeoman, born in the olden time'; worthy in all respects of the monument which was erected to him by public subscription, and placed over his body, in Thurnham Churchyard, in connection with the 'Mynn Memorial Fund' for decayed Kent cricketers.

The obituary notices in the sporting press were of course anonymous, but some were certainly written by men who had known the dead cricketer personally. 'Every one,' said *Bell's Life*, 'who had the pleasure of knowing Mr Alfred Mynn – and there are many thousands – knew him to be one of the most kind-hearted and generous of Her Majesty's subjects, and among his fellow-cricketers, particularly, he was much liked and esteemed.' The *Sporting Magazine* wrote that 'he was a universal favourite, and no wonder, for he overflowed with the milk of human kindness'.

Felix's tribute, as might be expected, was especially warm.

He heard the news of his old friend's death as he limped from church on the Sunday after it occurred. Soon after came a letter from Edmond Wilder giving the details, and Felix expressed his thoughts in a long reply which deserves quotation at some length:

No. 20 Montpelier Street Brighton
Nov. 5th. 1861.

Alas! then my dear Sir it is too true! Receive my warmest thanks for your dear kind letter wherein you have broken the force of the sad blow which has deprived us of one of the noblest specimens of manliness and courage combined with all that was becoming in a man. . . .

From the first moment of our introduction we chimed in together and every time we met only cemented our Friendship. I fought by his side and I have been enlisted to oppose him, but the same spirit of kindness ever prevailed, many a time he has bowled me a Ball, that as he said, would haved bowled six men out, and instead of feeling annoyed with me for stopping it (altho at that moment against him) would pat with his dear old hand and say 'well done my little man'. As you have truly said he had he could have had, no enemies. This same high minded sentiment prevailed throughout his character. . . . Oh! my dear Sir I have seen him under almost every circumstance of trial and trouble and his bearing was in strict accordance with all that has been written on the subject of tribulation working patience. With gigantic stature, unequalled symetry, there was combined the docility of a child – and many a time I have drawn a tear from his beautiful blue eyes when he has requested me to play him some favourite air on my Flute. I have a thousand fond recollections to call up all, all to his advantage. It was well for one or two who by their titles ought to have been above trifling with the feelings of so great and good a man of such noble temperament, else would he have lifted but his arm to seal their death. He would not, could not hurt a Worm. In the high toned sympathy of your ever feeling Heart you have hinted nay you have said, that such a Man whose loss we have now to deplore with deep deep grief ought not to pass to the silence of the Grave without some tribute being paid to his memory. More than once you have done me the honour to say you hoped to move my facile pen; I seem never before this to have felt the power of its weakness, nevertheless, if I thought for one moment that you wished it, I would contribute to the memory of my dear lost Friend and Companion any expressions consoling to the survivors or in proof to the World that a good and great Man has been called away from them, one whose example for nobility of sentiment and greatness of mind when alive was unequalled and whose very death by the last sweet smile is the envy of every Believer in One who has promised to intercede for those who put their trust in Him.

. . . How kind of you to go and see him only knowing that he wished to see you. 'Te aspicit in occulto, reddet tibi in propatulo'. Poor Walter Mynn subscribes as many broken Hearts have done before him and are still subscribing them-selves 'Yours gratefully'. How often and with what sincerity I have used this word when addressing you is known to Him from whom no secrets are hid. Once more my dearest Sir accept my warmest thanks for the trouble you have taken in communicating to me the sad intelligence and for the kind and considerate manner you adopted in conveying it. I cannot write any more. I know you will pardon this sudden withdrawing. As soon as all is quiet I will recall my shattered thoughts, the memory of the past will have its way. God in his mercy bless and preserve you, prays as ever,

Yours faithfully & gratefully,

N. Felix.

For Edmond Wilder Esq.

Felix's words were almost exactly echoed by Pycroft, who wrote of Mynn in a little-known booklet: 'He was a giant in stature, with the simplicity and good-humour of a child'.

But the best of all the panegyrics remains the one which, apart from the obituary notices, was the first to be published after Alfred Mynn's death. William Jeffrey Prowse was a young sporting journalist of high promise who had been a pupil at Felix's school at Blackheath and retained an enduring affection for his old master and his colleagues of the Kent eleven. The various verses of his valedictory poem have been quoted at the heads of the chapters of this book; but in a work devoted to Mynn they must be given once more in full, just as they appeared in *Bell's Life in London* on November 10, 1861:

IN MEMORIAM

Jackson's pace is very fearful; Willsher's hand is very high;
William Caffyn has good judgment, and an admirable eye;
Jemmy Grundy's cool and clever, almost always on the spot;
Tinley's slows are often telling, though they sometimes catch
    it hot;
But however good their trundling – pitch or pace, or break, or
    spin –
Still the monarch of all bowlers, to my mind, was Alfred Mynn!

Richard Daft is cool and cautious, with his safe and graceful
    play;
If George Griffith gets a loose one, he can send it far away;
You may bowl your best at Hayward, and whatever style you try,
Will be vanquished by the master's steady hand and certain
    eye;
But whatever fame and glory these and other bats may win,
Still the monarch of hard hitters, to my mind, was Alfred Mynn!

You may praise the pluck of Burbidge, as he plays an uphill
    match;
You may thunder cheers to Miller for a wondrous running
    catch;
You may join with me in wishing that the Oval, once again,
Shall resound with hearty plaudits to the praise of Mr Lane;
But the Gentlemen of England the match will hardly win,
Till they find another bowler such as glorious Alfred Mynn!

When the great old Kent Eleven, full of pluck and hope, began
The grand battle with All England, single-handed, man to man,
How the hop-men watched their hero, massive, muscular, and
    tall,

As he mingled with the players, like a king amongst them all;
'Till to some old Kent enthusiasts it would almost seem a sin
To doubt their County's triumph when led on by Alfred Mynn!

Though Sir Frederick and 'The Veteran' bowled straight, and
    sure, and well,
Though Box behind the wicket only Lockyer can excel;
Though Jemmy Dean as long-stop would but seldom grant a
    bye;
Though no novices at batting were George Parr and Joseph
    Guy;
Said the fine old Kentish farmers, with a fine old Kentish grin,
'Why, there ain't a man among 'em as can match our Alfred
    Mynn!'

And whatever was the issue of the frank and friendly fray
(Aye, and often has his bowling turned the fortune of the day!)
Still the Kentish men fought bravely, never losing hope nor
    heart,
Every man of the Eleven glad and proud to play his part;
And with five such mighty cricketers, 'twas but natural to win –
As Felix, Wenman, Hillyer, Fuller Pilch, and Alfred Mynn!

With his tall and stately presence, with his nobly moulded
    form,
His broad hand – 'twas ever open! – his brave heart – 'twas
    ever warm! –
All were proud of him, *all* loved him! . . . As the changing
    seasons pass;
As our Champion lies a-sleeping underneath the Kentish grass;
Proudly, sadly we will name him – to forget him were a sin;
Lightly lie the turf upon thee, kind and manly Alfred Mynn!

Tottenham, Nov. 7, 1861.   W. J. PROWSE, B.M.C.C.

STATISTICAL APPENDIX

BATTING

*

There are obvious difficulties in the way of presenting statistics in the modern manner relating to the career of a cricketer of Alfred Mynn's time. These difficulties chiefly concern bowling, but in batting too one is faced with the problem of what matches to include, since there was no established distinction between first-class games and others. One must decide on some criterion, and in the tables below I have worked out the figures from those matches recorded in Haygarth's *Scores and Biographies*; for this reason they do not necessarily agree with the figures published at the time and given in Chapter III, which were mainly based on the matches reported in *Bell's Life*. I have included all matches in which odds were given, but not single-wicket matches.

	Innings	Runs	Highest Score	Times not out	Average
1829	8	33	12	1	4·71
1831	1	8	8	0	8·00
1832	13	90	29	1	7·50
1833	14	79	29	0	5·64
1834	21	232	24	2	12·21
1835	15	209	53	1	14·93
1836	25	497	125*	4	23·67
1838	17	250	59*	2	16·67
1839	20	267	46	0	13·35
1840	31	297	37	1	9·90
1841	27	402	51	0	14·89
1842	25	441	61	0	17·65
1843	31	497	73	2	17·14
1844	29	396	48	0	13·66
1845	14	182	55	0	13·00
1846	38	480	51	1	12·97
1847	53	666	62*	5	13·88

	Innings	Runs	Highest Score	Times not out	Average
1848	45	484	72	3	11·52
1849	62	687	92	2	11·45
1850	55	413	69	5	8·26
1851	48	446	85	2	9·70
1852	46	464	53	5	11·32
1853	42	422	34*	8	12·41
1854	27	321	54	3	13·38
1855	19	272	47	1	15·11
1856	14	176	22	0	12·57
1857	15	65	22*	3	5·42
1858	3	22	19	1	11·00
1859	5	49	22	0	9·80
1860	2	2	2	0	1·00
1861	1	4	4	0	4·0
Totals	766	8853	125*	53	12·42

* Not out.

BOWLING

*

Bowling statistics present a far harder problem, owing to the haphazard manner in which the scores were kept. In most of the early matches the bowler was credited with a wicket only when the batsman was bowled. When his name came to be given for all wickets it was still some time before it was customary to note the runs scored off him; when this was done the total usually included extras. It follows from this that Mynn's total of wickets must have been considerably larger than as given below, while the number of runs scored off him (in those matches where details are given) must have been less. Even by the end of his career the totals of overs and maidens were so seldom given that I have not thought it worth while to include them.

	Runs	Wickets	Average	Wickets	Number Bowled	Total Ascertainable Wickets
	(In matches where details are given)			(Where no details of runs are given)	(Where no other details are given)	
1829					6	6
1831					2	2
1832				1	23	24
1833					34	34
1834					30	30
1835					43	43
1836				26	20	46
1838				5	43	48
1839	87	10	8·70	28	34	72
1840				45	42	87
1841				100	24	124
1842				94	9	103
1843	104	8	13·00	125	5	138
1844	658	85	7·74	57		142
1845	172	9	19·11	38	5	52
1846	454	38	11·95	104		142
1847	449	36	12·47	110	3	149
1848	128	29	4·41	79		108
1849	130	20	6·50	42		62
1850	117	29	4·03	30		59
1851	135	14	9·64	30		44
1852	271	18	15·06	18		36
1853	75	12	6·25	2		14
1854	270	28	9·64	17		45
1855	46	5	9·20	34		39
1856	21	0	—			0
1859	22	1	22·00			1
1861				1		1
Totals	3139	342	9·18	986	323	1651

For Kent Alfred Mynn made 2,147 runs, with a highest score of 92 and an average of 12·62, and took at least 346 wickets. For the Gentlemen against the Players he made 605 runs, with a highest score of 66 and an average of 15·92, and took at least 107 wickets.

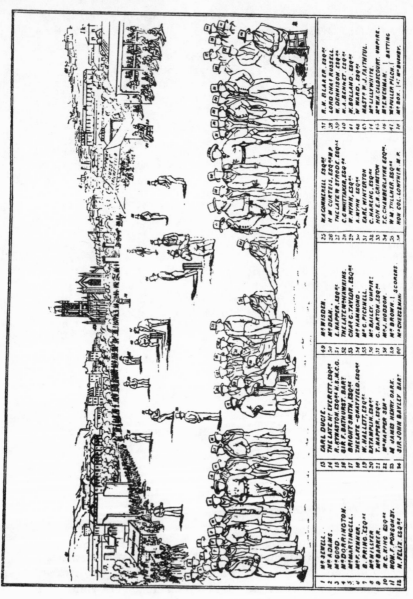

Key to W. H. Mason's engraving 'Sussex v. Kent' which is reproduced opposite page 177

NOTE ON SINGLE WICKET

*

The passage at the foot of page 148 was written before the announcement was made that a single-wicket knock-out competition would be held at Scarborough at the end of the 1963 season. These games, however, will differ considerably from single wicket as it was played in the first half of the nineteenth century. There will be a full complement of fielders, and the players will bowl overs from alternate ends, each being limited to a maximum of ten. At the moment of writing it has not been made clear whether hits behind the wicket will count for runs, but presumably they will. In other words the general principles of double wicket, as played in the new one-day knock-out competition, will be adapted to single wicket, without the special laws formerly in force.

BIBLIOGRAPHY

*

Alfred Mynn's daily doings in the cricket field are chronicled in *Bell's Life in London* and, in his last years, in the *Sporting Life*. I have also made use of the *Sporting Magazine*, the *New Sporting Magazine*, *Lillywhite's Guide to Cricketers*, *Cricket*, the various Kent papers and a few other provincial papers. The fullest account of the North *v.* South match at Leicester in 1836 is in the *Leicester Herald*.

The principal printed books and articles used are the following:

Altham, H. S. *A History of Cricket.* (Allen & Unwin, 1926).

Alverstone, L. C. J., and Alcock, C. W. *Surrey Cricket: Its History and Associations.* (Longmans, 1902).

Anonymous. *The Canterbury Cricket Week.* Vol. I (William Davey, 1865). (Vol. II was never published).

Ashley-Cooper, F. S. *Chats on the Cricket Field: Mr Edward Hodges.* (In *Cricket*, 1907). *Nottinghamshire Cricket and Cricketers.* (Saxton, 1925).

Bettesworth, W. A. *The Walkers of Southgate.* (Methuen, 1900). *Chats on the Cricket Field.* (Merritt & Hatcher, 1910).

Bligh, Hon. and Rev. E. V. *Former Kent Cricket* (written anonymously in the *Kent Magazine*, 1896).

Bolland, William. *Cricket Notes.* (Trelawney Saunders, 1851).

Box, Charles. *The Theory and Practice of Cricket.* (Warne, 1868). *The English Game of Cricket.* (The *Field*, 1877).

Brodribb, Gerald. *Felix on the Bat: Being a Memoir of Nicholas Felix.* (Eyre & Spottiswoode, 1962).

Caffyn, William. *Seventy-One Not Out.* (Blackwood, 1899).

Cochrane, Alfred. Mr Mynn ('By A.C.' in *The Cricketer Winter Annual*, 1929).

Daft, Richard. *Kings of Cricket.* (Arrowsmith, 1893). *A Cricketer's Yarns* (ed. F. S. Ashley-Cooper; Chapman & Hall, 1926).

Denison, William. *Sketches of the Players.* (Simpkin & Marshall, 1846).

Felix, N. *Felix on the Bat.* (Bailey Bros., 1845).

Gale, Frederick. *Echoes from Old Cricket Fields.* (Simpkin & Marshall, 1871). *The Life of Robert Grimston.* (Longmans, 1885). *The Game of Cricket.* (Swan Sonnenschein and Lowry, 1887).

Glover, William. *Reminiscences of Half a Century.* (Remington, 1889).

Grace, W. G. *Cricket.* (Arrowsmith, 1891). *W.G.'s Little Book.* (Newnes, 1909).

Harris, Lord. *The History of Kent County Cricket* (ed. Lord Harris; Eyre & Spottiswoode, 1907). *A Few Short Runs.* (Murray, 1921).

Harris, Lord, and Ashley-Cooper, F. S. *Lord's and the M.C.C.* (London & Counties Press Association, 1914). *Kent Cricket Matches,* 1719–1880. (Gibbs & Sons, 1929).

Hayes, S. F. *A Hundred Years* (in the *Cricketer,* 1937).

Haygarth, Arthur. *Frederick Lillywhite's Cricket Scores and Biographies of Celebrated Cricketers,* Vols. II–IV (1862–3). (Haygarth was the compiler; Lillywhite the printer). Arthur Haygarth's Cricket Scores and Biographies from 1855 to 1875, being a continuation of Frederick Lillywhite's Scores and Biographies from 1772 to 1854. Vol. V. (M.C.C., 1876).

Hole, S. R. *The Memories of Dean Hole.* (Arnold, 1892).

Knight, Albert E. *The Complete Cricketer.* (Methuen, 1906).

Leigh, Hon. Sir Edward Chandos. *Bar, Bit and Bridle.* (Murray, 1913).

Martineau, G. D. *They Made Cricket.* (Museum Press, 1956). *The Valiant Stumper.* (Stanley Paul, 1957).

Norman, Philip. *Scores and Annals of the West Kent Cricket Club.* (Eyre & Spottiswoode, 1847).

Parker, Eric. *The History of Cricket.* (Lonsdale Library, Seeley Service, 1950).

Pullin, A. W. ('Old Ebor'). *Talks With Old English Cricketers.* (Blackwood, 1900).

Pycroft, Rev. James. *The Cricket Field.* (Longmans, 1854). *Cricketana.* (Published as 'by the Author of *The Cricket Field*'; Longmans, 1865). *Oxford Memories.* Vol. II. (Bentley, 1886). Cricket: Reminiscences of the Old Players and Observations on the Young Ones (An undated booklet 'by the Author of *The Cricket Field*').

Rait Kerr, R. S. *The Laws of Cricket: Their History and Growth.* (Longmans, 1950).

Read, W. W. *Annals of Cricket.* (Sampson Low & Marston, 1896).

Rutter, Edward. *Cricket Memories.* (Williams & Norgate, 1925).

Small, E. Milton. *The Canterbury Cricket Week.* (Jennings, 1891).

Steel, A. G., and Lyttelton, Hon. R. H. *Cricket.* (Badminton Library, Longmans, 1893).

Tate, Rev. Harold A. *Cricket Champions: Mr Alfred Mynn* (in *Cricket*, 1906).

Taylor, Alfred D. *Annals of Lord's and History of the M.C.C.* (Arrowsmith, 1903).

Vizetelly, Henry. *Glances Back Through Seventy Years*. Vol. I. (Kegan Paul, 1893).

Warner, Sir Pelham. *Lord's, 1787–1945*. (Harrap, 1946). *Gentlemen v. Players, 1806–1949*. (Harrap, 1950).

Watson, F. I. *Sidelights on Cricket History* (in the *Field*, 1949).

Wilson, E. R. *One Hundred Years Ago* (in the *Cricketer*, 1949).

INDEX

*